INVENTION, COPYRIGHT, AND DIGITAL WRITING

INVENTION, COPYRIGHT, and DIGITAL WRITING

MARTINE COURANT RIFE

Southern Illinois University Press
Carbondale and Edwardsville

16   15   14   13   4   3   2   1

Library of Congress Cataloging-in-Publication Data
Rife, Martine Courant.
Invention, copyright, and digital writing / Martine Courant
Rife.
    p. cm.
Includes bibliographical references and index.
ISBN 978-0-8093-3096-6 (pbk. : alk. paper) — ISBN 0-8093-
3096-2 (pbk. : alk. paper) — ISBN 978-0-8093-3098-0 (ebook)
— ISBN 0-8093-3098-9 (ebook)
1. Copyright and electronic data processing—United States.
2. Online authorship—United States. 3. Authorship—Study
and teaching—United States. 4. Electronic publishing—Law
and legislation—United States. I. Title.
KF3024.E44R54 2013
346.7304'82—dc23   2012023690

Printed on recycled paper. ♻
The paper used in this publication meets the minimum requirements of American National Standard for Information
Sciences—Permanence of Paper for Printed Library Materials, ANSI Z39.48-1992. ∞

To Bill and Jeff

Contents

Acknowledgments

William Hart-Davidson deserves extra-special thanks for all of his professional advice and mentoring over the last several years. I could not have conducted the study or written this book without his time and attention. Dr. Hart-Davidson provided the intellectual framework for many of my ideas; his ideas, which he so generously shared, are peppered throughout these pages. I also extend special thanks to Jeffrey T. Grabill for his advice about the book-writing process specifically, and also for sharing feedback as I developed some of my ideas in this text. Special thanks also goes to Dànielle Nicole DeVoss and Bump Halbritter.

I also thank Ansel Courant for acting as a research assistant and teaching me Excel. I admit I tested the limits of his patience. I also thank my family of course, especially Mike and Olivia, for giving me space and time to write and rewrite this book. Also special thanks to Jim Ridolfo for reading and rereading these chapters and talking to me about, especially, the "author-function." I also thank the research participants, especially the interviewees, who are certainly the smartest and most cunning digital writers I know. They are also good people. I thank Kendall Leon for providing feedback on the survey. I generally thank the Michigan State University Rhetoric and Writing Program, including those idea-generating scholars I attended graduate school with, and the professors, particularly Malea Powell, as well as the undergraduate Professional Writing Program at Michigan State University for supporting this study in many ways. I also thank the Graduate School at Michigan State University for providing generous funding for my work. I thank the WIDE Research Center for its intellectual support.

I also want to thank those who have generally been supportive of my work over the years that I wrote this book—those folks include Kirk St. Amant, Dan Holt, Michael Nealon, Rick Reagan, Sue Webb, Angela Shetler, Amy Diehl, and everyone in the NCTE CCCC IP Caucus.

Copyright and Composing: Invention and Digital Writing

The Congress shall have Power . . . To promote the Progress
of Science and useful Arts, by securing for limited times to
Authors and Inventors the exclusive Right to their respective
Writings and Discoveries.

—Article 1, Section 8, U.S. Constitution

Copyright law and the issues around it increasingly intersect the interests of academics, and for that reason educators are not hesitating to participate in public forums where legal policy is made. An example of this participation is the recent letter submitted by the CCCC (Conference on College Composition and Communication) community pursuant to a national call for public comments. The call for public comments came from the newly appointed U.S. copyright czar Victoria A. Espinel (U.S. intellectual property enforcement coordinator), of the newly created intellectual property arm of the U.S. Office of Management and Budget. Espinel solicited public comments for purposes of shaping the Joint Strategic Plan as authorized by the Prioritizing Resources and Organization for Intellectual Property Act of 2008, Public Law 110–403 (Oct. 13, 2008). The Joint Strategic Plan (Espinel, 2010) shapes the future of education in copyright contexts because it embodies the U.S. federal government's current "landmark effort" to develop an "intellectual property enforcement strategy" such that "agencies charged with enforcing intellectual property rights" will be better able to "effectively and efficiently combat intellectual property infringement" (Federal register, 2010). Among sixteen hundred comments considered by Espinel is a letter put forward by a team of professor-researcher-scholars from the CCCC Intellectual Property (IP)

Caucus, including myself and others such as Mike Edwards, Charlie Lowe, Jeff Galin, Karen Lunsford, Traci Zimmerman, Kim Gainer, John Logie, Clancy Ratliff, Jamie Thornton, Jim Porter, and too many others to mention (see CCCC IP Caucus Letter for a list of the numerous supporters).

When finalized in June, the 2010 Joint Strategic Plan did acknowledge the importance of fair use and protecting the ability to exchange information for purposes of learning and teaching: "Strong intellectual property enforcement efforts should be focused on stopping those stealing the work of others, not those who are appropriately building upon it" (Espinel, p. 4). The plan is focused throughout on infringement of U.S. intellectual property rights by users in other countries rather than on the uses typically made in U.S. educational environments for purposes of teaching and learning. We have to believe that all the public comments received, such as the comments in the CCCC letter emphasizing the importance of fair use, were taken into account by Espinel and her team in shaping the Joint Strategic Plan.

The CCCC letter—first conceived during the writing of the introduction to an in-process edited collection, *Copy(Write): Intellectual Property in the Writing Classroom*, by Dànielle Nicole DeVoss, Shaun Slattery, and myself within a seven-day period— made its way into an e-mail posted to a list serve, then to the floor of the annual CCCC IP Caucus meeting by way of attendee Mike Edwards's laptop; the letter was displayed by projector onto a large screen and revised with the eyes and voices of about twenty caucus attendees. Over the next few days, this letter found its way to the CCCC IP Committee, and eventually I requested that the text be placed on CCCC letterhead—and it was—moments before formal e-mail submission by Barbara Cambridge, who was to be the first signatory, and who was the director of the Washington, DC, office of the CCCC/National Council of Teachers of English (NCTE). By posting to Facebook, Twitter, and various list serves, I also gathered almost one hundred signatures to add to the letter, from professors and graduate students in numerous disciplines across the U.S. Signatories of the letter also include organizations ATTW (Association of Teachers of Technical Writing) and WIDE (Writing in Digital Environments Research Center). This letter not only exemplifies the ways that writing now unfolds in the digital age, but also suggests how great a concern copyright law—the law of texts (Woodmansee and Jaszi, 1995)— is to a wide range of scholars across the disciplines. Likewise this book, the culmination of research begun almost five years ago, is offered as a discussion pushing copyright issues more solidly into rhetoric and composition studies—and in turn making the discussions of scholars in rhetoric and composition more useful and relevant to those interested in the law as an area of research and scholarship.

Other kinds of ongoing public policy issues around copyright law, such as the public discussion on the Joint Strategic Plan, have not gone unnoticed in academia. Scholars and researchers working in this area where law, rhetoric, and composition intersect include legal-oriented scholars such as Marjorie Heins and Tricia Beckles, Rosemary Coombe, Lawrence Lessig, William Fisher, Peter Jaszi, Martha Woodmansee, and William McGeveran. In rhetoric and composition, some of the many scholarly contributors to the copyright and IP conversation include John Logie, Lisa Dush, Steve Westbrook, TyAnna Herrington, Dànielle Nicole De-Voss, Jim Porter, Jessica Reyman, Kathleen Durack, and Clancy Ratliff. IP-focused scholarship written for broader audiences includes contributions by Charles Bazerman and R. J. Brockmann. Together this group of researchers have studied issues ranging from Logie (2006b) and Reyman's (2010) work on narratives and metaphors of intellectual property to Steve Westbrook's (2009) edited collection, *Composition and Copyright: Perspective on Teaching, Text-Making, and Fair Use*, as well as his *College English* piece theorizing upon the culture of fear created for writing teachers and students due to copyright issues (2006). This area of rhetoric and composition scholarship includes a wide range of work such as TyAnna Herrington's sustained scholarly focus on the impact copyright law has on educators and to Lisa Dush's study on the copyright/fair use knowledge students have upon arriving in her classroom (and they do not come as blank slates). In 2010–2011, three special issues, of *Computers and Composition*, *Technical Communication*, and *Technical Communication Quarterly*, are or will be published on themes around copyright, law, and writing/composing (see Rife, Westbrook, DeVoss, and Logie, 2010; St. Amant and Rife, 2010). In 2009, at the suggestion of then incoming chairperson Karen Lunsford, the CCCC IP Caucus began a monthly NCTE newsletter on IP issues,[1] and 2010 marked the caucus's fifth year of publishing the online edited collection "Top Intellectual Property Developments," which includes the largest collection ever of articles by new and established rhetoric and composition scholars (see Ratliff, 2007–2010).

Attention to issues around the intersection of copyright and education continues to grow for the general public as well. As Lawrence Lessig points out in his 2009 Educause conference keynote, it was only a couple of decades ago that copyright law occupied an extremely tiny area of legal studies—and most persons lived their lives without any concern or knowledge about copyright law. That all changed of course with the advent of the Internet and its accompanying architecture for digital writing. And so we have ongoing legal battles like the ones over the Joint Strategic Plan and exemptions to the DMCA (Digital Millennium Copyright Act), and concerning all kinds of issues around the practices of educational institutions, such as the Association for Information and Media Equipment's challenge to the University of California at Los Angeles's use of streaming video (see Kolowich, 2010a; Laster, 2010), the Google books case, and the Georgia State University lawsuit—where the college is being sued for "providing course reading material to students in digital format without seeking permission from the publishers or paying licensing fees" (Hafner, 2008). Effective July 1, 2010, the U.S. Department of Education's new regulations implementing filesharing provisions of the Higher Education Opportunity Act (HEOA) must be enacted by all colleges and universities "seeking continued eligibility for Title IV funds [student financial aid]" (7 things, 2010, p. 1; see also Rife, 2010d). While not changing copyright law, the HEOA requires colleges and universities wishing to maintain their funding to educate students (in filesharing contexts) on the implications for violating copyright law, and to have procedures in place to "combat infringement" (7 things, 2001, p. 1). The increased attention toward institutions of higher education with respect to copyright law might surprise some, but in reality this attention makes sense since, after all, "universities are among the world's largest producers and consumers of intellectual property" (7 things, 2001, p. 2). In the face of all this law-focused activity, Lessig reminds us that legal battles over copyright law's reach into webspace are battles between old and new, past and present. Lessig (2004) argues our culture is becoming less of a free culture and more of an unfree, permission-based culture—in large part due to the Internet, along with technologies that govern the ways we can access and copy texts. Unlike ten years ago, copyright law now touches the daily lives of many people.

Networked digital writing in turn causes those interested in composing process theory, writing teachers, others who work with writers, and writers themselves to return to initiating theories developed in the 1970s and 1980s by researchers such as Linda Flower and John Hayes, Sondra Perl, and Janet Emig.[2] Other composing theories that should be revisited include those relying on rhetorical invention but developed before networked digital writing. R. E. Young (1978) points to four such rhetoric-based theories: classical invention, Kenneth Burke's dramatistic pentad, Gordon Rohman's prewriting method, and Kenneth Pike's tagmemics (p. 35). As I saw it when I designed and implemented this study, my curiosity piqued, what better time to conduct a study of rhetorical invention in the context of digital writing and copyright law than when, due to digital writing environments, we are now presented with what Richard E. Young or even Thomas Kuhn might characterize as a crisis in the disciplines. This crisis is due to the unseating of existing inventional theories—those theories imagining a single author as a text's originating point and those composing theories based on alphabetic, paper-based writing. In the twenty-first century, we must update our understanding of composing process—invent new theories grounded in an understanding of writing where authorship is complex and multiple and includes digital and networked environments: writing that can instantly circulate the globe, as Foucault might say, without the filter of the "author." Examining and exploring composing process in contemporary digital writers not only illuminates the presence of any copyright heuristic at work but also helps "articulate the new models of composing developing right in front of our eyes" (Yancey, 2009).

This project came first and foremost from my wish to connect the two professional areas of my life—first, the law and second, the teaching and researching of rhetoric and composition. The ideas for this specific project came to me through my graduate school experience. I obtained my PhD in rhetoric and writing more than twenty years after obtaining my law degree and came to graduate school with a significant past of professional experience as an attorney with a scholarly interest in legal studies. During my time as a rhetoric and composition graduate student, I noticed inconsistencies in the pedagogies, curricular materials, and general approach to acknowledging and teaching about copyright law, and I noticed all kinds of interesting understandings and behaviors on the part of my fellow students with respect to the law. As part of my doctoral work, I returned to law school to take a couple of classes specifically on copyright, attended and even presented at legal conferences, and became aware of two very difference epistemological approaches across the disciplines as far as the legitimacy of how knowledge is created. So I decided to pursue this study, an empirical study that began with a desire to test and explore the copyright knowledge and understanding of digital writers, both students and teachers. I wanted a research design that could answer my research questions but might also appeal to audiences both from the law school and from rhetoric and composition—thus the empirical, mixed-methods approach. From this exploration grew the related examination of rhetorical invention in digital composing that eventually became central to my study; I realized that when writers are presented with a "writing problem" such as copyright law, they become inventive. And so my research originates somewhere in literatures at the intersection of work on composing process theory and scholarship on rhetorical invention. To my knowledge, no one has studied the copyright problem as a *problem of invention*. It is with this perspective I write this book.

Study Design

The book reports on an empirical study I conducted among digital writers, more specifically students and teachers in U.S. writing programs. The study explores U.S. copyright law's mediational influence on digital composing using, as characterized by John Creswell (2003), a sequential[3] transformative mixed-methods research design (see also Greene, 2007). The study is mixed methods because it uses both quantitative and qualitative approaches and because I approach the research with a certain frame of mind. Quantitative and qualitative approaches might be seen on a continuum, with quantitative methods often involving experiments, surveys, and counting (the use of numbers). Qualitative approaches in contrast depend more on narrative interpretations (although admittedly even the most numerical-based research methods rely on narrative to relay information to the reader). I used the quantitative survey to gather a broad view of the writers and the qualitative interviews to gather a narrower, deeper view. Rhetorical issues factored into my decision to use mixed methods because I want this study to be useful and acceptable to the maximum number of persons. Therefore I chose to use multiple approaches emanating from more than one knowledge claim, or what I call *rhetoric of truth*—I explain this more in chapter 3.

A major goal of the study is to investigate elements of rhetorical invention in digital-copyright contexts for writers in U.S. writing programs. A digital survey ($N = 334$) was administered to a randomly selected population of students and teachers, and discourse-based interviews were conducted with select writers as well. Among this population, some key areas examined are the role of rhetorical invention in digital writing, the status of knowledge and understanding of copyright law, and levels of "chilled digital speech" in light of copyright law. My research questions are:

1. What do writers know and understand about copyright and fair use?
2. How confident are writers in this knowledge?
3. Are writers unable to express themselves fully because of fear of copyright liability, that is, is their digital "speech" chilled?
4. How important do writers think knowledge of copyright and fair use is to their work?
5. What is the relationship, if any, between knowledge of copyright/ fair use, confidence in that knowledge, and levels of "chilled speech" in digital environments?
6. When writers create webtexts or write for the web, does their understanding of copyright law and fair use influence the choices that they make?
7. How do writers understand copyright law and fair use as they do rhetorical invention in digital writing?
8. How do writers reshape the law as written via their understanding (what happens as the external law becomes internalized)?

9. What other rhetorical topics are at work in writers' minds as they compose for the web, other than copyright and fair use?
10. What kinds of things do writing students need to know in order to be experts after they graduate or when they are writing outside of the educational setting?

Questions 1 through 5, and to a small degree question 9, are investigated in the survey. The interviews explore all the questions but are mainly focused on questions 6 through 10.

Prior to completing the full study that is the topic of this book, I also completed a 2006 pilot study with Dr. William Hart-Davidson (at the time I was a graduate student, and Hart-Davidson was my advisor): "Is There a Chilling of Digital Communication?" The pilot study was used to test and refine the research design used in the full study—the survey method and the discourse-based interview. However in the pilot just one writing program was studied—with a total participant number of twenty-three to twenty-seven students and four writing faculty (see Rife and Hart-Davidson, 2006 for a report on the pilot). The pilot was administered in face-to-face environments and a sixty-nine-question paper survey was used. The small study examined how understandings of copyright law and fair use shape student and teacher web writing and also examined levels of copyright knowledge. The pilot found certain gaps in knowledge existed among both students and faculty, but both thought knowledge of copyright and fair use was important. From the interviews, it was determined that copyright law functioned as a sort of inventional heuristic, like a design heuristic. (The pilot study is important to keep in mind because I do sometimes refer to it in this book.) To summarize the overall findings in the pilot, we found:

- Participants were aware of copyright and fair use issues.
- Some students had more copyright knowledge than some teachers (but overall teachers had slightly more knowledge).
- Writing students (and teachers) think copyright/fair use instruction should be part of their education.
- There is substantial confusion about the difference between the ethic of antiplagiarism and copyright/fair use.
- There are some misunderstandings about the differences between authorized and unauthorized use, that is, the nature and coverage of the fair use doctrine.
- There is misunderstanding about the government document exception to copyright.

Once the pilot was completed, I undertook this full study in order to further test, explore, and explain the findings of the pilot study—seeking a heuristic that might help visualize rhetorical invention in digital, copyright-imbued environments. In chapter 4, more specific details about discourse-based interviews along with a specific "walk-through" example and details on how I selected interviewees are provided.

The research for the full study was conducted primarily in cyberspace via the online survey and for the interviews primarily in a conference room at a midwestern university where participants attended as students. I chose to conduct the research with this population since I taught writing for ten years and digital writing about seven years; I am familiar with and interested in the population. The study population, that of U.S. writing programs and the students and teachers in those programs, was also selected because it self-identifies as having expertise in digital writing. Additionally, I offer this book as a sort of marker in time of where the field is with respect to its expertise on fair use and copyright, and of how important it actually thinks such issues are.

Digital Survey

I conducted the study in two phases; phase one is the survey, and phase two is the interviews. In the survey phase, I created a stratified, randomly selected population of 155 writing programs and writing majors taken from STC (Society for Technical Communication) and ATTW membership lists, and NCTE writing major lists as of September 2, 2007. As of this writing, these writing programs and majors do not have a single definitive publication listing, rating, and categorizing member programs. Therefore, in order to gather a full-view of such programs, I pieced together a master list of 232 programs based on the membership lists of three lists.

Programs were divided into five categories: PhD programs, MA programs, four-year programs, two-year programs, and certificate programs. For stratification of these five categories in the population and a comparison between the entire population of programs and those programs that had confirmed presence in the survey data, see table 1.1. Pragmatically, in order to conduct the random selection, I segmented the list of 232 programs into four random lists reflecting the program stratification of the larger list; students and teachers in programs appearing on three lists were administered the digital survey. The randomly selected stratified population was created by taking approximately 20% of the population in each of the five categories.[4]

In order to collect data with the digital survey, students and teachers in the 155 randomly selected programs were contacted directly with recruitment and reminder e-mails. E-mails included a link to the online survey. Between September 17, 2007, and November 2, 2007, a total of 1,935 recruitment e-mails were sent by me, with a total response rate before

Table 1.1. Comparison of stratified populations

Programs	Entire population (no.)	(%)	Survey population (no.)	(%)	Difference in survey population (%)
PhD	29	13	17	27	+14
MA	61	26	19	30	+4
Four-year	99	43	26	41	–2
Two-year	37	16	1	1	–15
Certificate	6	2	1	1	–1

survey attrition of 23%. A total of 446 digital writers began the survey, while 334 finished the entire survey. Sixty-four writing programs and/or writing majors confirmed response, for a programmatic response rate of 41% with 334 students (41%), teachers (47%), and "others" (12%) completing the entire twenty-nine-question digital survey (see appendix 1 for a list of participating institutions). The survey contained fifteen one-part and fourteen two-part questions and asked participants about knowledge and understanding of copyright law, confidence in that knowledge, and levels of chilled speech. For details on the survey findings, see chapters 2 and 3. Appendix 2 contains a copy of the survey; appendix 3 contains the answer key. In chapter 7, I discuss some very pragmatic ways to use the survey and its answer key as portable teaching tools.

Discourse-Based Interviews

About the time the survey was closed, I began phase 2 of the study, interviews with seven digital writers as we together examined their web compositions and the choices they made while composing. Discourse-based interviews use retrospective accounts of writing, are semistructured, and use strategies of stimulated elicitation (Odell, Goswami, and Herrington, 1983; Prior, 2004). Prior to interviews, sample texts were collected to provide a focus for interview questions. Interviews explore the research questions and interviewees' general understandings about copyright law and fair use in the context of digital composing, and interview data is used to add depth to and pull out details from the survey. Interviews are interpreted for relationships to survey results and connections to existing research on rhetorical invention such as discussed by Haller (2000). In the final stage of data analysis, I synthesize and transform the survey and interview data together—this synthesis is the focus of chapters 5 and 6.

The interviewees are (pseudonyms used to protect privacy):

- Leslie, a PhD candidate in rhetoric and composition on the job market
- Rob, a second year PhD student in rhetoric and composition studying in the U.S. but with Indian citizenship
- Jessie, a master's degree professional writing student finishing up her thesis and about to enter a PhD program
- Carey, a master's degree professional writing student who also works full-time at the educational institution where she studied
- Sarah, a recent master's degree professional writing graduate working in her own start-up web design business
- Amanda, a recent undergraduate professional writing degree holder, working for a national health organization
- Heather, a junior undergraduate professional writing major

As a method of data analysis, interview data was used to create multimedia vignettes of the participants as digital writers. The vignettes also record a marker in time of current digital writing practices. I include all seven of these vignettes in chapter 4.[5] Because the probing questions asked of each interviewee differed significantly, each interview creates a kind of portrait of a single digital writer at a single moment in time. For example, one student, Rob, is an international student, and so issues of international law arose during our discussion. Another student, Sarah, had recently graduated and was working as an independent contractor writing websites for nonprofit organizations and was also completing gift writing; copyright issues in this work arose. Amanda, another student, was working as an employee for a nonprofit health organization, and so work-for-hire and corporate authorship issues arose. Like the survey takers, interviewees were offered no payment or other remuneration although I sent them a short report on the study as well as an answer key for the survey.[6]

From the pilot study, I had derived the first five themes or "rhetorical topics" listed below, and after the full study, I developed all seven rhetorical topics as those subthemes emerging from digital writers' motivations and intentions in the composing choices they made:

1. Probabilities: Thinking/calculating of probabilities, risk, weighing consequences, strategizing that doesn't fit in the other categories.
2. Copyright: Using, applying, referencing copyright law such as asking permission, originality, and so on.
3. Fair use: Referencing fair use or the four-factor fair use test of Section 107 (fair use elements such as educational use, amount used, size, and so on).
4. Ethics: Ethical/political considerations including considerations of attribution.

5. Design: Issues of design/content rather than issues of copyright as influencing composing choices.
6. Culture: Reasoning based on one's cultural background or faith.
7. Employer requirements: Reasoning based on the demands or requirements of one's employer.

The seven rhetorical topics I list mediated digital writers' choices, and as I proceeded with data analysis, I hunted for ways to situate these rhetorical topics in relation to each other. I looked for evidence of patterns as well as the ways that these rhetorical topics might be embedded in each other and/or prioritized in writers' minds.

Methodology

Invention, Copyright, Digital Composing

The theoretical approach I used for the research entailed combining several strands and theories under an umbrella idea of an empirical mixed-methods study. To design the study and analyze data, I relied on a synthesis of classical and more contemporary theories in rhetoric studies, including theories on rhetorical invention, along with activity theory (AT), the work of Michel Foucault, and actor network theory (ANT). My approach going into this research after completing the pilot study is that rhetorical theory can be easily applied to a study involving copyright law because the law, like design guidelines and ethical considerations writers draw upon, functions within a guiding heuristic comprised of rhetorical topics. Connections have even been previously drawn between the classical topics and "actual arguments made by judges, philosophers, politicians, and others" (Bizzell and Herzberg, 1990, p. 1066). As a parallel example, Haller (2000) shows how design heuristics are similar to rhetorical topics because like topics, design heuristics generate invention, are applicable across a number of situations, and, like the special topics described by Aristotle, are bound to certain audiences. Similarly, copyright law is a heuristic or list of considerations at work if one wishes to know the legality of a use. Copyright law is an abstract concept but is applicable across a number of situations. U.S. copyright law (Copyright Law, Title 17, USC), enacted through Congress's constitutionally granted power under Article 1, Section 8, U.S. Constitution, is applicable to digital composing because this law provides automatic protection to any work that is *fixed* and *original* at the moment of its fixation. Something "original" and subsequently protectable under Section 102, Title 17, U.S. Copyright Law must have "origins" and must have those origins in an identifiable source, usually a single individual, an "author." Of course the "author" can also be an organization or a group of individuals, but nonetheless, there must be a single originating point, at least in theory, in order for copyright law to make sense. Pragmatically, if the author or his assigns are not locatable and that work is appropriated, no one will object, and so copyright law is irrelevant. Work having no author is work we might consider "common knowledge," community-owned knowledge, or knowledge in "the commons." "The commons" as a theoretical space is extremely complex, and so I take some time to map out "the commons" in chapter 5.

In the U.S., any original text, visual work, sound work, and so forth published to the web is automatically copyright protected (and throughout this book I refer to U.S. law unless otherwise expressly stated; references to "Section" are to a section within Title 17, United States Code). Protected works include notes, webpages, software, computer code, e-mails, reports, patterns, tutorials, instructions, manuals, visual works, video, audio works, and works in all other "fixed" media. Virtually all digital publishing then is going to invoke copyright law. Under current law, a copyright holder has the exclusive right to copy, distribute, perform/display, and create derivative works. Fortunately, relief from the copyright holder's monopoly is provided through the fair use doctrine as codified in Section 107 of the U.S. Copyright Act, Title 17, United States Code. This doctrine provides an exception to the copyright holder's exclusive rights and is heavily relied on in educational environments as students and teachers complete remixes, critical analysis, research, and mash-ups for purposes of teaching and learning (DeVoss and Webb, 2008; Dush, 2009; Ridolfo and DeVoss, 2009; Rife, 2006, 2007a, 2007b; Westbrook, 2009).

Section 107 provides the fair use heuristic. Fair use is defined as "reproduction in copies . . . or by any other means . . . [for uses] such as criticism, comment, news reporting, teaching (including multiple copies for classroom use), scholarship, or research." The four factors courts use to make legal determinations regarding infringement are listed in the statute and function as a legal heuristic guiding not only judges but also attorneys, users, authors, and others who attempt to make everyday composing decisions. Those four factors ask that one consider:

1. The purpose and character of the use, including whether such use is of a commercial nature or is for nonprofit educational purposes;
2. The nature of the copyrighted work (nonfiction has less protection that "creative" work);
3. The amount and substantiality of the portion used in relation to the copyrighted work as a whole; and
4. The effect of the use upon the potential market. (Section 107)

Copyright law provides a heuristic device to assess the legality of using another's copyrighted materials, and like Aristotle's special topics, copyright law is bound to a special audience, usually in the purview of copyright lawyers, but increasingly in sight of digital composers.

I rely primarily on the theory of Cynthia Haller and Janice Lauer for a theory of heuristics needed in this study in order to map out the mediational rhetorical topics drawn upon by digital writers. As Cynthia Haller (2000) points out, rhetorical considerations and design heuristics overlap, and I argue rhetorical considerations and copyright law overlap because like design heuristics, *copyright law is a system of invention organized by rhetoric*. Intellectual property issues are especially appropriate to examine with rhetoric because IP laws are formal systems of invention; Haller (2000) echoes McKeon (1998) in suggesting that "all systems of invention . . . are ultimately organized by rhetoric. . . . Aristotle's art of forethought governs both [rhetorical invention and design] processes" (Haller, 2000, p. 356). The U.S. "legal" system of invention exists in codified laws governing copyright, patent, trademark, and trade secret, and as such is organized by rhetoric. This system of invention embeds itself into rhetorical invention and the texts subsequently produced (as suggested by Bazerman (1999) and Brockmann (1988, 1998, 1999). In other words, a system of invention may leave traces in the texts it produces. These traces may be discovered and explored through research like mine, and if the researcher relies on a theory of heuristics, as I do, then the traces may be extracted, categorized, and theorized by developing and/or visualizing an inventional heuristic.[7] This work is the main focus of chapter 6.

J. Lauer (1970) suggests heuristics can be useful in developing a metatheory of rhetorical invention. According to Lauer, heuristics should have the elements of transcendency, flexible direction (that is, provide a "clear sequence of operations"), and generative power (J. M. Lauer, 1979, p. 268).[8] Two of Haller's observations can be mapped onto Lauer's invention-based metatheory for heuristics: generative power (Haller asserted design heuristics generate invention) and transcendency (Haller said that design heuristics are applicable across a number of situations); this leaves Lauer's concept of heuristics as a series of steps or a sequence of operations (flexible direction) as an addition to Haller's description. Based on my research with digital writers over the last several years, I also add that a heuristic might be evaluated by its ability to provoke the weighing of probabilities, a systematic weighing and balancing of elements, especially when composing in copyright-imbued digital environments.

In this study, I begin with a working understanding of heuristics as mediating rhetorical invention and as drawing upon rhetorical topics.

This inventional heuristic I seek, when invoked by digital writers, should include qualities of (1) transcendency, (2) flexible direction (it has steps, sequencing, or a hierarchy), and (3) generative power, (4) enabling the creation of arguments of probability based on the weighing and balancing of numerous variables (probability thinking), and finally, (5) (for special topics) connection to special audiences. The metatheory of invention I am seeking in my research develops with the idea that an inventional heuristic will contain these five qualities.

My question moving forward in this research centers on examining invention in a digital context in order to see how invention might look now, when our writing environment has changed so much from what it was even two decades ago. Rhetorical invention is a particularly apt concept with which to study digital writing because according to Richard E. Young (1978), it is thought of as *central* to traditional composing processes. Some theories of rhetorical invention put forward by scholars such as Janice Lauer, Cynthia Haller, Richard McKeon, Carolyn Miller, Richard Enos, and Robert Scott support the idea invention is not limited to simply providing strategies for arranging, drawing from, or discovering existing information, but rhetorical invention can also be used to create new, even novel information.[9] As Young points out, current-traditionalists are infamous for their rejection of invention as a central component in composition theory, relying instead on the idea that invention should come from other disciplines. But Lauer (Young's student; he sat on her doctoral committee) argues that if freshman English studies doesn't develop theories of invention applicable outside first-year writing, it "will never reach the status of a responsible intellectual discipline" (J. Lauer, 1970, p. 396). Young suggests theories of rhetorical invention could inform our understandings of writing in many contexts across the disciplines and in civic life.

The discussion on differences and overlap between the inventional concepts of discovering and arranging existing information or creating something novel is one rhetorician Carolyn Miller (2000) both explains and complicates in the framework of classical rhetoric. It's useful to delve into Miller's discussion because the novelty-discovery dichotomy can be mapped onto issues around copyright law, and I rely on Miller's concept of "the hunt" as well as her related discussion of *metis* in theorizing digital writing processes, especially in chapters 6 and 7. As she writes, the Latin and Greek verb *invent* originally held the sense of both novelty and discovery; the Aristotelian concepts of topos or topics and commonplaces as interpreted by Richard McKeon (1998) and Miller (2000) left space for both managerial (discovery) and generative (invention) functions; with origins in "place," literally, the Aristotelian concept of topos serves as a spatial metaphor and connects to Aristotle's term *ethos*, "its early sense being 'haunts' or 'the places where animals are usually found'" (Miller, 2000, p. 139). The conjectural paradigm "may be the oldest act in the intellectual history of the human race: the hunter squatting on the ground, studying the tracks of his quarry" (Carlo Ginzberg qtd. in Miller, 2000, p. 138). Carolyn Miller (2000) carefully links the use of hunting imagery to Renaissance vocabulary of invention (relying in part on Ong). She connects the hunt to the venatic or conjectural worldview and the quality of *metis*, "a quality frequently attributed to Odysseus, the polymetic, or many-skilled, the paragon of craftiness and cunning" (p. 138).

Venatic imagery persists in Cicero's, Quintilian's, and Aristotle's work (Miller, 2000, p. 139). The hunting imagery reminds us of invention's original conception as a habit of mind that brought together both the familiar and the unfamiliar—one hunts in a familiar location for something one expects to find—but has not yet found. Yet sometimes when hunting for thing A, a person instead finds thing B. However the finding of thing B is not totally unexpected, although it might be surprising. The act of hunting, like the act of researching, like the act of digital composing, is an act of *discovery in context*. As Carolyn Miller (2000) argues, "To be rhetorically useful, then, as well as comprehensible, novelty must be situated. Rather than offering the radically new, it must occupy the border between the known and the unknown" (p. 141). Miller's careful argument makes visible that "invention [as in novelty] and discovery are not so different. . . . What the hunter finds is never completely unexpected but may often be startling or surprising" (Miller, 2000, p. 143).

The Commonplace

That discovery and novelty are not so different is also illustrated in McKeon's (1998) observation of the paradox in commonplaces. A rhetoric-based theory of the commonplace is also important to this project because I discuss webtexts as commonplaces in chapter 4. Richard McKeon refutes the traditional notion that commonplaces serve only as catalogs of "prior knowledge and fixed clichés" (qtd. in Miller, 2000, p. 132). Instead, as does Miller, he sees the topos as places potentially leading to insights and novelty. Commonplaces are literally places where the familiar and unfamiliar can be brought together—through an exploratory combining of the new with the existing; McKeon argues that the commonplaces concept contains a paradox where the topoi can be both generative and managerial, novel and serving decorum, inventing and rediscovering, simultaneously (Miller, 2000, p. 132). Janice Lauer further documents differing theoretical views on the purpose of rhetorical invention ("to lead to judgments, reach new insights, locate arguments to support existing theses, solve problems, achieve identification . . . locate subject matter for texts" [J. M. Lauer, 2004, p. 3]), but all existing theories fit neatly into the two senses of rhetorical invention discussed by Carolyn Miller (2000): invention-as-novelty and invention-as-discovery.

Miller discusses ancient rhetorical concepts in the context of the hunt, but these concepts connect to contemporary theories of copyright law in a very fundamental way. The issue of whether a text is novel or original is pertinent to copyright law because the law protects original, fixed expression: the new, the novel. However copyright law also protects fixed work that isn't completely original as long as the new work has sufficiently transformed the previous work it draws upon. In order for a use to be "transformative," it must derive from an artifact that preceded it, thus the "discovery" element of copyright law. Just as in rhetorical theory, copyright law tacitly acknowledges there are degrees of originality or novelty, and that when a work moves far enough along the continuum toward pure novelty (in the U.S. there must be a "modicum of creativity" for a baseline finding of "originality" in the legal sense; see *Feist*, 1991), the work will be protected by copyright. Work that incorporates or draws upon preexisting and copyrighted work and does not transform that work enough might be deemed to have infringed the copyright of the previous creator. Both in Miller's interpretation and in the tacit workings of copyright law, inventing is the act of discovering the novel in context; it is like the hunt, arising from a certain way of making knowledge and then fixing that production in a tangible form of expression. When the digital writers I study make pragmatic content and design decisions in their web writing, they engage in a behavior similar to hunting. They "hunt" for content, and for reasons to make the "right" content decision. They use a set of guide marks, or heuristics, when making these decisions. This heuristic, guiding their "hunt," is a rhetorical-inventive heuristic.

Acknowledging this tension between the new and the old, the novel and the transformative, a number of scholars such as Dànielle Nicole DeVoss, Jim Ridolfo, and Lawrence Lessig have put forward theories of "remix" writing (see also DeVoss and Porter, 2006a; Gaylor, 2008). The idea of remix writing connects to the traditional theories around the commonplace and its relationship to invention. In the digital age, those specializing in writing are acknowledging the remixed nature of most texts, especially since the Internet allows quick access to information and others' work (but we have very little empirical evidence on this remixed nature of writing). Remix writing is a writing behavior and results in a finished product containing bits and pieces of other texts. This finished product stands in relationship to those other texts. Both the past and the present appear simultaneously in remix writing, and there's an element of anticipation (Ridolfo and Rife, 2011; Rife, 2008, 2010c). Those who remix might anticipate their own texts being continually revisited and appropriated by others. I extend my discussion of remix writing in chapters 4 and 5.

Activity Theory

Activity theory (AT), or the theories of Lev Vygotsky and followers Yrjo Engestrom and A. N. Leont'ev, was crucial in both my study design and data analysis. AT is a good fit for the research design because activity theory tries to provide a research paradigm that bridges the problem in research between "macro" (the survey) and "micro" (the interviews) units of analysis. There are two specific reasons for the use of AT in this study. The first is that in the study's phase 2, Vygotsky's research methodology is helpful. While I approach authorship with a basic understanding that writing takes place in a system with many actors, and does not just emanate from a single human being, I did interview *individual* writers just as did Flower and Hayes, Emig, and Perl. Of course for purely pragmatic reasons it would be very challenging if not impossible to simultaneously interview all the "authors" of a webtext, ever, because one would not be able to hear their voices in the din of multiplicity. For this reason, Vygotsky's activity theory is useful because according to Vygotsky, an individual's ability to write comes through "mastery of an external system" (1997, p. 133). In order to write, a child internalizes the external system. This system is a product of cultural development.

Since individuals, under the Vygotskian activity theory view, have internalized the system, a researcher is not required to exclusively study the system to learn about or acknowledge the system at work; elements of the system or architecture can be teased out from interactions with the individual (interviews, observations, screen-capturing, study of compositions) during a research project. While activity theory researchers and scholars such as Roth and Lee (2007) and to a greater extent Spinuzzi (2003, 2007) have used activity theory to study large systems, Vygotsky himself studied *individuals* in order to trace development, what I term invention, within the larger culture—thus his theory is very useful for justifying my research methods as well as analyzing the data.

Vygotsky's basic method of researching individuals, what he called development and what I call invention, included placing individuals in situations where their routine was disrupted (giving a child a broken pencil and asking him to create a drawing); providing more than one route to problem solving (placing candy on a shelf above the child's reach but providing a number of everyday artifacts the child might use to reach the candy); and posing for participants a task that exceeds their knowledge (giving memory quizzes in which artifacts are available that participants might organize and use to recall information). Similarly, copyright issues potentially interrupt and complicate composing for the web. So an examination of the law's intersection with web writing provides a readymade research scene leveraging the research tools Vygotsky used to explore what those in rhetoric and composition call invention. The copyright problem disrupts routine writing methods, provides more than one route to a solution, and depending on writers' knowledge, poses a task exceeding writers' knowledge and abilities. To research the presence and influence of copyright law on digital composing choices is to insert oneself into the inventional process. I discuss my reliance on Vygotsky's research methods and their relationship to researching invention in more detail in chapter 7.

The second reason I rely on AT is that it offers the concept of mediation, which is very useful as I theorize the way copyright law might factor into composing choices. Mediation assists the researcher who wants to complicate issues of control—the operation of power, in a given research situation, beyond the simple explanation of cause and effect. In figure 1.1, the traditional social psychology model for understanding human behavior shows the two components that influence behavior—one the person, or two, the environment. An example of how legal literature tries to explain the fact that individuals violate copyright law appears in an article by legal scholar Jessica Litman (2004). Litman argues individuals violate copyright law because it is *human nature* to "share." Biology or "inherent free will" are the only explanations offered (Engestrom, 1999, p. 29). Lev Vygotsky developed his theory *as a refutation of the stimulus-response view* of human behavior. Under AT, human (writing) behavior merits a more complex explanation—artifacts like copyright law mediate behaviors rather than cause simple nonreflective actions as I discuss in chapter 6.[10]

In early composing process/inventional theories, an explicit discussion of mediation, or the "invisible" role of inventional heuristics, in actual

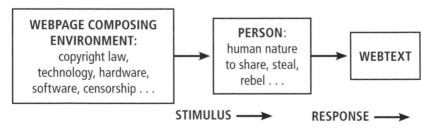

Figure 1.1. A traditional social science stimulus-response model. In a traditional social psychology framework, the person (as a container of variables) coordinates a task (creating a webtext) with the environment. The environment or human nature, or both, causes the person to make composing choices. Copyright law is part of the environment, one of many parts that the actor takes into account when composing for the web. Contrast this to the activity theory triangle in figure 6.2.

composing processes is lacking.[11] Lauer states how we might evaluate inventional heuristics, but she did not show us how such inventional heuristics might mediate writing. While other composition theorists such as Emig, Perl, and Flower and Hayes imply that their inventional models kind of *float in space* rather than function as a "stimulus" to a writer's response, they never really theorize this aspect of their ideas, and they certainly do not discuss the concept of mediation. I hope this book extends the work of our original composition theorists and scholars who brought us light years ahead of where we were at the time by simply providing (or so it seems simple in hindsight) models where writing processes could indeed become the subject of serious research. AT and its accompanying concept of mediation is increasingly used by those studying composing processes (see, for example, Hart-Davidson, 2007; Geisler and Slattery, 2007). The concept of mediation is additionally useful for explaining behavior, cultural movement, cultural change, and even individual change and learning that is unexplainable in the traditional social science stimulus-response model. Explanations grounded in activity theory assist understandings of digital writers' lawfulness or unlawfulness (why won't digital writers obey copyright law?). Activity theory also assists in understanding political action in the area of copyright restraints on free expression, and changes or proposed changes in the copyright law itself.

Foucault with ANT in the Mix

In addition to using the theories and methods of Lev Vygotsky, my research design, analysis, and interpretation of data depends heavily on the work of Michel Foucault for two main reasons. The first is the nature of Foucault's work; his methodological analysis, based in genealogy and archaeology, is very helpful in an exploration of authorship, which is ultimately a search for origins, a tracing of networks, an excavation into the contributions and motivations that make up a webtext. Since, as Gutter points out, most of Foucault's books are histories, Foucault returns to the issue of origins in many of his works, and I will further explore this concept and its relationship to digital writing in chapter 5. It is very helpful that Foucault's most famous essay, "What Is an Author?"—an essay containing ideas Foucault continued to develop in subsequent writings (Gutting, 2005)—is specifically focused in large part on unpacking the traditional understanding of literary authors—one person and his book. Foucault's theory then can help inform traditional composing process theories that have not yet necessarily taken into account the digital age.

However actor network theory was also important to clarify and remediate Foucault's discussion of authors and origins because ANT, also a theory examining the operation of power, more clearly authorizes the acknowledgment, through its ideas of radical symmetry and actor networks, that things (like copyright law and the technologies and architectures of digital writing) and entities as well as people can be actors—and, by deduction, can be authors. As I will explain in chapter 5, Foucault does authorize this view as well, but he is not very clear about it, and he tends to always return to a focus on linguistic structures or discourse. In fact, commentator Gary Gutting proposes that Foucault had a "fascination with avant-garde literature" (2005, p. 19). Though Foucault's acknowledgement of the agency of "things" is present in his work, it tends to be more tacit than how such theory is presented in the work of John Law and Bruno Latour. And so by blending together Foucault's idea of the "author-function" and ANT's ideas of actor networks and radical symmetry, I move forward in this project with an understanding of "author-function" both as an activity occurring prior to the formation of "author" and as an operation working to reconstitute the author after he has emerged within a network. This view of author-function that I have developed comes out of data analysis and interpretation as well as my working with both Foucault's theory and ANT. I further discuss these ideas throughout the book, but especially in chapter 5.

The second reason Foucault's work is relied upon in my project is that Foucault's theory of how power works as both a productive and disciplinary force is appropriate to use in the context of a study about law and the writers I examine who are working at least in part within the structure of the educational institution. In copyright contexts, Foucault offers a new lens through which to understand how copyright law and events like stakeholder antistealing media blitzes function. Foucault offers two examples of how power works to produce discourses. His two examples are the communities or colonies created by leprosy and the separating and dividing caused by the plague (Foucault, 1977, p. 198–99). In the twenty-first century, the "binary branding and exile of the leper" is compared to branding individuals as copyright violators, (copyright) terrorists, (copyright) criminals, and hackers (see Reyman, 2010; Logie, 2006b). And the disciplinary mechanisms as products of fear of plague are the same kinds of mechanisms that arise via stakeholders' fear of copyright violators. The "existence of a whole set of techniques and institutions for measuring, supervising and correcting the abnormal brings into play the disciplinary mechanisms to which the fear of the plague gave rise" (Foucault, 1977, p. 199). The increasingly potent disciplinary mechanisms of U.S. copyright law have arisen from the fear that one's property will be unjustly appropriated in such a fashion as to deprive stakeholders from what they perceive as due profit. Notice that here the fear on the part of copyright holders produces more and more copyright restrictions; this is in contrast to the fear on the part of student writers and their teachers of violating copyright law

(Westbrook, 2006). Fear is powerful on either side of the copyright debate.

The dividing techniques that Foucault refers to are seen in copyright laws' categorizing of behavior and enumerated set of punishments (higher damages for willful and wanton infringement). This is true with all formal U.S. laws, not just copyright laws. In a less negative context, the coexisting community building and individual sustaining nature of U.S. law is easy to locate. The Constitution of the United States preamble begins: "We the People of the United States, in Order to form a more perfect Union, establish Justice, insure domestic Tranquility, provide for the common defense" (1787/1991, p. 1). The "people" are a union, a community like those isolated in leper colonies, but comprising the union are individuals—like those with the plague, marked, separated, and counted each night. The construct of the individual, like the construct of the author, according to Foucault, realizes the political dream of a disciplined society. A disciplined society contradicts "all forms of confusion and disorder" (Foucault, 1977, p. 199) Constructing the individual counters potential chaos. The Fourteenth Amendment is an easy place to find a reference to the individual: "nor shall any State deprive any person of life, liberty, or property, without due process of law" (1787/1991, p. 26). The U.S. courts and legislatures thus spend much time balancing the interests of common good against the interests of preserving individuals' rights. Every time this effort is sought through law, it reinscribes the categories of individual and union.

Foucault's discussions of how power produces discourses that serve to regulate human behavior are useful when examining the law's influence on digital composing because Foucault flattens the connotations and disconnects existing relationships that might cloud a researcher's observations (in this Foucault's purposes are similar to the goals of ANT). But Foucault does not clearly connect the law-function and the author-function in his discussions of what might be very simply described as cultural dividing activities and grouping activities that are continually bumping up against each other. The grouping practices that rounded up the lepers and placed them in a colony were used to exclude others, but also to build a community. The dividing practices that marked off those with the plague and separated them from others both disciplined and individuated but were also used to group. Both the dividing and grouping practices Foucault discusses function to organize meaning, organize knowledge production, and counter potential chaos. If Foucault had more clearly connected his discussion of law-function and author-function as similar functions emanating from activities organizing meaning, we might have been able to derive a more robust understanding of the cultural activities and operations that produce the "author." In chapter 5, I try to further develop this understanding.

Brief Chapter Summaries

Chapters 2 and 3 focus specifically on the study's first phase, the digital survey. Chapter 2 outlines basic survey findings, while chapter 3 further discusses survey outcomes in the context of the rhetorical construction of truth. Chapter 4 focuses on phase 2 of the study, the interviews. Details on the discourse-based interview method are provided, as are individual multimedia vignettes of the seven writers I studied in the interview phase. Chapters 5 and 6 synthesize both study phases, with chapter 5 developing a remixed theory of authorship relying heavily on Foucault. Chapter 6 provides a visualization and accompanying discussion of the inventional heuristic emanating from the study and draws upon AT and ANT. I conclude the book in chapter 7 by discussing implications from this project—implications for research, teaching, curriculum design, and public advocacy towards changing copyright law.

2

The Meaning of Misunderstanding among Digital Writers

In this chapter, I analyze the survey data gathered in the first phase of the study by examining the presence of certain variables such as number of students, teachers, and other participants; levels of copyright knowledge among the population; and levels of chilled speech. In the next chapter, I continue the discussion I start here and examine possible differences between the presences of certain variables in particular populations, such as the difference between knowledge levels among students and teachers. It is in the context of examining differences that I discuss the rhetorical nature of statistical analysis in a comparative context. In the next chapter, I also examine the relationships between the occurrences of certain variables. I discuss whether or not my stated hypotheses and research questions are supported and answered. This chapter and the next are concluded with a discussion of implications based on survey results.

The digital survey, phase 1 of the mixed-methods study, examines a large population's attitudes, knowledge, and behavior in the context of copyright law. I also use the survey to learn more about the population. The twenty-nine-question survey is broken into six subsections (see appendix 2). In the first three sections, A, B, and C, survey participants are asked a few screening questions on whether they accept the terms and whether they ever composed and published to the web. In section C, the "digital writing" section, participations are asked the "ethics question," whether it is more important to obey the law or follow one's conscience. In this section, they are also asked about their educational level. The survey's fourth part, "Section D: How Chilled Is Your Speech," contains six questions measuring whether or not one's digital speech is chilled. In the fifth section of the survey, on knowledge and understanding" (hereinafter referred to as "section E"), participants are asked a total of fourteen substantive questions on basic copyright law and the fair use four-factor test of Section 107. These questions also explore participants' knowledge of the differences between unauthorized use via fair use and authorized use though permission and licensing. For example, a question that tests participant's knowledge of how fair use applies only in the case of unauthorized use reads: "If you ask a copyright holder for permission to use their material in your own original web composition, and they say no, this means you absolutely cannot use the copyright holder's material under fair use."

The best answer is false because fair use does not require permission and is often relied upon when permission is not given, as in the case of the requester's desire to create a parody (copyright holders are unlikely to agree to permit someone to parody their work) or even when the copyright holder's demanded usage fee is deemed unreasonable by the permissions seeker (see *Bill Graham Archives* [2006] and *Campbell v. Acuff-Rose* [1994] for examples). Some questions in this part are based on existing online quizzes, but many also echo Waller (2006a, 2006b) and Howard's (2004) fair use inquiries (see Dush, 2009 for a recent treatment of the student-copyright-knowledge issue). In formulating the questionnaire, I also used my training as a lawyer specializing in intellectual property (particularly copyright), as I am admitted to practice in two states with an active license in one. It's worth noting here that section E of the survey is intended to be a portable teaching tool and, like the rest of the survey, could as well be used as a future research tool. While I analyze the survey results here and in the next chapter, in chapter 7 I specifically focus on how section E and derivations of it can be used in the classroom.

After each knowledge question in section E, participants are asked how certain they are in their answer, with 1 being "very certain" and 5 being "not certain at all." The idea here is to examine whether a correlation exists between understanding and confidence levels. I explore whether any empirical data might emerge supporting the general statement that individuals are confused and uncertain about copyright law and/or fair use, an argument used to support the assertion that such individuals are thus fearful of fully expressing themselves when composing for the web (that is, their speech is "chilled"). In the final four-question section of the survey (section F), participants are asked how important they think knowledge and understanding of copyright law is to their work as digital writers. They are also asked how they primarily describe themselves, as student, teacher, or other; they are asked to specify their institution, and finally students are asked if they are willing to participate in an interview. Survey responses are anonymous unless participants volunteer identities.[1]

In a mixed-methods study, the goal is to synthesize the findings from the qualitative and quantitative methods (in this case, the interviews and the large survey). I will do that. But because of the survey's novelty,

I discuss the survey in this chapter as a kind of stand-alone study in order to provide a view into the first layer of examination. The survey results make visible well-defined areas of misunderstanding and understanding about copyright among writing students and their teachers. In my analysis, I reason through these misunderstandings to show that in some respects they make sense. In other words, misunderstanding as evidenced by getting an objective knowledge (cognitive) copyright question incorrect may be evidence that understanding copyright is not going to derive from drill and practice because "misunderstanding" is more than just "being wrong."

As evidenced in results from section E, areas of marked misunderstanding among the survey population (writing students, teachers, and "others"— "others" are those not self-identifying as either students or teachers and are likely recent alums of writing programs) include confusion on the difference between plagiarism and copyright, confusion on the difference between authorized and unauthorized use of others' copyrighted materials, not knowing about the U.S. government's exception to copyright protection, and misunderstanding that U.S. copyright law gives "creative" work more protection than "factual" work. An area of clear *understanding* among the survey population is that derivative works are protected under copyright law.

Other findings emerge from the survey as well. For this group of writers, ethical considerations trump legal considerations, that is, the majority of survey respondents are willing to break the law on exceptional occasions if the law is wrong. Further, while there is some discussion about how much fear copyright is striking into the hearts of writers/researchers (Ad Hoc Committee, 2010; Fisher and McGeveran, 2006; Heins and Beckles, 2005; Hobbs, Jaszi, and Aufderheide, 2007; Porter, 2005; Westbrook, 2006), ultimately research here finds writers express themselves although perhaps not in the fashion they most prefer. In other words, copyright law did not chill speech to the extent there is silence, but it did shape speech. Digital writers are not as "uncertain" about their knowledge of copyright and fair use as some might predict. They have a relatively stable confidence level regarding their own understanding of the law. Overwhelmingly, the survey finds the writing community believes knowledge of copyright is important to their work as digital writers.

On a pragmatic level, the survey's administration makes visible that a survey is a piece of writing, and while this may seem obvious, it often is not. Surveys are usually viewed as the purview of social scientists and are not normally coupled with writing instruction or expertise in writing.[2] Since conducting this study, I examine the writing quality in surveys, and often it is severely lacking. I am referring to basic tenants of good writing like adequate focus, organization, conciseness, and clarity. This is an area for further research, but in the next chapter, I offer some basic pointers as far as constructing a well-written survey, one that folks will not find too confusing or time consuming.

For the survey, I wrote screening questions (appearing in table 2.1) to screen out anyone who had not created and published a web composition. A couple of keys points arise from these survey question results. The first is regarding the population. While the population consisted of what I name "students, teachers, and others," the one quality these individuals all share is that they are writers, digital writers who have published to the web at least once in their life. In addition to their participation in writing major and/or institutional websites across the U.S., the fact that they are digital writers is the singular commonality that holds them together as a "population." The other key point that arises from these initial screening questions is that, as illustrated in table 2.1, the reported results throughout this chapter show a changing N due to survey attrition. When the N changes, the reliability of the results and propriety of generalizing the participants to a larger population also changes. The greater the N, the greater the reliability. This is why larger populations are desirable; they give more certainty in the results.

Table 2.1. Two screening questions

	Yes (%)	No (%)	N
1. Have you ever completed a web composition such as a web page, web space, wiki, blog, page on facebook/myspace, or other social networking software application?	91	9	437
2. Has the web composition been posted to the web such that it's available to at least some people (other than yourself or your teacher) with Internet access and a computer?	98	2	395

I am going to discuss statistics here, but I want to give my discussion a rhetorical frame, further expanded in the next chapter. For this I rely in part on the work of Derek Rowntree (2004), particularly his book *Statistics without Tears*, a book introduced to me during a quantitative research methods course I took in graduate school (see also MacNealy, 2009; Hacking, 1991). I did take this course outside of the Rhetoric and Writing Program, and outside the College of Arts and Letters, where I worked on my PhD. This is just a small factor that points to the lack of attention to quantitative research methods in rhetoric and composition and other humanities-focused disciplines. I reiterate here that the reason I am taking care in discussing statistics through a rhetorical lens in the context of my survey is to illustrate to those readers who might be a bit resistant to the idea of a legitimate place for such methods in the humanities that all research methods have a substantial rhetorical component in their constitution. I am trying to address the concerns of readers who are skeptical about these types of methods as fitting properly in rhetoric and composition. A "battle" has been documented in composition and rhetoric over the "trustworthiness between a number and a narrative" (Johanek, 2000, p. 16). Johanek argues the narrative currently wins simply because that particular method of producing knowledge is more highly valued in the field.

In contrast, some might plausibly argue that collecting observations via the personal narrative provides less accurate and subsequently "less true" information than quantifying observations. For example, Rowntree (2004) argues that scientists are more honest than others about the chances that their assertions are erroneous. I cannot say I agree with him on his assessment of honesty levels among scientists as compared to lawyers, writing teachers, writing students, and so on, but it is clear that in science, an effort is made to explicitly quantify, describe, and put out in the open, if you will, the probability of error. Rowntree (2004) insightfully writes, "There is no such thing as absolute 100% proof in science (or out of it). All we have is probability and levels of confidence. People with a claim to be scientists are simply more honest about it than others—at least when they are acting scientifically. The risk of error is quantified and stated" (Rowntree, 2004, p. 121). While likely not intentionally doing so, Rowntree discusses statistics rhetorically—pointing to how statistics in fact make use of the argument from probability, the ancient method studied by George Kennedy.

With reference to table 2.1, an N of 437 yields a confidence level of plus or minus 4.9%, while an N of 395 yields a slightly lower confidence level (Lauer and Asher, 1988). For example, if 91% of the respondents had completed a web composition, we can be confident that 91% of the entire population also completed a web composition, plus or minus 4.9% (86.1%–95.9% in the entire population thus created a web composition). By the end of the survey, the N falls to 334, yielding a confidence level of about 5.6%. Therefore, throughout the survey the confidence level is between 5.6% and 4.9% with an overall response rate of 23%.

The Variables

Generally, a survey can gather information about individuals and take measurements of their attitudes, cognition, and behavior (Babbie, 2004; Backstrom and Hursh-Cesar, 1981; Rife, 2010a, 2010b, 2010c). In order to keep the survey as short as possible and thus as little intrusive as possible, I kept my gathering of demographic information to the bare minimum. Demographic variables measured in the survey include educational level;

the participant's status as student, teacher, or other; and the participant's institutional affiliation. Attitude about copyright law is measured by asking participants how important they consider knowledge of copyright/ fair use. Participants are further asked to indicate their attitude towards whether ethics is above the law in some cases, that is, are they willing to break the law on exceptional occasions, or should the law be obeyed without question. The "cognitive" questions in the survey's section E are the knowledge questions (what do you know about copyright . . .) and fit into two categories: (1) objective knowledge, and (2) confidence in that knowledge. In the objective knowledge category, I designed fourteen questions and used those questions to test participants' objective knowledge of copyright/fair use. In the confidence category, participants' confidence in their knowledge is tested with a five-point scale offered (very certain, somewhat certain, undecided/can't answer, not too certain, not certain at all). Following each of the fourteen knowledge questions is a confidence question: "How sure are you that your answer is correct?" In addition to surveying students, teachers, and others in writing programs on demographics, attitude, and knowledge, I also tested their copyright behavior by asking them six questions measuring levels of chilled speech. The question of whether or not digital writers' speech is chilled due to copyright law turned out to be a little more complicated than I originally anticipated, as I will discuss momentarily.

Analysis of the Survey Data

I begin this analysis with demographics so that you know a few details about the survey population, the digital writers. Regarding the respondents' educational level, as table 2.2 illustrates, the survey data shows that 20% of the respondents are undergraduates, 13% are master's students, 25% are PhD students, 1% are undergraduate degree or certificate holders, 40% are graduate or professional degree holders, and 1% are "other." This question asks for the highest educational level and appeared early in the questionnaire (question 5 out of twenty-nine questions). Based on this data, almost 60% self-identify as students of some sort, and 40% self-identify as graduate degree/professional degree holders.

Near the end of the survey, participants are asked to self-identify as either students, teachers, or others: "How would you primarily describe yourself?" Between the beginning and end of the survey, survey respondents went from almost 60% students to 41% students, indicating that the attrition rate is higher for students than teachers. The reason for this cannot be known with certainty, but it could be that the content questions are a little long and complicated, and students may have been involved in other kinds of coursework that had priority over the survey. It could be that only

Table 2.2. Educational level

Please pick the choice that best describes your *highest* educational level:

Under-graduate student	Master's student	PhD student	Undergrad degree/ certificate holder	Graduate/ professional degree holder	Other/ can't answer	N
20%	13%	25%	1%	40%	1%	384

the more savvy students decided to stay in the survey for the duration or that teachers better understood the benefits of taking the entire survey as far as generating knowledge. Ultimately though, by the end of the survey, the population of students to teachers is almost equal—providing a good measure of how the population as a whole understood copyright.

As I noted earlier, the survey tests attitude about copyright by asking whether respondents would obey their conscience rather than the law if the right circumstances arose and also asks respondents how important they think copyright law is to their work as digital writers. Table 2.3 shows the results of what I call the "ethics question." This survey question examines whether a variable might be at work outside the law. If ethical considerations influence digital writers more than legal considerations, that could influence the lawfulness of digital writers: their "copyright behavior." It may also influence their copyright attitudes and even their knowledge of copyright (or motivation for obtaining that knowledge). A single question is not adequate to truly measure how lawfully a respondent might act in a given situation, but the response might indicate the need for further investigation or provide support for interview data.

The question I use, appearing in table 2.3, is taken directly from the GSS Social Science 1972–2000 Cumulative Codebook (GSSDIRS). Questions from the codebook have been tried and tested thousands of times, and other comparison data sets are often available. The question is also available through an International Social Survey Program ISSP ("a continuing annual programme of cross-national collaboration on surveys covering topics important for social science research") (Collins, 2007). According to Collins, many countries use these survey questions to make local and international comparisons. The codebook questions are also used in social science and statistics classes because free datasets are available. In the digital writing population studied, 73% would follow their conscience, 14% would obey the law, and 13% could not answer. This might be compared to a 1983–1984 British survey that compares weekly churchgoers with those of no religion. In that survey, 57% of the weekly churchgoers said they would obey the law, while 44% of the no-religion participants selected that same answer (Gill, 1999). Robin Collins (2007) reports results of this question's use to compare individuals in the U.S. and Canada in the context of deference to authority, free speech, and democracy. He reports that at one time the question was administered by blind ballot to an audience of twenty "humanists" where 100% selected that one should "follow their conscience." This question has been administered to the international community with global comparisons available. Some examples of results include the U.S., where 42.7% would obey the law without exception, while 57.3% would follow their conscience. In Canada, 25.1% would obey the law while 74.9% would follow their conscience. In France, 15.2% would obey the law, while 84.8% would follow their conscience (Collins, 2007). Perhaps folks in my study are more humanist than the general U.S. population. However data also shows that as educational level in the U.S. increases, so does the willingness to follow one's conscience over the law on occasion (Collins, 2007). My study results support these findings since a significant number of individuals taking the questionnaire had advanced degrees, and all had at least some formal education—and are situated in a field often associated with the humanities. The results from my survey then should not surprise anyone.

Table 2.3. Obeying the law (the ethics question)

	Obey	Follow conscience	Can't answer	N
In general, would you say that people should obey the law without exception, or are there exceptional occasions on which people should follow their consciences even if it means breaking the law?	14%	73%	13%	384

In another attitude question, I measure how important respondents feel knowledge and understanding of copyright and fair use is to their work. As illustrated in table 2.4, only 1% think such knowledge is not important. Almost 100% believe that such knowledge is at least somewhat important, with 79% stating that knowledge of copyright is either important or very important. Almost half of those participating thought that knowledge and understanding of copyright is very important. This coincides with my experience teaching writing over the last decade at more than one higher education institution. As years pass, copyright becomes a greater focus, and at this point both writing students and their teachers want to know

Table 2.4. How important is knowledge of copyright?

How important do you think it is, as a digital writer, that you have some knowledge and understanding of copyright and fair use laws in the United States?

Not very important	Somewhat important	Neutral/ can't answer	Important	Very important	N
1%	19%	1%	31%	48%	334

more. Information on copyright and fair use has started to appear even in first-year writing courses. My survey provides empirical data that this is an area of interest to individuals associated with U.S. writing programs.

Next I am going to discuss results from the cognitive or "knowledge" questions, those questions testing participants' knowledge and understanding of copyright law as well as confidence in that knowledge (section F). The fourteen knowledge questions are organized to test three areas. Eight questions are devoted to whether the writer understood the basic elements and protections of fair use per Section 107 of the statute. Five questions examine digital writers' understanding of the differences between the right to use someone else's materials in context of authorized versus unauthorized use. For example, the questions explore whether writers knew the difference between using with express permission, using under a license like Creative Commons, using texts that are not copyright protected, and using under the fair use doctrine. One question explored writers' understanding of the difference between the ethic of antiplagiarism and the considerations of the fair use doctrine. I have named this the "plagiarism question."

For global views of this populations' scores on the section F knowledge portions, I include only those who finished the entire survey (N = 334). The average score for the entire fourteen-question set on copyright/fair use knowledge is 63%. Based on a traditional grading rubric where 70% is around a 2.0, or adequate, the average score for the entire population falls short of "passing." On the other hand, considering the complexity of the subject matter and the questions themselves, and considering I tested *writing* students and teachers (not *law* students and professors) on an area some see as the exclusive domain of $300 per hour intellectual property lawyers, 63% is a remarkable accomplishment. With respect to confidence levels, the average certainty score for the entire population is 2.3—that is, somewhere between "somewhat certain" and "not too certain," indicating that as a whole, the population has awareness of its lack of knowledge (if the average certainty score is closer to 1 [very certain] with an average test score of 63%, we would have much more cause for concern). In a utopian world, 100% of the survey respondents would have received 100% on the knowledge scores and a 1 on the certainty score. That is, they would have high knowledge and lots of confidence. But for 100% of each of the fourteen questions, the majority of respondents answered "somewhat certain" (a 2 on the 5 point scale) regarding their confidence level.

Although some previous scholarship might cause one to predict that digital writers would be quite uncertain about their own level of copyright knowledge (see, for example, Ad Hoc Committee, 2010; Hobbs, Jaszi, and Aufderheide, 2007; Westbrook, 2006), the data here indicates that individuals are neither very confident nor very uncertain about their own knowledge level but instead are somewhere in the middle. If respondents are in fact extremely unsure, the data should show a lower average certainty score—perhaps closer to 5: "not certain at all." If respondents feel extremely lost and confused, we should be seeing the majority selecting "not too certain" rather than "somewhat certain" in at least some locations of the survey. It can be stated though that to the extent existing scholarship states writing students and their teachers have uncertainty about their own understanding of copyright law, my survey supports that (since respondents almost unanimously answer in between "somewhat certain" and "not too certain"). These digital writers on average are neither extremely confident nor extremely confused about their own knowledge level (although in some areas as I discuss momentarily, they are extremely confused about the provisions of U.S. copyright law). However the individuals who responded to the survey are probably more tech savvy and knowledgeable about copyright and fair use than those who did not respond since they may have had an interest in the topic when they received the recruitment e-mail. Further, those who took the survey are those already publishing to the web—a group likely more knowledgeable and confident on issues around copyright and fair use. That may explain the relatively high confidence level of this particular population of survey respondents.

The Meaning of Misunderstanding

The average score for the five questions on licensing versus fair use, or authorized versus unauthorized use, is 51%. This is also one cognitive area that interviewees (in the qualitative portion of the study) note is of concern for them. The average score for the eight fair use questions is 71%, indicating greater understanding in this area. On the other hand, in responses to the "plagiarism question" (table 2.5), less understanding is expressed about differences between the ethical doctrine of antiplagiarism and its requirement of attribution, versus fair use, which does not require attribution. On the plagiarism question, 49% of respondents are wrong, yet 60% feel at least somewhat certain their answers are correct. The meaning of the misunderstanding might be explained by looking at the kind of cultural capital circulating in academia. Attribution of one's work, one's contribution to the field in advancing knowledge, is what propels one forward under disciplinary metrics. Using another's texts or creations is strongly favored in academia if and only if that use comes alongside attribution. The confusion between antiplagiarism's requirement for attribution, first and foremost, and copyright's limitation on the simple right to copy makes sense in the academic community. The ethic of antiplagiarism might easily be characterized as having the force of law in disciplinary life. In fact, the survey data shows the requirement of attribution is conflated to a legal requirement and meshes together with whatever restrictions copyright law might impose upon a creator. Although there is a marked misunderstanding for half the population, the remaining half of the population did see the significant difference between copyright and the ethic of antiplagiarism. Yet half of the population's having this kind of misunderstanding, especially among individuals who are supposed to be experts in writing, is significant and certainly is something to be addressed either through curriculum or professional development or both.

Table 2.5. Knowledge and understanding: the plagiarism question

The single most important thing U.S. courts look at when deciding whether a particular use is fair is whether the original author has been attributed or credited.	True	False	Best Answer	N
	49%	51%	False	340

Confidence level	Very certain	Somewhat certain	Undecided/ can't answer	Not too certain	Not certain at all
	14%	46%	14%	21%	5%

Such particularly focused misunderstanding between copyright and the ethic of antiplagiarism also develops and informs Foucault's "author-function" concept and helps theorize the operation of power in this particular instance (by considering the author-function as an activity that deploys certain strategies that organize and even impede what would otherwise be a free flow of information). Understanding Foucault's theory (his theory the way I remediate and remix it in order to bring it into the twenty-first century) under this new light might help in the teaching of and theorizing about writing. Copyright law supports the author-function because it says who can and cannot speak and in what context. Plagiarism also does the same; citation practices reinscribe the idea of a single author by reminding us of him forever and ever. The requirement to cite impedes the flow of information because it slows us down in our writing practices. We further have been conditioned and expect to see citations in the materials we read so that we can understand where the material came from. The author and the citation operate as a screen through which information must first pass before we can properly receive it. The fact that a significant number of participants are confusing copyright and plagiarism seems justified and predictable when we consider that both copyright law and citation practices and the expectations around these two networks work both to produce the "author" and then, post-production, continually to remind us that somewhere along the way, there has been an "author," although each strategy uses different methods to do so.

Further, we even have at least one instance where a U.S. court conflated the notions of plagiarism and copyright infringement—further setting the stage for confusion between these concepts within the larger population. In the *Bright Tunes* (1976) case, George Harrison was sued by the copyright holder Bright Tunes over Harrison's alleged copyright infringement of the Chiffons' 1962 song "He's So Fine," written by Ronald Mack. At issue was Harrison's 1970 song "My Sweet Lord." After the court elaborates in its judicial opinion on the inventional processes going in to the composing of "My Sweet Lord," and notes that Harrison not only admitted having awareness of the original song but also that "He's So Fine" had been number 1 on the Billboard charts in the U.S. and England for extended periods of time, the court decides that copyright infringement did take place due to Harrison's subconscious "plagiarizing" of the Mack-Chiffons' song. The court states: "It is clear that My Sweet Lord is the very same song as He's So Fine with different words." In the short opinion itself, the court actually uses the term "plagiarism" in two places, even though the legal action is one on copyright infringement. Here we can explain the court's confusion as well since at the time the case was decided, the U.S. had not yet enacted its current statutory version of copyright law (the case was decided in August 1976 and the current copyright law was enacted that same year in October)—a statute wherein the word "plagiarism" is never used. So if even courts themselves conflate the two terms, certainly it is understandable that the larger population might easily do so as well.

In addition to the clear area of misunderstanding on the differences between plagiarism and copyright, there are additional marked areas of misunderstanding in the population, including a lack of awareness about the U.S. government exception to copyright protection (see Section 105, Title 17 USC for details), about the fact that U.S. copyright law protects creative work more than factual work, and about differences between authorized and unauthorized use of another's copyright work. The survey question that tests knowledge of the government exception reads as follows: "Mary, a law-abiding citizen, decides to use five pages of a seven-page Ninth Circuit Court decision in her website. She legally obtains this unedited opinion directly from the court's website. She wants to cut and paste all five pages directly onto the html page she is composing. She will not edit or comment on the court opinion, nor does her webpage allow comment by others. Before using the text in her website, as a conscientious, law-abiding person, she should be sure she is within fair use." While the amount used is normally an issue in a fair use determination (five pages of a seven-page opinion), in this case that should not matter because an unedited Ninth Circuit Court decision is a government document and thus in the public domain.[3] In a fair use determination, normally it matters how much synthesis the new author conducts, and whether the use is for research or critique. While the question points out that Mary is not doing any of that, it should be irrelevant because a U.S. judicial opinion is in the public domain. Therefore the best answer in this case is false because Mary does not need to do a fair use analysis even if she is a law-abiding citizen. In fact, a law-abiding citizen would know about the government document exception to copyright in the U.S.

Yet 68% of the respondents say that Mary should do a fair use analysis, and 67% are very or somewhat certain that they are correct in their answer. Pragmatically, it might not be that important to digital writers that they can use most federal government–authored materials without concerning themselves with copyright and fair use. But on a more political level, I think this misperception is important. In the U.S., as distinct from other democracies or other forms of government (monarchies, for example), federal government documents generally are not copyright protected. The fact that the savvy and educated participants taking the survey are not hearing the words of Lincoln's Gettysburg Address ("government of the people, by the people, for the people") as they consider authorship of government documents is troubling since the authorship status of government documents in the U.S. is one of the clear markers that separates the U.S. from other countries. A copyright information website sponsored by York University agrees that "documents prepared by the [U.S.] government are generally considered to be in the public domain," but in contrast, in Canada, "the Crown owns copyright in government documents" ("Copyright and You"). One wonders whether the implications of living in a democracy have been minimized due to the political climate engendered by the Bush administration and its legacy—that is, government-sanctioned wiretapping, Guantanamo Bay, government-sanctioned "torture," the Patriot Act, and so on. In the current political climate, some of us, especially the humanists, feel very detached from U.S. government–authored actions. One wonders whether this sense of detachment also seeps into our perceptions of who owns the government (and the knowledge it produces).

This area of misunderstanding can be layered into the participant responses to the ethics question. The survey shows 73% would follow their conscience rather than obey the law on exceptional occasions. From a humanist perspective, one's conscience is ideally under the individual's ownership, while the law is a product of the government. If this is a theoretical separation for these participants, it again makes sense that something authored by the government is not seen as something authored by oneself, and thus it is logical that a digital writer in this context needs to either have permission or be within fair use. Of course, since government documents are in the public domain, fair use is inapplicable because fair use applies only to unauthorized uses. Items in the public domain can be used without considering fair use or permission.

The misunderstanding evidenced by the answer to this question provides clear contrast to a question on the ability to create derivative works from another's copyrighted materials: "The owner of a copyrighted novel has failed to make this novel into a play. You decide to do so without the copyright holder's permission. Your derivative work, the play, closely follows the plot and characters in the novel, but is likely to be a fair use because it is different than a novel." The best answer here is false since the play is obviously a derivative work based on the novel and impairs the original author's future market. A novel is also a creative work and so has more protection than something like a factual report. The participants overall had a very clear understanding of the derivative-work issue, as 95% out of 350 selected the best answer. The clear understanding perhaps emphasizes the academic economy of symbolic capital via attribution and the ability to control the destiny of one's creative works. It might be that the survey respondents feel they are stakeholders along with the novelist but are removed from items authored by the government (even though in a sense, U.S. citizens are coauthors of government documents).

The "author-function" concept is relevant to this analysis. In his famous and oft-cited "What Is an Author," Foucault spent more than half of the essay focusing on our understanding of literary authors. But a little over halfway through the piece, Foucault admits that "up to this point I have unjustifiably limited my subject" (1979/1984, p. 113). He proceeds to discuss a much more abstract concept of "authors" as "founders of discursivity." These types of authors (he names Marx and Freud and contrasts them with novelists) are different than the author one imagines as a literary author. Thinking of an author as a founder of discursivity, under Foucault's view, enables us to view authors' activities as those initiating a "discursive practice . . . heterogeneous to its subsequent transformations" (p. 155). Such "authors," according to Foucault, create "a possibility for something other than their discourse, yet something belonging to what they founded"

(p. 114). A creative work, under U.S. copyright law, would be linked to the first type of author Foucault discusses in his essay—someone who has what we might traditionally think of as a perpetual surging of innovation—a genius—and U.S. copyright law gives greater protection to those types of authors. But as for the second kind of author, founders of discursivity, the entire concept of author can be opened out to include something like the "U.S. government." The U.S. government as author initiates a discourse that is heterogeneous to that founding act; for our purposes, the texts created by the U.S. government can be internalized by subjects who then are disciplined in certain ways to perform as (hopefully) upstanding citizens.

In *The Archeology of Knowledge and the Discourse on Language* (1972), chapter 2, "The Original and the Regular," Foucault categorizes two discursive fields of concern to the history of ideas, mapping out the relative importance of authors (p. 141). The first field of discourse concerns formulations that are "highly valued and relatively rare," that "serve as models for others," and that are associated with and regarded as "creations" (p. 141). Authors, especially famous ones, are of course highly valued, relatively rare, and thought of as "creative," and so authors are more important in this first field, what I'll call the "author-heavy" field. Thinking of Foucault's all-too-brief discussion of authors in "What Is an Author," literary authors are situated in this first field of discourse. However the second field of discourse Foucault describes in "The Original and the Regular" is one revealing history as "inertia and weight," and with a diminished importance in the "author's identity." Instead what is important for this field of discourse are the groups in which its statements circulate and the extent of their "repetition in time and place" (1972, p. 141). I'll call this second field the "author-light" field because in it authors are less important. Foucault's discussion in *The Archeology of Knowledge* (where he does frequently discuss and allude to books, collections of works, and authors) is consistent with his discussion in the earlier "What Is an Author" as far as imagining multiple types of authors as nodes in a network, produced by activities upstream and prescribing activities downstream, with authors operating by different rules and expectations depending on the field of discourse. So in one field of discourse, named authors matter a great deal (author-heavy), but in another field, authors are less important (author-light), as what is more important is how ubiquitous the statements supporting the discourse become.[4]

The U.S. government as "author" does not prohibit the dissemination of government documents, and copyright law functions to facilitate, or at least not impede, the circulation of government-authored documents and discourse. The law itself circulates in an author-light field of discourse. U.S. government documents are not owned by a "Crown" and thus can be more easily disseminated. But U.S. copyright law privileges and reinscribes the creative genius, the individual novel writer (by providing more protection to creative works), and so the law itself, while circulating in an author-light field, helps produce the author-heavy field, the field of discourse where authors *are* more important. (I map these ideas out in more detail in chapter 5). Considering Foucault's discussion of the economy of discipline in a culture that no longer allows public torture, hangings, and death by guillotine, it makes sense that in order to properly discipline citizens, the texts that take the place of physical disciplining, that is, the law, must have the ability to circulate widely (the authors of the law are then founders of discursivity). Copyright law serves an economy of discipline because when freely circulating, public domain, government-authored documents are internalized by subjects, it is hoped that the messages within it will control from the inside, to produce virtuous citizens rather than incorrigibles, without resulting to "the hold on the body" (Foucault, 1977, p. 10). Perhaps it is the humanist impulse in digital writers that resists the unimpeded flow of government-authored texts by seeing the need for permission or fair use to use such documents even though the law has no such requirement.

What I am saying here is that U.S. copyright law and its provisions placing government documents in the public domain serve a government-sanctioned economy of discipline that results in the government's having a potentially more ubiquitous presence than it might have if it locked down its own textual productions via copyright law. Instead it sets these textual productions free. "Most hegemonic texts were products not of original individual writing but of transcription of the divine word" (Henry, 2000, p. 142). Further evidence illuminating this perspective is provided by one survey taker who also participated as an interviewee in phase 2 of the mixed-methods study. Rob,[5] an international PhD student attending a university in the U.S. but whose home is in India, informed me that certain texts he called the "Vedas" were "ancient Hindu texts" . . . said to be the word of God given to some sages and [that] we never came to know which sage said what." Because of this diminished emphasis on individual authorship in his home culture, according to Rob, cultural practices involving "remixing, remediating and reinterpreting" became the norm—thus permitting the Vedas to spread widely and interject themselves in other discourses; specifically Rob said that the Vedas had over time gained a great "relevance to contemporary ethics." Rob's theory is that knowledge was not permitted to be owned by any single individual in India, "by any author flexing copyright over it," so that in turn the message within the ancient texts could take hold in many places.

As (1) Jim Henry (2000) documents, (2) Foucault theorizes regarding fields of discourse, and (3) research participant Rob confirms, a sure way to weight the scales in favor of a text's becoming hegemonic, in favor of the message of the text growing over time, is to disconnect it from the individual, and instead to set it free to circulate as a kind of "common knowledge." U.S. copyright law, by donating government documents to the public domain, tips the scales, whether intentionally or not, in favor of government ideas circulating, taking hold, and disciplining without impediment. The meaning of misunderstanding in this area among digital writers may signal tacit resistance to this "disciplining" in its present form. The writing students, teachers, and others who responded to the survey may tacitly *not* want to internalize government generated discourse even though they could do so unimpeded since copyright law holds no bar.

Another clear area of misunderstanding among the survey population is about the difference between creative work and factual work in the eyes of copyright law. The question read: "Using someone's 'creative' work (i.e., fiction, drama, poetry, art, artistic designs, music) without their permission is just as likely to be a fair use as is using their 'factual' work (i.e., nonfiction, unaltered photographic representations, news items) without permission." While the correct answer is false since creative works receive *more* protection under copyright law than factual work, a clear majority of survey participants were not aware of this difference, with 58% answering incorrectly and indicating they believe creative and factual work are equally protected by copyright, while only 42% thought that creative work would have different protection than factual work. Courts look at this issue in the context of fair use determinations under Section 107, and specifically courts conduct their analysis based on the second fair use factor listed in the statute: "the nature of the copyrighted work." For example, in *Stewart v. Abend* (1990), the court focused on copyright protection of the owner's exclusive right to create derivative works and did not find fair use. Cornell Woolrich is the author of the story "It Had to Be Murder," and *Rear Window* is based largely on Woolrich's story. When MCA rereleased the film, suit was brought. The court held that the film was not a "new work" falling under the protection of fair use. Three of the four factors are taken into account by the court: The infringing work was commercial (factor 1, purpose of the use); the original work was creative rather than factual (factor 2, nature of the copyrighted work); and the rerelease harmed the copyright holder's ability to find new markets (factor 4, effect on market). In this case, the creativeness of the infringed work was one of the factors that, added with the others, caused the court to find this use was not fair.

The misunderstanding held by the majority of survey respondents could derive from the rhetoric and composition community's tendency to deconstruct concepts like "creative" and "factual." It could also derive from these digital writers' more sophisticated understanding of genre. If any group challenges traditional notions of "creative" writing, it is the students and teachers in U.S. writing programs, who are inclined to postmodernism. While the master narrative defining creativity might label it as producing items like poetry, paintings, short stories, sculpture, novels, and so on (poetry and fiction are the exclusive domain of the "creative writing" course at my institution), anyone who has either produced or critiqued an instruction manual appreciates the vast creativity involved in constructing a text that appeals to and is understandable by a broad audience. Yet in the U.S., the more traditional definition of creativity arises in determinations for purposes of copyright protection and fair use. This increased protection of "creative" works maps very well onto Foucault's categorization of the ways that authors function in the two fields of discourse he described in "The Original and the Regular." U.S. copyright law is meant as an incentive to create in a couple of ways: It does protect texts in that field of discourse where *authors* are more important but in the field of discourse where *dissemination* is of greater importance, copyright law does less to impede circulation.

Is Digital Speech Chilled?

One of the major findings in the overall study (survey and interviews) is that while digital writers' speech might be influenced, informed, and mediated by copyright law, their speech is not chilled to the extent they are not able to express themselves (but then recall that the vast majority of these digital writers are willing to break the law if their conscience tells them to). In this section, I discuss specifically the survey results with respect to the "chilled speech" issue (section D; appendix 2). The survey finds that for the majority of this population, digital speech is not "very chilled" although it is clear that copyright law is having a negative impact on or is restricting digital writers. As illustrated in table 2.6, "chilled speech" is measured by six questions. In summary, the six questions explore whether writers were asked to take others' copyrighted material down from the web, voluntarily did so, or reflected on using copyrighted materials and decided not to even though the web composition may have been improved. The six questions further ask whether writers in general feel unable to express themselves due to restraints of copyright law. From these six questions I created a metric where a score of 0–2 means "not chilled," a score of 3–4 is "somewhat chilled," and a score of 5–6 is "very chilled." Taking a global view of the responses under this metric shows only 2.42% of the population has "very chilled" digital speech. In contrast, 80.38% of the population has speech that is "not chilled." Of the respondents, 17.2% have "somewhat chilled" speech. Notably, only 6% of the population ($N = 373$) has been asked to remove web materials by a copyright holder or alleged copyright holder.

Table 2.6. Chilled speech index

	Yes (%)	No (%)	Can't Answer (%)	N
1. Have you ever been asked to take down something (text, audio, image) you had posted to the web by a copyright holder or alleged copyright holder because the text, audio, image, etc. was allegedly infringing on the owner's copyrights (for example, via a communication by way of a take-down notice or a cease-and-desist letter, or even an e-mail)?	6	94		373
2. If so, have you ever actually taken down such material because of this request?	5			
3. Have you ever voluntarily taken something down, on your own initiative, that you had posted to the web because you felt you might be subject to copyright liability even though you never actually received a request to do so?	18	78	4	373
4. Have you ever not posted something to a web composition you were creating because of fear of copyright liability?	46	50	4	373
5. Have you ever felt that the purpose or message of a web composition you were creating would be better, clearer, or more aesthetically pleasing to the audience if you could use others' copyrighted materials without fear of legal liability?	58	34	8	373
6. Have you ever felt that you weren't really able to say what you wanted in a web composition because you were afraid if you said it the way you wanted, someone might sue you for copyright infringement?	14	82	4	373

Survey participants are influenced and even restricted by copyright law, but the law does not prohibit them from expressing themselves. While 58% felt that "the purpose or message of a web composition [they] were creating would be better, clearer, or more aesthetically pleasing to the audience if [they] could use others' copyrighted materials without fear of legal liability," only 14% felt they "weren't really able to say what they wanted in a web composition because [they] were afraid if [they] said it the way [they] wanted, someone might sue [them] for copyright infringement." Yet 14% is a significant amount of the population even though it is not the majority. We must recall that this population is likely the tech-savvy component of rhetoric and composition, and among the less technologically sophisticated members who did not take the digital survey, the number whose speech is chilled could be much, much higher. It is helpful to remember that my two screening questions appearing at the survey's beginning eliminated any participant who had not published to the web. It is possible that those folks who do not publish on the web at all are the ones with the highest levels of chilled speech.

We should as well take note that a majority of 58% felt unable to express themselves in a fashion that is as aesthetically pleasing as it could be because of fear. Almost half of the population had not posted something to a web composition they were creating because of fear of copyright liability. Almost 20% voluntarily took materials down from the web on their own initiative because of fear of copyright liability even though they never actually received a request to do so. So although the metric I developed in order to provide a global snapshot of chilled speech levels indicates the majority of participants don't have "very chilled" speech, upon examination of individual question responses, there is evidence that speech is chilled in certain contexts.

The first chilled-speech question indicates 94% of the population has not received a take-down notice or otherwise been asked to take materials down from the web, confirming another empirical study showing that copyright stakeholders are not coming after the educational community yet (Fisher and McGeveran, 2006). Because copyright stakeholders may not be pursuing those in the educational community (such as writing students and their teachers), this very forbearance could explain the lower levels of chilled speech among this population. The lower levels of chilled speech in some areas could also be due to writers' low level of knowledge about copyright law. However even 14% to 58% of a population having chilled speech in some specific areas expressed in the survey, especially considering this is the United States of America (the land of the free), and especially considering these writers are all working in educational contexts, we should really question if this is acceptable. My opinion is that these levels of chilled speech are too high, especially when we acknowledge there is a possibility of lessening this fear by a change in copyright law, a change that might expand fair use and limit copyright liability in digital-writing in educational contexts. Further, by increasing knowledge and understanding of the law by this population, we could also lessen the fear.

On this last point, I really have to agree with Lawrence Lessig, who says that as a law professor, he is "a little surprised by the respect that non-lawyers typically give the law" (2010). I believe the reason nonlawyers give the law so much respect[6] is that they don't understand all the ways that the law can be challenged and strategized against, at every turn, or can be leveraged for one's advantage. Also as Latour (2010) points out, like scientists, legal experts are very sure about the way they produce knowledge—lawyers' and legislators' posturing represents the law as something to be reckoned with. Judges expect their legal orders be obeyed. The law, like science, presents itself as a certain type of truth to be revered. But I have to agree with Lessig that as lawyers, we are taught to expect and do "constantly ask and demand of the law that it explain to us: How does this make sense? And we never presume that we happen to have a body of regulation that makes sense" (2010). This is especially true when one digs around and figures out how laws are created, the hundreds of rhetorical turns and compromises made in the process of any law's creation, the midnight deals, and so on. When the law makes sense, we encourage others to follow it, but when it doesn't make sense, "our perspective is that the law needs to be changed" (Lessig, 2010). It's this really deep critical engagement with the law that I think we want to work for as a cohort of professional writers, students, teachers, and others alike. In other words, we do not want our students to take the law at face value. We should question the law.

Certainly, the survey shows that digital writers are considering and addressing copyright and fair use in their writing processes, something that might be time consuming and frustrating, but ultimately they are able to express themselves although perhaps not in a way that is as aesthetically pleasing as they would have liked. The data clearly shows there is absolutely no doubt copyright law considerations are layered into digital composing choices, at least for this population. In the next chapter, I take this analysis further by using a rhetorical lens to discuss survey response differences between the population of students, teachers, and others and correlations between variables such as chilled speech and levels of copyright knowledge.

3

The Rhetoric of Truth

This chapter takes a rhetorical view of the survey findings and methodology. I spend time elaborating on this rhetorical view because a survey is typically seen as a quantitative method—it permits counting and objectification of the data it elicits. Because there has been controversy about the need for and legitimacy of quantitative methods and those research methods that rely on numbers and counting in rhetoric and composition as well as other fields (Johanek, 2000; MacNealy, 2009), I illustrate in this chapter that statistical methods, like other methods of generating knowledge and truth, have a significant rhetorical component. A statistical analysis of survey results, evidence offered up in legal proceedings, a "classical argument," and even a personal narrative have something in common. All these knowledge-generating, truth-seeking methods have certain mechanisms in place that attempt to quantify or at least describe the "probability of error" (Rowntree, 2004, p. 21; see also MacNealy, 2009). In statistical analysis, the probability of error is calculated numerically and labeled with agreed-upon terminology; "statistically significant," for example, indicates a low probability of error. In the legal arena, differing standards of evidence refined in case law apply in different legal contexts. Proof at the level of "beyond a reasonable doubt" might be required in a capital case, while in a civil case the lower standard of "preponderance of the evidence" might apply. In a classical argument, the counterargument and rebuttal provide the reader with an assessment of the probability of error being made by the writer, and in personal narrative, the writers' ethos often provides a method by which to judge their credibility and their chances of being erroneous in whatever tales unfold. Another similarity is that the survey, evidence in legal proceedings, the classical argument, and even the personal narrative all rely on "data" if we agree with Derek Rowntree's assessment that data is just technical jargon for a *collection of observations* (p. 14). Each of these methods of generating knowledge though relies on different rhetorical constructs, constructs aligned with community preferences, that play upon the audiences' willingness to accept the interpretation of data as "true."

Claims to knowledge or truth based on inferential statistics, like claims to knowledge in any other discipline, are rhetorically constructed. Since I discuss differences among members of the population with respect to knowledge of copyright, attitude towards the importance of copyright law, and the "ethics question," some theories from inferential statistics provide additional understanding; inferential statistics help understand differences. When examining differences between populations using inferential statistics, the inquiry is framed with the question of whether the null hypothesis should be rejected. From a rhetorical point of view, the null hypothesis means different things in different contexts, but it proposes the presumptive is true—in this case that there is no real difference between the averages in two populations (students and teachers, for example). When examining differences between the averages or means of two populations, each population will have a dispersion of data points that creates the average. So the question is whether the difference between the averages is a real difference or is due to random variation that exists in the different distribution of means. For comparison, one might think of the null hypothesis as a kind of skepticism that any honest researcher has, especially one who goes into a research project with some expectations. A qualitative researcher who enters a research project with few expectations or predictions is kind of accomplishing the same ends as is accomplished by approaching a statistical analysis framed with the null hypothesis. Both strategies resist the bias one inserts into the data—that secret desire to find the thing you thought you would find.

The "alternative hypothesis" contrasts with the "null hypothesis" and proposes the relationship between variables that the researcher is trying to test. The alternative hypothesis is the researcher's hypothesis—for example, one of my original hypotheses is that "the more knowledge one has in copyright law, the less chilled one's speech is." In order to accept this hypothesis as the alternative hypothesis, the probabilities must be great enough that it is true and small enough that there is error. If such probabilities are met, the null hypothesis can be rejected in favor of the alternative hypothesis. If not enough support is available to reject the null hypothesis, then the alternative hypothesis instead must be rejected. Inferential statistics provides parameters that guide the decision on whether to reject the null hypothesis.

Rowntree (2004) discusses the two risks encountered as the researcher decides whether to reject the null hypothesis. The risks are in making either a type I or a type II error. A type I error is rejecting the null hypothesis when it should not have been rejected, and a type II error is not rejecting the null hypothesis (and accepting instead the alternative hypothesis) even though it should have been rejected. Rowntree (2004) makes a useful comparison between these types of statistical errors and errors that might occur in a court of law. In court, if weak evidence is accepted to convict, then the risk is that an innocent person ends up serving time. On the other hand, if only the strongest evidence is used to convict, a guilty person could go free. To guard against the type I error, one can require a higher level of significance (say that there is only a 1 in 100 chance that the difference between means is random rather than a 5 in 100 chance). But when the level of significance is increased, the chances of making the type II error also increase (not rejecting the null hypothesis when it should have been rejected).

Rowntree (2004) points out the difficulty here; "since there is no way of knowing whether the null hypothesis is 'really' true or false," it can never be conclusively determined which type of error we are making (p. 120). I add to this an analogy from my legal background, also relevant to my discussion here on copyright law and its influence on writing. In the law's administration, differing theories or burdens of proof are at work in legal determinations (some which can be life-and-death decisions, just like the decisions made in science). While inferential statistics uses terminology like "significant," "highly significant," and "very highly significant," burdens of proof in law are described by words such as:

- *beyond a reasonable doubt:* "Fully satisfied, entirely convinced, satisfied to a moral certainty" (*Black's Law*, 1979, p. 147).
- *clear and convincing:* "More than a preponderance but less than is required in a criminal case" (*Black's Law*, 1979, p. 227).
- *preponderance of the evidence:* "Evidence which is of greater weight or more convincing than the evidence which is offered in opposition to it; that is, evidence which as a whole shows that the fact sought to be provided is more probable than not" (*Black's Law*, 1979, p. 1064).
- *scintilla of evidence:* "A spark of evidence. A metaphorical expression to describe a very insignificant or trifling item or particle of evidence; used in the statement of the common-law rule [to avoid a directed verdict] that if there is any evidence at all in a case, even a mere *scintilla*, tending to support a material issue, the case cannot be taken from the jury, but must be left to their decision" (*Black's Law*, 1979, p. 1207).

The law employs different burdens in different contexts just like inferential statistics, but Rowntree would probably argue that science is more conservative: "they demand significance levels that ensure we are far more likely to *fail* to claim a result that (unknown to us) would have been justified, than to *claim* a result that is illusory. . . . The emphasis is on avoiding Type I errors" (Rowntree, 2004, p. 121). The law, I think, takes the context into account to a greater extent than inferential statistics since the burden of proof depends on the type of case or issue at hand (criminal, civil, and so on.). Below is Rowntree's summary of significance levels from inferential statistics.

- 5% *significant*: 5 in 100 chance that the difference is random (arising merely because of sampling variation)
- 1% *highly significant*: 1 in 100 chance that the difference is random/by chance
- .1% *very highly significant*: 1 in 1,000 chance that the difference is random/by chance

One can imagine how crucial it might be whether the differences are significant or not—if a life-saving vaccine is tested, not to be released unless the differences between the population who received the vaccine and those who did not is significant enough to justify producing and marketing the vaccine. The legal burdens used in courts of law similarly become crucial because decisions based on them mean the difference between an innocent person being executed or a serial killer walking free. In statistics, the bigger the difference between the means of two populations, the more confident one can be in rejecting the null hypothesis. But to place the descriptors of significance in context, Rowntree reminds us that they are only verbal labels and ultimately only mean what we want them to. The labels of significant or not significant "really add nothing to what is shown in the figures—though they may make the researcher feel happier that he has produced something worthwhile" (Rowntree, 2004, p. 118).

After using inferential statistics to analyze differences between students, teachers, and others in survey data, very few differences are found. Specifically, I examine the survey participants' responses with respect to copyright knowledge levels, willingness to break the law if their conscience requires it (the "ethics question"), and attitude towards importance of understanding copyright law in digital writing contexts. Regarding differences among the population on copyright knowledge, as shown in figure 3.1, teachers' average score for knowledge of copyright and fair use is 68%, while students' is 57%. Those who self-identified as "other" have knowledge levels between teachers and students at 62%. While there is a statistically significant difference between students' and teachers' knowledge scores, the key point is that there is only a small actual difference in knowledge levels between students and teachers (9%). On the extremely complicated subject of copyright and fair use, authorized use and unauthorized use, the student and teacher population hardly varied.

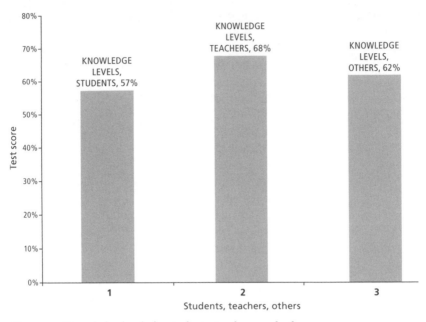

Figure 3.1. Knowledge levels for students, teachers, and others.

Neither the ethics question nor the question on how important knowledge of copyright is revealed any statistically significant differences among the population. On the topic of the willingness to disobey the law, 14% of students and 16% of teachers stated they would obey the law without exception, while 86% of students and 84% of teachers said they would follow their conscience even if it meant breaking the law. There is no statistical difference between these populations, and as Collins (2007) indicates, writing students and their teachers alike trend toward the humanist perspective. According to the survey data, for the vast majority of survey participants, regardless of whether they are students or teachers, knowledge of copyright law is at least somewhat important to their work as digital composers. The differences between students, teachers, and others regarding attitudes on how important copyright law is to their work shows that those differences are not statistically significant.

Analyzing Relationships

In this section of the survey data analysis, I examine the strength of relationships between variables, or the correlations. I also discuss regression, or the nature of that relationship, positive or negative (Rowntree, 2004). There are three kinds of correlations: positive, negative, and zero.

A "positive" correlation means that the more there is of one variable, the more there is of the other. A "negative" correlation indicates that the more there is of one variable, the less there is of the other. A "zero" correlation means that there is no apparent relationship between two variables and their frequency of occurrence. For a "zero" correlation, the relationship *approaches* zero because it is almost impossible to find two variables that have no relationship. Also just because a correlation exists, it does not mean there is causation. A correlation between two variables could be coincidental. (While it might seem like washing your car causes it to rain, when this occurs, it is simply coincidental).

Some examples of correlations (taken from Rowntree, 2004) are:

- rainfall and attendance at football games (a negative correlation—the more rainfall, the less attendance at games)
- age of a car and its value (a negative correlation—the greater the age of the car, the less its value)
- length of education and annual earnings (a positive correlation—the greater years of education, the higher the earnings)
- ability to see in the dark and quantity of carrots eaten (no correlation!)

Rowntree (2004) notes that the correlation between two variables is a fact, but it is a matter of interpretation whether that relationship is good, bad, weak, or strong. The verbal labels that have been assigned to the various correlation coefficients are:

Correlation Coefficient

0.0 to 0.2	very weak, negligible
0.2 to 0.4	weak, low
0.4 to 0.7	moderate
0.7 to 0.9	strong, high, marked
0.9 to 1.0	very strong, very high

While Rowntree does provide these descriptors, he notes that they are *not used consistently* and that ultimately one must make his or her own interpretation based on the data.

Now, in the context of my study prior to collecting data via the survey or interviews, I formed some hypotheses, *alternative hypotheses*. I wrote out sentences that described what I thought was going to happen once I collected survey data and conducted analysis. These hypotheses, all which predict a certain relationship between variables such as "knowledge" and "chilled speech" are:

H1 The more knowledge one has about fair use, the less one's speech is chilled.

H2 The higher the educational level, the higher the knowledge about fair use.

H3 The higher the knowledge of fair use, the more likely one is willing to see exceptions to obeying the law.

H4 The higher the knowledge of fair use, the higher the certainty one's knowledge is correct.

H5 The more certain one is in his or her knowledge, the less one's speech is chilled.

H6 Persons who believe in exceptions to obeying the law will have lower levels of chilled speech.

With respect to the first hypothesis (H1), this assertion is not supported by the data because the correlation between the variables of knowledge and chilled speech is −.075, showing a "very weak" or negligible relationship. This weak relationship might be because over 80% of the population did not have chilled speech to begin with. While the relationship between the variables (education level and fair use knowledge) in the second hypothesis (H2) is also very weak (.28), it is stronger than the relationship between the variables in the first hypothesis; but it is not strong enough to support the hypothesis. However the relationship between education level and fair use knowledge is indirectly supported by the higher scores teachers received compared to students on the copyright and fair use knowledge test. So we know there is some relationship between education and fair use knowledge.

The third hypothesis (H3) predicted that the higher one's knowledge of fair use, the more likely one would follow his or her conscience rather than strictly obey the law. The data again shows a very weak relationship between these variables (.042). This may have been because more than one half of the population would follow their conscience. The fourth hypothesis (H4) posits the higher the knowledge of fair use, the higher the participant's confidence level. The correlation coefficient between these two variables showed a stronger relationship than that in H3, but still a weak relationship (−.223). The correlation is negative because higher certainty received a lower score (a 1 is very certain). Therefore, the higher the test score, the lower the certainty score—the more respondents know, the more confident they are. The correlation is better than "very weak" or "negligible" but not as great as "moderate." None of the relationships allow us to reject the null hypothesis. Figure 3.2 shows the dispersion of scores of knowledge and certainty for participants. Also included is a trend line showing the weak nature of the relationship. In strong relationships, the trend line is more vertically slanted.

Is There a Chilling of Digital Communication?
Knowledge and Certainty Trends

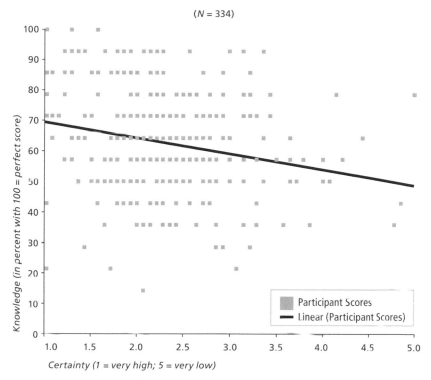

Figure 3.2. Showing the relationship between knowledge and certainty in that knowledge.

The testing of the fifth and sixth hypotheses (H5 and H6) also shows very weak relationships between the specified variables. H5 expects a relationship between certainty and chilled speech but yielded a very weak correlation (−.081). H6 posits that persons who believe in following their conscience will have lower levels of chilled speech but also had a very weak relationship between the variables (.097). However it is difficult to find correlations in these variables because this population—writing students, teachers, others—is very homogeneous both in its low level of chilled speech and in its willingness to follow its conscience. Because of this, trends are difficult to establish based on the measures provided by this data. So the kind of differences imaged in these hypotheses is not present, and, as stated, the null hypothesis cannot be rejected in any of these cases. However we do know that Collins (2007) found with a different population and a different survey a 30% increase in willingness to follow their conscience for U.S. degree receivers. The data here has not provided anything to negate Collins's findings.

Answering the Research Questions

As a reminder, the research questions geared towards the survey (as opposed to the interviews) are:

1. What do writers know and understand about copyright and fair use?
2. How confident are writers in this knowledge?
3. Are writers unable to express themselves fully because of fear of copyright liability, that is, is their digital speech chilled?
4. How important do writers think knowledge of copyright and fair use is to their work?
5. What is the relationship, if any, between knowledge of copyright/ fair use, confidence in that knowledge, and levels of "chilled speech" in digital environments?

With respect to the first two research questions, what writers know and understand about copyright and fair use and how confident they are, we can say that on this complicated topic, writing students, their teachers, and others have a decent understanding (63%) of the issues, more understanding in the area of fair use compared to understanding in the area of licensed use. Regarding the second question, the population has self-awareness of the limits of its knowledge. The differences in knowledge levels between students and teachers is minimal, pointing to the ways that cyberspace possibly challenges those subject positions.

With respect to the third question, whether copyright law is causing such fear that writers cannot fully express themselves, my data does not support that. Less than 3% of writers had very chilled speech, only 6% had been asked to take anything down from the web, and only 14% felt unable to express themselves due to fear although writers acknowledged that their web creations may have been more aesthetically pleasing if they did not have to worry about copyright. Note that it is possible speech is less chilled than we might expect for three reasons: (1) digital writers are not fully aware of some of the legal risks they are taking (with an overall score of 63%), (2) copyright stakeholders are not coming after the educational community yet (Fisher and McGeveran, 2006), and (3) the population taking the survey may be the least fearful and most knowledgeable on these issues. As far as the fourth research question, asking how important writers think knowledge of copyright and fair use is to their work, hands down, the majority of students and teachers think it is at least somewhat important, with almost half indicating they think it is very important. Regarding the last research question, question 5, the survey data did not provide evidence of any significant relationships between these variables possibly for the reasons discussed above—mainly that the population is very homogenous.

Things to Be Learned from the Survey

In addition to exploring the research questions, some issues with the survey administration itself might inform us.[1] The overall response rate is 23%, which is acceptable for a digital survey, but it could be higher. Some of the reasons for the relatively low response rate (compared to paper surveys especially) might be as stated in empirical survey research: lack of cohesive community, technological ability, or that e-mail is associated with spam (see Groves, Cialdini, and Couper, 1992; Schillewaert, Langerak, and Duhamel, 1998; Rife, 2010b; Swoboda et al., 1997; Yun and Trumbo, 2000). My experience administering this survey supports the idea that the particular population studied lacks cohesiveness or community in three ways. First, as I constructed the study population, in order to obtain the master list of programs, I had to create a bricolage between three membership lists, and those lists are not exclusive. The lack of a definitive publication listing and categorizing of U.S. writing programs can plausibly be connected to a lack of agreement within the writing program or major community about how to gather and list such programs. The existence of several lists indicates the possibility of more than one perspective, lack of a single tool to measure and categorize writing programs, and possibly lack of resources or the unwillingness or inability to pool resources in order to produce a definitive list that all agree on. Second, the problems I encountered simply trying to locate contact information for faculty, and especially students, also points to what is possibly a serious problem with the "community" and who is allowed representational space in the field (see Knight et al., 2009 for a detailed discussion of this). And third, there is already existing research that indicates survey response rates are low when a sense of cohesion is low among the community studied (Yun and Trumbo, 2000). Lack of cohesion among the population may map on to a lack of motivation to complete the digital survey. I had a relatively low response rate, so this third point is supported.

Grabill (2001) defines community as a group that has shared values, networks, relationships, shared meanings, and socially constructed boundaries created by shared norms. But in the field of rhetoric and composition, plenty of debates abound on whether such shared norms and values exist. For example, Connors (1982), Dobrin (1983), Durack (2004), and Rutter (1991) (among others), outline debates within the field regarding how the field defines itself as a profession, what matters to the profession, and what issues are researched within that profession, while writers such as Charney (1998, 2004), Haswell (2005), Johanek (2000), North (1987), and Phelps (1988) document debates on appropriate methodologies and resistance to the use of typical "social science" and/or "empirical" research designs in rhetoric and composition studies. The scholarly debates within rhetoric and composition about methodology point to what might be a serious problem with the population/community of writing students and their teachers since *methodology is the very essence of a population's identity and sovereignty.* Accepted methodologies within a community dictate the kinds of rhetorical constructs required in order for one to claim truth (statistical significance, preponderance of the evidence, or personal experience, for example). I certainly would not venture into the traditional scientific community and offer my singular personal experience as evidence of truth, nor would I advocate before my local courtroom judge that he should rule in favor of my client because the arguments I have presented him are statistically significant.

From my view, the relatively low response rate I received at least tentatively supports the notion that writing programs or writing majors do not coagulate together as much as they could, in the sense of moving forward as a serious field of study. The response rate may be indicative that there is not as full a sense of community, at least with respect to digital writing, as one might hope. Further, the response rate might provide evidence of resistance to the survey method. On the other hand, regarding the population that did respond, Grabill (2001) at least implies that a researcher may facilitate the construction of community. Perhaps as the eleven weeks went by when I collected data, the act of researching the "community" created ad hoc networks, connecting individuals. By selecting sociocultural activity theory to frame my exploration of the field, I did impose a certain shape on it—thus creating a stronger community than existed previously. Whether the community I examine exists only on the AT triangle[2] or as well in some other space external to my study remains something to be explored.

The single identifying factor holding my study population together is their quality of being digital writers regardless of whether they are students, teachers, or "others." But when designing and writing surveys, if there is not a significant amount of cohesion amongst a population, it is difficult to create a survey that will appeal to a large number of people; they may have little commonality. The researcher selecting his or her population has to be a good guesser because until the data is collected, the researcher may not know enough about the population to assess whether or not it is cohesive enough to really be a community in the full sense of the word. In contrast, as my data analysis supports, if a survey population is too homogenous, it might be difficult to pull out differences among subcategories (students and teachers) within that population. I did not realize until after the data was collected exactly how homogenous writing students and their teachers are, at least with respect to attitudes, knowledge, and behavior in copyright contexts. Of course extracting and analyzing differences is only important if the research questions seek such inquiries. My survey data provides a view of web writers in U.S. writing programs—but because of the 23% response rate, we have only a glimpse of some members in the larger educational community. Ultimately, learning about the field as a collective will prove difficult from a research perspective if its members do not participate in studies that examine collective practices.

While it may seem obvious, another one of the key things learned from administering the survey is that a well-crafted survey is a well-crafted piece of writing. Although the response rate to the e-mail–digital survey is not high compared to paper-administered surveys, it is a normal response rate with respect to e-mail surveys, and it is a high response rate as far as surveys administered to students and teachers in writing programs. A well-written survey makes data analysis easier too. Just like writing, peer review, and revision works for the traditional essay, writing, piloting, and revising a survey is extremely beneficial. Prior to administering the twenty-nine-question digital survey, I piloted a paper version that contained sixty-nine questions. I received a great deal of feedback on the paper survey (as well as a number of well-intended complaints from the unpaid participants about the time it took—over an hour). Since multiple-choice survey questions are very good at measuring the presence or absence of variables, writing hypotheses before designing the survey made survey construction much easier. The writing of hypotheses first, to frame and organize a survey, is a similar strategy to writing an outline before drafting the essay. The survey literature states that survey questions should ask about only one variable at a time, that the survey be short, that there should be reminders, and so on (Babbie, 2004; Backstrom and Hursh-Cesar, 1981; Rife, 2010b; see also Singh, Taneja, Mangalaraj, 2009; Watson and Anderson, 2005). I really considered the time commitment I requested from the unpaid participants, and I tried to be as efficient with their time as possible. I have talked to individuals writing surveys who put questions in their surveys without knowing why they are asking the questions other than that such questions are usually in surveys (like race, gender, class, and so on). This is something to be very wary of because once the question is asked, the researcher then needs to do something with that data.

Even though individuals in rhetoric and composition are writing specialists, there is very little, if any, field literature on writing good surveys. This is definitely an area that could be developed, theorized, researched, and worked into various curriculums. The ability to craft and administer a good survey is a very useful skill to have since surveys are used all the time in community work, political activities, and even writing program evaluation. As experts of writing, folks in rhetoric and composition could helpfully add to the existing literature on surveys. Surveys are a place where rhetorical theory and composition theory have room to roam and make a contribution (Rife, 2010b).

In addition to drawing out the possibilities of mapping rhetoric and composition theory onto the construction of surveys, the survey results themselves offer further implications. The findings of the survey show that the vast majority of writing students and teachers believe that knowledge of copyright law is important to their work as digital writers. Yet they scored only 63% overall on the knowledge portion of the survey. We might explore the idea that explicitly teaching copyright law to digital writers in educational contexts should become the norm. In the interviews, it is found that students (and recent alums) wanted to learn and experience *all* the various laws that impact digital writing, such as privacy law, defamation law, and contract law. Teaching copyright might be folded into a core course where the laws of public writing in general are taught, but taught through a rhetorical lens.

Because there is a lot of interest in copyright and legal issues in digital writing, some writing programs might be very smart to explore developing a concentration within, for example, a four-year undergraduate professional writing major specifically in "law, rhetoric, and community" or "law, culture, and community." Such a concentration could be helpful for students who want to continue in a legal career, work as journalists or consultants, or become legal experts in their organizations, including nonprofits. Such a concentration would be very helpful for students who want to advocate for others via their writing, as many professional writing students do desire. Students graduating with such concentrations may contribute to an expanding research trajectory in law, composition, and rhetoric. The data shows students sometimes know more than their teachers about copyright, and also the interviews show students are doing very complicated digital writing outside of the classroom. We have empirical evidence of this now. I think that these findings should shape writing pedagogies and invite explorations in this area by other scholars.

The mixed-methods approach is very promising for researchers working in rhetoric and composition (Sullivan, 2008). Quantitative methods render rhetorically constructed probable knowledge just as do classic hermeneutical interpretations. Thus rhetoric and writing researchers should not fear using quantitative methods such as surveys because we have the understanding and skill to unpack their rhetorical nature. Yet we also do not want to let go of our qualitative traditions. Mixed methods allow us to do both. Because we can do both, I think we need to exercise much more caution in claims that we make unless those claims can be backed up by empirical evidence or otherwise substantiated. The data shows digital speech is not chilled to the point where writers are silenced. While students and teachers have concern over copyright law, based on the survey and interviews, I am not sure I can go so far as to say that *all* of the population is living in a "culture of fear" (Westbrook, 2006). The overall population might very well be living in a culture of fear, but my study alone does not provide enough evidence that I am comfortable asserting that. However I do agree that *some* digital writers are indeed living under a cloud of fear about possible copyright liability. For example, Jessie is a survey participant selected for an interview. While discussing a video remix she created, one that incorporated others' copyrighted materials, although this video remix was posted on the web and was presented by Jessie in numerous public forums, she said: "I also in the back of my mind think that the copyright police will come after me someday, but you know." Yet this is a population willing to break the law if their conscience tells them it is acceptable to do so. If the population is willing to break the law, as far as chilled speech levels, it follows that the law is going to be a lot less restrictive than one might otherwise imagine. The mixed-methods approach allows a broad view of a particular area of inquiry and might be implemented more frequently in order to explore and verify some claims made in current scholarship that have not been executed in an empirical study.

Possibilities in curriculum development suggest places for opening collaborative spaces between legal studies and rhetoric and composition. Clearly, students and teachers in writing programs want to learn more about copyright. Developing such curriculum might be done in collaboration with legal studies. In turn, the kind of contributions researchers in rhetoric and composition studies could make to legal studies and practice is immeasurable and almost completely unrealized. I think rhetoric and composition scholars could inform theories of law school writing pedagogies and legal writing, including judicial opinion writing. Rhetoric and composition theories might inform legal methodologies and analysis with respect to the rhetorical moves made to achieve justice. In turn, scholars in legal studies could localize some of their scholarly conversations for those in rhetoric and composition who are teaching and researching writing in a law context. These two fields are not presently connecting very well in their respective literatures.

Other spaces for collaboration could center on changing notions of authorship and how the law might reflect that. Research on digital writers' actual composing practices might better inform possible changes to the law. Having 14% to 58% of a population fearful of publishing content to the web even though they are working in educational contexts is unacceptable.

Writing students and teachers need more freedom from possible legal liability in order to learn and be inventive. Changes in copyright law to protect the educational community are merited. Lawrence Lessig (2010) most recently laments that copyright law may not change: "I'm sorry to report that I think this is a hopeless strategy today" (p. 36); however I have to reject his (hopefully strategic) stance and move forward with the belief that changes to copyright law are still possible. Just recently, the United States Government Accountability Office has admitted that the claims made regarding economic harm based on digital piracy are in fact relatively unsubstantiated (2010). With the Obama administration in place and the new focus on education, I do continue to move forward believing copyright law can and will change. The new and favorably expanded DMCA exemptions for educators, issued in July 2010, show that change can occur (Librarian of Congress, 2010; Peters, 2010; Rulemaking, 2010; for commentary see Aufderheide, 2010; Kolowich, 2010b; Jaszi, 2010; Mittell, 2010; Rife 2010e, Tushnet, 2010). But in order to create change we need to be able to offer the kind of evidence acceptable to stakeholders in a position to make policy and legislative decisions.

In May 2009, I took the data from this survey to Washington, DC, and along with thirty-seven other educators and organizations such as the EFF (Electronic Frontier Foundation), testified at the tri-annual rulemaking hearings before the register of copyright at the Library of Congress on the need for an exemption to the provisions of the DMCA (Digital Millennium Copyright Act, section 1201[a][1], USC Title 17).[3] The DMCA prevents fair use of media that is protected by anticircumvention technologies such as CSS-protected DVDs (Copyright Law). Fair use is prevented because potential users violate the law by circumventing technological measures in order to take clips from such DVDs even though the use of such clips may fall squarely under Section 107.

In the 2010 decision, based on the 2009 hearings (Peters, 2010), the arguments of educational and noncommercial stakeholders were successful. But during the hearings, it became clear that witnesses/copyright stakeholders such as the MPAA (Motion Picture Association of America), RIAA (Recording Industry Association of America), AAP (Association of American Publishers), ASMP (American Society of Media Photographers), AVA (Alliance of Visual Artists), BSA (Business Software Alliance), DGA (Directors Guild of American), ESA (Entertainment Software Association), PACA (Picture Archive Council of America), Time Warner, and the DVD Copy Control Association had a vastly different view of writing than did I based on my training in and understanding of composition process theory. The content industry argues that digital writers wishing to create remixes with such technologically protected media should simply seek permissions.

However composition process theory clearly shows that writers do not work linearly. During my testimony on May 6, 2009 I stated:

> Since no one has ever appeared from my field, writing studies, I can explain that permissions, the idea of permissions or asking permissions to be, to use or be sent movie clips three to five days ahead depends on something false, which is a linear model of writing process. Writing is not—we have research in our field going back 30 years that clearly demonstrates writing is not linear, but it's recursive, and the writer revisits and revises decisions multiple times continuously synthesizing information and changing things around, and here I cite the work by Flower and Hayes, Janet Emig, Sandra Pearl [sic], Lee O'Dell. (Rife, 2009a, pp. 188–90)

During the testimony and in submitted documents I provided my data on chilled speech emphasizing the negative influence copyright law is having on writers even though they are working in educational environments. The U.S. Copyright Office understood my empirical data. In her recommendation, M. Peters, the register of copyrights, reminded us that in order to successfully request an exemption, a "preponderance of the evidence" must show a need, and that evidence cannot be "speculation alone" (2010, p. 10). She demanded a showing that a "substantial" harmful impact is likely if the exemption is not granted (p. 10). The rhetorical construct of "the survey," with its exploration of variables and its rather large N, is one understood and valued in that discourse community. I also had information from the interviews I presented at the hearings, including a sampling of an interviewee's[4] multimedia work (a colorful, spectacular video montage critiquing popular movies for the racial stereotypes they perpetuate). This research participant's work, which would not have existed but for the writer's willingness to violate the DMCA in order to obtain clips, was shown on a big screen before the panel and the audience. So I had multiple types of evidence, both quantitative and qualitative, to offer the register and her panel of experts from the Copyright Office.

What educational stakeholders/witnesses argued for is an extension and expansion of the 2006 DMCA exemption achieved by University of Pennsylvania film studies professor Pete DeCherney. In 2006, DeCherney successfully argued for a DMCA exemption for "media studies or film professors," allowing them to hack CSS encrypted DVDs in violation of the DMCA for purposes of teaching and learning (see "Statement of the Librarian," 2006). The 2006 exemption reads: "Audiovisual works included in the educational library of a college or university's film or media studies department, when circumvention is accomplished for the purpose of making compilations of portions of those works for educational use in the classroom by media studies or film professors" ("Statement of the Librarian," 2006). And the new 2010 exemption language issued is:

> (1) Motion pictures on DVDs that are lawfully made and acquired and that are protected by the Content Scrambling System when circumvention is accomplished solely in order to accomplish the incorporation of short portions of motion pictures into new works for the purpose of criticism or comment, and where the person engaging in circumvention believes and has reasonable grounds for believing that circumvention is necessary to fulfill the purpose of the use in the following instances:
>
> > (i) Educational uses by college and university professors and by college and university film and media studies students;
> > (ii) Documentary filmmaking;
> > (iii) Noncommercial videos. (Peters, 2010)

This new expanded exemption reflects a huge leap moving forward from 2006 and addresses broader needs of college-level stakeholders—including documentary filmmakers and noncommercial video makers ("vidders"). In fact, the new exemption is nothing short of a victory for the college and university crowd. This example shows concretely how changes to the law *can* occur. The exemption that DeCherney, a faculty member and not a lawyer, admirably gained for the academic community in 2006 was set to expire in December 2009 and was not only extended by Peters but was substantially expanded.[5] College teachers and their students now enjoy and benefit from broader protection from legal liability as they are teaching and working in digital environments. These new exemptions provide more peace of mind. Yet changing the law by conducting and sharing research on composing processes, attitudes, behaviors, and understanding is a possibility that is almost completely unexplored in rhetoric and composition despite rhetoric's deep history with public engagement and advocacy (for a persuasive argument that scholarship itself can be a form of activism see Reyman, 2010, appendix A, pp. 153–54).

Before moving on to a discussion of the digital writer interviews, I report that all findings from my 2006 pilot study are further supported in this survey. I won't repeat those here since they are listed in chapter 1. But the survey findings I've outlined in chapters 2 and 3 are supported in two studies that took place about two years apart. Therefore we can feel confident that these findings are accurate. The interviews I discuss in the next chapters, the vignettes I paint of each digital writer I interview, further enhance our understanding of writing in the digital age as well as copyright law's mediational influence on the composing process.

4

Seven Digital Writer Multimedia Vignettes

> Writers know more fully what they mean only after having
> written it.
>
> — Sondra Perl, "The Composing Process
> of Unskilled College Writers"

Once I administered the large-scale digital survey examining respondents' knowledge of, attitudes toward, and behavior involving copyright and digital writing, I moved on to the interviews. Using criterion-based sampling, I selected seven survey respondents for participation in discourse-based interviews. All interviewees were students who had taken the survey; all were from one university (but spanned a broad range of student-subject positions from undergraduate, to recent alum, to a PhD candidate on the job market); all had some interest in copyright law; and all were known to be responsible and reliable people (that is, they would show up for the interview—on this prediction I was 100% correct). After locating interviewees that met the criteria, I contacted participants by sending them a recruitment e-mail. Interviews were conducted between November 14 and November 30, 2007.[1] Interviewees include Leslie, Rob, Jessie, Carey, Sarah, Amanda, and Heather, as introduced in chapter 1. For purposes of constructing interview questions and as a memory-provoking topic of discussion during the interviews, participant-authored web compositions were collected.

In the interview recruitment e-mail, I asked for participant-authored web compositions by requesting "a URL of some sort of something you've published to the web, or composed for the web—a digital portfolio, teaching materials, Facebook profile, webpage, or something of that nature."

In response to the prompt, interviewees provided me with an amazingly wide variety of web writing: "gift writing" (web writing done for a family member or friend at no or low cost), course project writing, professional portfolios, writing completed as an employee while also a student, writing that had transformed from student writing to teacher writing, social network spaces, and a national teacher database of digital teaching material, to which I had limited access.

Upon receipt of web compositions from each interviewee, I analyzed them to generate discourse-based questions regarding potential tacit copyright-focused motivations and/or tacit copyright knowledge. I examined each web composition or web portfolio containing webpages with or without visuals, videos, flash movies, and PowerPoints, looking for examples where copyright law may have shaped content selection. I looked for small thumbnail images rather than entire, full-size images; I looked for the use of small snippets of materials, as in collages, and links to others' websites rather than the wholesale appropriation of others' materials, downloaded. I looked for content that may have been made or written "from scratch" rather than content that appeared extremely polished and commercial. I looked for originality and novelty—content that was new to me; I looked for familiar trademarks and content that I had seen or read previously, somewhere. In other words, *I looked for material in student web writing that was written by someone other than the student.* As webtexts were examined, questions asked of each text were:

1. What is the context for this webspace?
2. Who authored the components of this webspace?
3. Is there material present that might be copyrighted by others—text, visuals, sound?
4. If not, why not?
5. If so, how has the student synthesized these multimedia materials with other material?
6. Were strategies used to avoid negative copyright implications? Examples might be generic representations of name brand items, low-pixel or smaller-than-normal visuals, partial and/or short quotations, collages, visuals/sound files that have been modified from what might have been their original form, digital materials that appear to have been constructed from "scratch," attributions, copyright or use information (Creative Commons licensing, copyright symbol, terms of use, and so on).

In this chapter, I first provide additional details on the specialized interview method I used by walking through this process step-by-step with a specific example from the interview I conducted with Shauna, a participant in the 2006 pilot study. Shauna's interview provides some stellar, quintessential examples of the strengths of discourse-based interview strategies. And it was in the pilot study that I tested and developed this method. After the procedural details on the interview method, I describe the vignette as a method of data analysis and present visual and textual vignettes (that is, multimedia vignettes) of the seven interviewees who participated in the full mixed-methods study. I present these by first listing the interviewees' pseudonyms, then providing a visual vignette of their web writing, and finally summarizing the interviews with each writer. I conclude the chapter with some initial observations.

The Discourse-Based Interview: A Step-by-Step Example

Based on the methods offered by Odell, Goswami, and Herrington, discourse-based interviews were used in hopes of eliciting tacit[2] knowledge and better understanding writerly motivations behind specific choices made during the digital projects. Generally, discourse-based interviews ask interviewees about choices they made in their writing by offering alternative choices and requesting a rationale. A question might be: "I see here that you used a thumbnail image. Would you instead consider using a larger image or linking a pdf of that material?" The purpose of this question is to learn whether the writer was trying to avoid copyright liability by using the thumbnail image. Since the interviews were semistructured, parts of the discussions between myself and the interviewee were freeform or naturalistic, especially when I probed certain issues that arose with individual participants.

The discourse-based interview technique is good at helping interviewees retrieve motivations they might not be otherwise in touch with. During the approximately thirty-minute interviews, each interviewee's web composition was referenced as participants were asked to revisit specific choices made during writing that involved copyright/fair use issues (for example, use of images, videos, text) and were offered alternative choices meant to explore how that issue factored in making composing decisions (see appendix 4 for the interview protocols—sample interview questions). Figure 4.1 is a screen capture from Shauna's webtext. Shauna focused especially on *design* issues underlying her composing decisions, even expressly denying early in the interview that copyright influenced her decisions in any manner. But when asked about alternative choices, she acknowledged that copyright was a consideration. In her web composition, Shauna had chosen visuals of generic media, a visual of a generic jump drive, and when she was asked if she would choose something with a trademark or visual branding instead, she responded that she had carefully chosen the jump drive and other images because they were generic in order to avoid copyright liability.

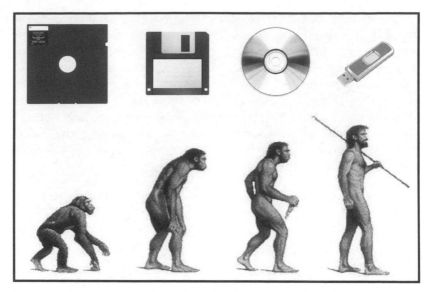

Figure 4.1. A screen capture from Shauna's webtext used to formulate interview questions before our meeting.

The screen capture in figure 4.1 is an extract of a larger webpage that included Shauna's picture and text. Before meeting with Shauna, as with the other interviewees, I collected a webtext and reviewed it with the above questions in mind. I knew that the webtext under examination was a part of this writer's professional digital portfolio. Upon examining the webtext, I deduced Shauna had probably not created from scratch any of the visuals depicting media (the floppy disc, jump drive, and so on). Since the "evolution-of-man" sequence looked familiar, I decided that Shauna probably had not created that either, but that the sequence had been created by someone else and the writer had matched together the media visuals and the evolution-of-man depiction. Based on my review of Shauna's web composition, I developed questions regarding composing choices. This is how I formulated the questions in each case. Since I wanted to avoid biasing my interview analysis, I did not examine participant survey scores until I finished analyzing their interviews, but I include those survey scores along with the vignettes. Interviews were digitally recorded and transcribed.

To further clarify the rhetorical topics that were part of the inventional heuristic I was seeking, I offer a few specific examples. Shauna's web composition featured in figure 4.1 provides an example of interview data portraying the rhetorical topic "copyright." Shauna chose the particular "evolution-of-man" image (a monkey gradually and linearly standing upright and turning into a man) because the audience might find these images very familiar. Because the evolution-of-man images were so commonplace, Shauna felt they were not original enough to be copyright protected—she felt they were common knowledge. That these images were widely available on the web also informed Shauna's content-selection process. In the event Shauna's use of the images was challenged, she thought she could argue that the "exclusive" rights of the copyright owner, if any, were in vain. It was her view that her use did not infringe on others' copyrights, and although she used existing material, it was in a way that created something "original" and fixed such that Shauna herself would now own the copyrights in the remix. As an example of the "probabilities" topic, Shauna carefully considered the use of others' work in her site and made sophisticated decisions on what kind of author or owner of copyright would be more or less likely to attempt to enforce copyrights against her educational use.

As an example of interview data portraying the rhetorical topic of "ethics," web writer Shauna applied her own moral judgment by cracking (circumventing) the anticircumvention code on film discs in order to take clips and incorporate them into a digital remix, a montage she'd created critiquing popular movies for their perpetuation of racial stereotypes. She said she knew it "is supposed to be illegal to circumvent the copyright protection on the discs." Even though she knew it was illegal (a violation of the DMCA), she said, "I circumvented that because the law prevents fair use which I don't agree with so I sort of use my own judgment about breaking that and that is the policy that I follow." Shauna carefully conducted a complex fair use analysis, then considered which laws it was ethical to follow and which laws she would break for ethical reasons.

When analyzing the interview data for purposes of mapping it onto the rhetorical topics, filling in the inventional heuristic I imagined, I also drew upon my former training as a lawyer and my experience conducting *legal reasoning* (Latour, 2010; Tiersma, 2008). Tiersma defines legal reasoning accurately as an analytical process that requires looking across texts for evidence of certain salient features, pulling these features out, and from this technique, formulating some kind of rule(s) or principle(s). As Tiersma points out, legal reasoning tends to be more conceptual than textual. For this stage of the analysis, I thought of the seven rhetorical topics listed as concepts rather than textual artifacts. How the concepts interact together and any conclusion that might be drawn across interviews are analyzed with legal reasoning. Legal reasoning is very similar, if not the same, to what Janice Lauer (J. Lauer, 1970; J. M. Lauer, 1979, 2004) describes as heuristical thinking, that is, having some frame of reference that one draws upon as one conducts analysis, solves problems, or invents; or in the reverse, heuristical thinking can be examining a text and extracting its rules or principles (see Rife, 2009b for a discussion of this latter technique).

This same kind of inventional process is at work when I conduct interviews, as when in the case that I used my former experiences interviewing clients (or witnesses) as a frame of reference. When interviewing clients, I had a certain heuristic in mind of which they were unaware. This heuristic might include, depending on the circumstances, the strength of the client's case based on the elements required to meet the definition of a certain legal concept. In the personal injury setting, if an injured client visited me, this legal concept might include negligence. Negligence includes elements of both causation and reasonable foreseeability. In order for a defendant to be deemed negligent, he must have caused the plaintiff's injury, and that causation must have been reasonably foreseeable. Part of this inventional process relying on heuristics also includes the weighing of probabilities in the sense of cost-benefit analysis—even if negligence is present, is the potential monetary award substantially greater than the costs of proving the case? Even if there is clear negligence, will the rules of evidence allow a fair chance of proving the case? Practicing law is usually a for-profit business, and so this kind of evaluation must occur when one is interviewing clients in for-profit environments. Similarly, when I interviewed study participants, I had a heuristic in mind that included the elements of fair use and the elements of copyright infringement, as well as the seven rhetorical topics listed. During data analysis, I attempted to categorize and fit the interview data into these heuristics.[3]

The Multimedia Vignettes

I chose to use vignettes as part of the interview data analysis for five reasons. The first reason is that this method of data analysis creates a small historic record of what writing was like in 2007 for this handful of digital composers. Considering the rate at which writing has changed over the last ten years, it is plausible that during the next ten years digital writing environments will change just as dramatically. Someone might want to repeat this study in the future and compare. The second reason is that the vignette permits additional opportunities to look across cases for principles. Vignettes help the researcher formulate key issues towards the researcher's theory of what is happening (Miles and Huberman, 1994, p. 81). The third reason is that using vignettes allows me to let all of the interviewees have a presence in this book, and that is very important. Each vignette raises key but diverse issues with respect to digital writing in the twenty-first century. Vignettes are a solution to an analysis problem where small pockets of data might otherwise be ignored (Miles and Huberman, 1994). The fourth reason I decided to write seven short vignettes is that they are similar to longer profiles (Miles and Huberman, 1994; see also Seidman, 1991), and I have experience writing newspaper profiles from interviews I conducted back in the 1990s in the community where I reside. I can thus draw on this experience with some expertise.

And finally, the fifth reason for using vignettes is that while the literature discusses vignettes with the assumption that vignettes are produced with alphabetic text, I decided to also incorporate visual vignettes of student webtexts to offer an interpretation and also protect participant privacy as best I can. My method in creating the visual vignettes is similar to my method for creating the alphabetic vignettes. With both, I took bits and pieces of the interviews, including bits and piece of interviewee digital writing, and wove these together in order to create a single coherent piece. The visual vignettes, like the textual vignettes, are minicollages representing the interviewee and his or her work. Such visual vignettes offer a brief impression of digital writers' work that might enhance readers' understandings. The multimedia vignette as a method of data analysis allows me to bring a standard research method into the twenty first century, taking into account the mixture of visual and textual writing that most folks in rhetoric and composition now experience on a daily basis with the advent of the web.

Vignettes are "vivid, compelling, and persuasive" (Miles and Huberman, 1994, p. 83), usually narrative and story-like; the researcher must use caution in order to avoid misleading. Because, as Erickson (1986) points out, a single vignette cannot provide interpretive validity within the vignette itself, Miles and Huberman (1994) summarize that "multiple vignettes and accompanying commentary are needed" (83). I therefore decided to create vignettes for all seven interviewees, along with commentary. It is imperative in this approach that the researcher make sure not to pull out only the most sensational or unique events, and not hide data that is inconclusive or contradictory. For example, Sarah expresses dissatisfaction with how copyright law was covered in her education, but Amanda is mainly content. Sarah goes to great pains to abide by copyright law, but prudent Leslie said she complies only if it is easy to do so.

In addition to the frame provided by the seven meditational rhetorical topics (probability, copyright, fair use, ethics, design, culture, employer requirements), I created an outline to shape the multimedia vignettes. This outline includes (1) context for the digital writing; (2) writers' motivations; (3) multiple roles of writer; (4) description of the writer's digital composition, its purpose, audience, and complexities;(5) the writer's aspirations or works in progress; (6) the writer's general attitude about copyright law as it intersects digital writing; and finally, (7) information, if any, the writer wants readers of the study to know about copyright and fair use in the context of teaching, learning, and working. In this area of the analysis, I examine each interviewee as a writer, his or her motivations and purposes in writing. This allows me to draw some conclusions about how digital writing might change our notion of "writing," and how such changes might impact teaching, learning, working, and research. In later chapters, I try to draw out issues raised in the vignettes as well as synthesize the vignettes with the survey data.

"Leslie"

Leslie was a PhD candidate teaching first-year writing at a doctoral university as she completed her degree requirements and entered the job market. The webtext depicted in figure 4.2 is a screen capture of the course webpage Leslie created for her first-year writing students. She was interested in using a theme for her writing course that might draw upon her students' interests while simultaneously involving the study of digital writing. Leslie said, "I wanted to have a cool site for them, when they first signed up." In her web writing, Leslie plays the roles of graduate student, teacher, and potential job seeker and employee. This webspace serves the pragmatic function of housing teaching materials, incorporating work Leslie did as a graduate student, and also showcasing Leslie's web design abilities and innovative pedagogies for potential employers. The gaming control and visuals were blended together by Leslie in a graduate visual rhetoric course, where she received feedback and even a grade from her professor. By the time Leslie taught this course, though, the gaming-control visual as a graduate course project had detached from its origins and was acting simply as a teaching and marketing tool for Leslie. By considering Leslie's multiple audiences, and how she fashioned this webtext over a period of time (more than one year) and with multiple underlying motivations illustrates the commonplace at work—a place of convergence of the past (graduate student), the present (graduate teaching assistant), and the future (faculty member at a new institution).

On a very practical level, Leslie's webtext illustrates a commonplace in remix writing, by bringing together the familiar with the unfamiliar. During our interview, Leslie explained to me that at the time she composed her digital remix, she had just learned Photoshop and "was playing with [her] new knowledge . . . doing cool things." She emphasized to me that her web composition was "made up of like 100 different pieces." Her remix-writing process was extremely complex. As she explained to me that the main portion of the digital composition focuses on a PlayStation component, a console, but she replaced the portion where one would "normally see the video game" with a "composite image" that includes "the name of the class" in fonts "developed for a particular game, Grand Theft Auto. It's called Price Down." Leslie divided up the composition visually into sections based on an idea she saw "somewhere else. Somebody had a

Figure 4.2. Visual vignette of Leslie's web writing.

book cover that had like little pieces divided up into little frames, sort of almost like stained glass, and I wanted to do something similar." In her web composition, Leslie wanted to emphasize how people use games rather than the games themselves. She obtained almost all of the images used to create the composite from flickr.com. "I searched for video games, and I got pictures of real people playing video games, and then I cut out just the people that I wanted. . . . I traced, cut out the people, and I ran them through some kind of filter to make it look funky like they do. They look kind of stylized, almost like video games." She then "assembled them into these little frames, and put them in there."

Leslie took things familiar to students— a game control, game fonts, a look of "stained glass," people playing games, a portable PlayStation, typical webpage navigation elements, an image of notebook paper, a list of office hours—and then blends those items together with the newness of a college course, creating an unfamiliar medium for a syllabus, making unusual connections between games and formal education, a combination of familiar game control and webpage navigation links and what to the new student is the great unknown of first year college writing, and brings all of these images and allusions into a new light. This is the commonplace, the digital remix. And it triggers all kinds of copyright issues.

Fonts can be copyrightable and usually are in the context of gaming and branding; gaming control designs are copyrightable. All the visuals Leslie took from flickr.com may well have copyrights owned by others. Leslie did all this without permission. She was far less worried about copyright than about protecting peoples' privacy, especially for the younger individuals featured playing games. That was one of her main motivations for applying the filters in Photoshop. She said, "I wasn't really worried about copyright. I didn't think anyone would come after me for taking their flickr pictures." She did say she would be more careful about using these materials to make her remix if she were going to sell this image for a profit. But in the context of educational use, "I think for not for profit, for educational purposes I think that would be pretty low on anyone's list of priorities for anyone to come after me about it." Leslie's multimedia vignette shows how the webspace as commonplace triggers rhetorical invention and begs for an examination of whether copyright is influencing writerly decisions.

Leslie is one of the participants least concerned about copyright—the law did not stop her from inventing and being creative. She concerns herself with copyright only if it is easy to do so and still accomplish her pedagogical and creative goals. For example, when asked about the possibility of posting copyright protected articles and teaching materials in an open webspace as opposed to a password protected one, Leslie explained that she "probably would, if that was the easiest thing to do. I would worry a little bit about copyright violations, but you know I would weigh that against what my options were. If I had an easy option to make it password protected I would do that but if I don't have an easy option . . ." Leslie made this web composition her own by cutting, pasting, applying filters, adding text, and synthesizing her own interpretations and ideas with others' materials. In Leslie's case, it turns out inventional decisions were made to protect peoples' privacy and for design reasons—to intrigue her students—rather than to abide by copyright law. Leslie took the old and turned it into the new.

Chilled Speech Score (0–2 not chilled; 5–4 very chilled):	3.0
Fair Use/Copyright Knowledge Score:	50%
Level of Certainty Score (1 very certain; 5 not certain at all):	3.0

"Carey"

Carey was a master's student in a professional writing program. She was also an employee of the institution where she was a master's student (not a student employee). I do not provide a visual vignette of her web composition because all she offers me is a social network site page fairly devoid of content. Before her interview, I wondered what we would talk about because she had not sent me a web composition that triggered any copyright issues. However when I arrived at the interview, we began talking about her nonstudent work with a national database that encourages teachers to share teaching and testing materials. Carey's involvement with this database is central, and she is directly involved in the design of the database's interfaces. She also provides technical support and training for the university-supported project. The teachers she works with include high school teachers as well as university teachers from all over the U.S. I cannot provide visual depictions because they are in a password-protected area.

Regarding her work as an employee, she stated that the users she works with usually do not choose to lock down their own information in the system, although they could. She believes this is because it is easier for them to leave their materials open to others. She explained that the CMS she manages is open source, and permits instructors to create, for example, a remixed physics course "out of homework that they created themselves, another colleague's at [the same university] . . . someone else's at [another university] . . . , and problems from the textbook they are using." Users can then choose to publish system wide, or lock it down in any way they see fit. According to Carey, textbook publishers regularly give all the images from textbooks to requesting teachers, who then publish these images to the entire network. Carey expressed concern about whether publishers know the images will be published in this way. Carey's general impression is that teachers are concerned about who might be able to access their self-created teaching materials. These same teachers are less concerned with any implications for sharing textbook materials or images with others who may not have purchased that book.

It turns out there is a logical explanation for the bareness of Carey's social network site. The main reason is that she feels responsible to the institution for her professional identity especially as it intersects with her knowledge of copyright. She feels that as someone working in a technology enhanced area where others' materials are shared, and as a student in a professional writing program that has a focus on digital writing, she should also be an expert on copyright. She is concerned about the design of her social network page with respect to code and errors in code. If she enhances her social network site, errors in the code will be visible to her colleagues who are scientists or web programmers.

In order to increase her copyright knowledge and because she has special interest in the topic, Carey took a special copyright course, not part of her regular curriculum, at the college library—offered for employees and students. Carey admitted that with respect to the social network site she uses, "I actually read those forms and I found out, like early on, when I first signed up, it says like oh you grant them your copyright—oh what a bunch of bull!" And so because of that, she hesitates to place anything that might be of value on her social network space. She says she would not place any "excellent" material she might have in her social network space because of the copyright ownership issues. Further, she doesn't add materials to her social network space because "I'm like snobby with my code, and I can see errors, and so many of them don't work on a Linux machine because they are not coded correctly, and I just get! So it ends up looking like that." In her webspaces, Carey occupies the roles of tech-savvy employee, graduate student, and family member. She and her husband are friended through their social network software profiles. While Carey is exceedingly knowledgeable about copyright issues, she does not feel totally confident about her abilities, and thus she prefers to keep a low profile on the web.

Carey is not doing a lot of reflection about copyright or fair use with respect to her social network site because she has decided to keep her site clean. After reading the social network site's terms of use, she did worry about having her own materials exploited. Yet the main reason she keeps her site clean is to control her professional identity, not necessarily to avoid copyright liability. With respect to the teacher CMS she maintains and supports, it is her employer's requirement that she allow teachers to share their materials. I am not sure that the institution has invested Carey with the authority to police these teacherly exchanges for copyright violations. She does not seem to think she has that kind of authority. My impression is that the institution that maintains this teacher exchange site looks the other way with respect to the technicalities of copyright. While Carey worries about copyright and ethical issues, she does not let that stop her from supporting others' use of the CMS. She does not act as a police officer with respect to how others use the system and remains very enthusiastic about the service. Carey wants teachers to use this system to share their materials. She did have a very strong reaction to the ethics question on my survey, which asks whether it is acceptable to break a law on occasion if that law is wrong. To this she answered a resounding "yes," explaining to me, "because I mean we wouldn't have all the civil rights, the law now, we wouldn't have it unless people stood up to the law."

Chilled Speech Score (0–2 not chilled; 5–4 very chilled):   1.0
Fair Use/Copyright Knowledge Score: 71%
Level of Certainty Score (1 very certain; 5 not certain at all):   3.2

"Rob"

Figure 4.3 is a visual vignette I created from the numerous web compositions (URLs) Rob supplied to me in anticipation of our interview. Rob was a second-year PhD student in a rhetoric and writing program. He was an international student, having come to the U.S. from India. Rob supplied me with numerous webpages he created both while still in India and while a student in the U.S. Rob constructs webpages for family and friends and previously worked as a web designer in India. He described this as doing

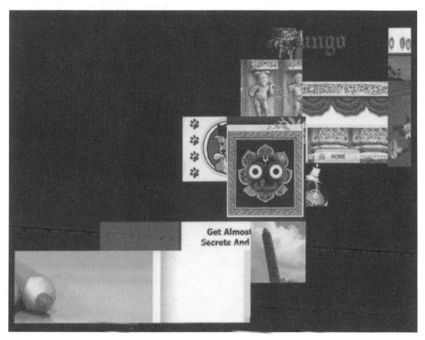

Figure 4.3. Visual vignette of Rob's web writing.

"outsourcing" work. In India, he created websites for people all over the world. He also offered websites he created as a graduate student featuring some his PhD coursework. So in webspace, he occupies the roles of family member, friend, student, and employee. I created a visual vignette of Rob's work partially to protect his identity, but also to impart an idea of the vast array of digital composing this writer completes.

The purposes and audiences for Rob's work varies greatly. He is very concerned about copyright, but that is a newfound interest after coming to the U.S. He noted that when obtaining his master's degree in India, reference pages and lists of works cited were not required. He did not consider copyright law in his work previous to entering the U.S. graduate program and learning about these issues as part of a course. Rob describes his pre–graduate school thinking as solidly based in the cultural norms of India. He theorizes: "There could be a historical/cultural reason why we Indians do not think about [copyright] much. Knowledge is a community-owned thing in India, and this concept dates back to the time before written language." He goes on to say, "Every aspect of politics, relationship, customs, dress, art is encoded in the scriptures. We use them and re-use them to suit our times. The question of asking permission to use them never arises." Interestingly, Rob's summary of India's cultural attitudes, that knowledge is owned by all, has been recently confirmed in the most recent (2010) IP Watchlist. In the context of their ability to provide citizens with access to knowledge, India is ranked number one within the top ten countries. Rob went on to explain that in India, he could just mention "any author" in his "university exam answer" but was not required to "add a reference to formally acknowledge the author, because to us, it is not the author, but the new knowledge that is more important." The ways that Rob character- izes this field of discourse in his home country of India (even though in academia) would fit into the second field of discourse described by Fou- cault in "The Original and the Regular" (the chapter in *The Archaeology of Knowledge*)—that author-light field where the statements supporting the discursive field should circulate widely and authors are less important.

After his extended stay in the U.S., Rob came to believe that copyright is very important, but he believes that if he obtains all his images from flickr. com, those images are free from copyright. That is not completely true, as many flickr.com images are restricted in some way by the owner. A user has to read each license, which can be exceedingly complicated. However Rob definitely tries to do things correctly. He is the only interviewee who experienced having his own web materials—photos and text—appropriated by someone else. One day Rob was searching the web and found a site that had taken his materials. But in this case, it was materials from the website of an professional Indian dancer he was writing for (gift writing), and she was happy someone had taken her images because it gave her additional publicity. Again, here the dancer's attitude shows us her images are circulat- ing in the "author-light" field, where the photos' author, the photographer, is less important. What is more important is dissemination of the photos' content, images of the dancer. So in that case, Rob did not have any worries about others using his material. But I asked what he might do if another person appropriated his webspace design, the design where he posted the dancer's pictures. I asked him if someone took his design and used it, sim- ply switching in different dancers' pictures, what would he do? He said he would "scream" and wanted to know if he could sue for something like that.

Rob is willing to share the dancers' text and pictures as long as it is ac- ceptable to the dancer. But as for his design, he expects others to respect his work and not use it without asking. Rob's attitude in this instance indicates he considers his web composition—the architecture and design of his composition—to be circulating in the author-heavy field. He wants credit for his work, and he does not want others to appropriate that work wholesale. He also tries very hard to use materials that are copyright free, are within fair use, are properly licensed, or have a low risk of triggering legal liability. He is very appreciative of learning about intellectual property issues in U.S. graduate school courses and discusses these issues as well with the first-year writing students he instructs as a teaching assistant at the university. Rob does consider copyright law and fair use as he composes for the web. He is also very concerned about ethical issues in the context of using others' materials, including proper attribution, and he of course considers design issues as he composes for the web. In the background of Rob's composing practices is his experience in India. This prior experience provides Rob with a rich contrast from which he can compare situations and practices in the U.S., making Rob very reflective and thoughtful about using others' materials. His Indian background presents a different cultural norm for remixing. This contrasting cultural norm is the basis of some of Rob's pre–graduate school practices for composing for the web. I have tried to capture this "cultural collision" in the visual vignette, although I am not sure I have done so.

Chilled Speech Score (0–2 not chilled; 5–4 very chilled):   3.0
Fair Use/Copyright Knowledge Score: 64%
Level of Certainty Score (1 very certain; 5 not certain at all):   2.3

"Sarah"

Sarah was a recent graduate of a professional writing program, having earned her master's degree just over a year ago. When she was not working on her novel, Sarah spent her time completing webpages for family members as well as church organizations that originally connected with her through family members. This work is completed either for free or at a very low cost. At the time of the interview, it appeared Sarah's "gift writing" was developing into a web design business that would continue to increase. She was thinking about charging proper amounts and developing legal contracts to govern her work. Sarah's primary web identity is a relatively invisible one, as she creates materials to promote others' endeavors—in the typical fashion of a technical writer. One of her relatives received a national book award, and Sarah created a website for this person at no charge in order to promote both the author and the book. This website is a total remake of a previous website and will continue to expand over time: "There is going to be five books total, and the second book is due out in spring, and then we will add another whole page, just on the second book, and the third book and the forth book and the fifth book." Sarah's digital work is represented in figure 4.4, a visual vignette providing a sampling of the kinds of work Sarah has recently completed in her role as digital composer. Her special focus is writing for others.

Sarah's work illustrates the idea of a commonplace, a mixing of the past, the present, and the future all in a neat package of one website. Sarah also created a website for a church at a low cost and is working on another

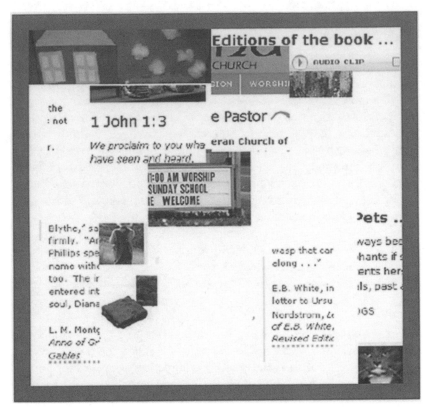

Figure 4.4. Visual vignette of Sarah's web writing.

church site, plus has additional jobs in the pipeline. She thus composes for a range of audiences. Of the seven interviewees, Sarah (along with Jesse) is one of the most reflective about her use of others' materials. She cares deeply about using others' materials ethically and goes to great lengths to try to use materials that do not require either permission or attribution. Sarah reads licenses and tries her best to understand them. She is very interested in copyright and fair use and strives to learn more and keep up to date on such matters. She also knows the flipside of copyright, in that her relative who received the book award has a proprietary interest in earning income from her book, and Sarah thus works to protect that in her web design. When asked whether she would consider including a link to a pdf of the entire book rather than a short audio excerpt imported from a commercial site, she said: "Well it would be bad business for her, I don't know if a pdf of the entire book exists, which means I would have to do it. As an employee of hers, I wouldn't suggest it because it wouldn't make sense to the purpose of the website, which is to advertise and publicize her book."

Sarah, as an independent contractor, also worries about protecting her clients from legal or ethical problems. For example, she carefully considers the use of others' photographs on the church websites (the church gave her photos of church members and events) and checks that these individuals have given some kind of permission. Although Sarah would have loved to have forms and perhaps a contract that she could have her clients sign, at the time of our interview, she was working under informal verbal agreements. The website "was for a whole church that I've never met before, and the idea of letting them down or getting in trouble was pretty nerve racking for me, because they trusted me, and I tried to be the best I could but I honestly didn't feel equipped, you know." These issues of privacy protection, contract negotiation, and detailed copyright in for-profit environments were not in the curriculum in the professional writing program where she obtained her master's degree. "I love the different things we learned in school, but the focus was really on work you do in the classroom." Sarah said that she reflects on "all the time we were building stuff in class where I wished we had pretended we were doing it for commercial reasons." She said that instead, the issues around digital writing in for-profit environments was "sort of ignore[d] . . . because we were safe then."

In other words, Sarah believes that her program did not really prepare her for entrepreneurship or operating an independently owned web design business. Undoubtedly, "fair use" plays a larger role in educational contexts. Its role is much less prominent in for-profit environments. In our talk, it is clear that Sarah does not feel she can rely on "fair use" in for-profit environments in the same way she could while still a student. And while she wants to further develop her web design business, she hesitates. She does not feel confident about working on her own in "independent web design" because of the uncertainly she's experienced working on websites for family members. She thinks she could only go forward doing more commercial web design if she were working with a group "because I feel like it's just a little too much, gray for me. On my own, you know."

The web compositions Sarah creates do use others' materials. Much of the content is given to her, some she locates, and some she creates from scratch. For example, for the relative's promotional site, Sarah was given quotes (including quotes from well-known authors that somehow connect to this new book), images, and text from her relative. Sarah herself takes entire book reviews and audio samples from commercial websites and incorporates those into the site. "She [Sarah's relative] wanted to quote, and she took them all herself, and listed them and I just put them all [on the site]. I really hadn't thought about it until now, but I can't imagine that there would be a copyright issue." Sarah also creates part of the design and text from scratch. This kind of remixing is also present in church websites she is working on. When asked whether she considered just grabbing some images from a Google image search, Sarah explained how she created a logo for a church website. First, she pointed out that she would certainly not just do a random web search in order to obtain images because it would be "blatant copyright [violation]." Instead she used iStockphoto, where she was able to download sample pictures. After doing that, she "changed it up in Photoshop, and made it more like a painting, then a photograph, and changed the colors to make it more vibrant." Once she did that, she showed it to her client, "and they really liked it." So she now returns to iStock to purchase images for a one-time licensing fee. She then bills her clients for this amount. By way of classic strategies of remix—webspace as commonplace—these multiauthored "100 different pieces" of content came together under Sarah's hand and converged in the web compositions Sarah shared with me.

Chilled Speech Score (0–2 not chilled; 5–4 very chilled): 3.0
Fair Use/Copyright Knowledge Score: 64%
Level of Certainty Score (1 very certain; 5 not certain at all): 2.3

"Jessie"

Jessie was transitioning from master's to PhD student. At the time of our interview, she was finishing up her master's in professional writing and applying to PhD rhetoric and writing programs. Soon after our interview, Jessie was accepted into a PhD program and was planning to continue her studies in this area. As a digital writer, Jessie maintains web identities as graduate student, graduate teaching assistant, teacher (having taught at other institutions), and applicant to PhD programs. Again I see the past, the present, and the future converging in Jessie's commonplace, her digital portfolio. The digital portfolio she shared with me contains all the basic elements like CV, teaching philosophy, classes taught, and so on. Jessie teaches web design and multimedia writing, but even in the first-year writing courses she teaches, she implements some type of major multimedia component. In the courses she teaches, Jessie always discusses and teaches fair use and copyright issues. Jessie might be called a copyright activist; she has a great deal of interest in preserving and expanding fair use. She developed some materials for teaching copyright and some theories and has presented these at numerous conferences and as a guest speaker in others' classrooms and has published on fair use/copyright in a major journal in computers and writing. Jesse's digital composing is represented in figure 4.5—a collage I pieced together from the webwriting she provided me as part of our interview.

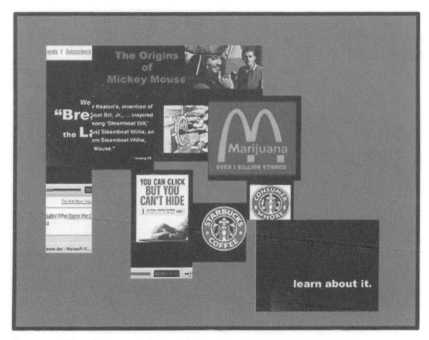

Figure 4.5. Visual vignette of Jessie's web writing.

Our talk centered on a movie she had created (Jessie refers to this as a PowerPoint essay). The movie is a multimodal "remix" presentation incorporating music clips, images from popular culture, and theories from researchers in legal studies and rhetoric and composition. This presentation argues for activism in the area of fair use and changes in the law. She hopes that the movie will increase public awareness. Having spent 100 to 150 hours creating the single movie, Jessie explained the genesis, development, and inventional process underlying her web composition. She tells me that her movie "started to be a book report about Larry Lessig's book *Free Culture*." She was supposed to present the book report for a graduate seminar; however Jessie's son had simultaneously "made a PowerPoint that ah, was an automatic, you click it one time and it played all the way through and it played to 'Wake me when September ends.'" Jessie said this inspired her. She decided she wanted to try to recreate the same kind of presentation and use it instead of the book report.

Once Jessie had her basic idea, she began composing and recalled "an old song called 'Breakin' the Law.'" She decided that song was about appropriation and fit her purpose: "It just kind of grew from there." The entire movie is ten minutes and contains three background songs. When asked about where she obtained the materials for her webtext (the movie), she answered: "Google.com." Unlike Sarah, who took the stance that lifting images from Google would be "blatant copyright violation," Jessie did not hesitate to use the Google search engine. In contrast, Sarah spent countless hours searching out licensable material and refused to take materials from Google. A key difference though is that Sarah worked on a web composition for a third party, and she did not want her own composing choices to bring liability to others. Jessie, on the other hand, was appropriating images from Google for her own use. The different purposes in composing then could explain the different stances of these two authors.

Jessie provided a detailed rationale for taking materials from Google. com. She said: "I mean I knew that ah, one of Lessig's examples was when Walt Disney remixed Steamboat Bill into Steamboat Willie, or got his idea for Steamboat Willie, Mickey Mouse's first cartoon from a movie that was called Steamboat Bill. So that's kind of where that started." She tells me it was "easy enough to go to Google and do an image search" and locate images for her to "highlight" what she presented in the movie. She took images of popular movies and "many a logo" in order to illustrate the need for freedom of expression. "So I show a logo of Star Bucks and someone's remixed it to consumer whore logo. I show a logo of Coca Cola and someone remixed it into a enjoy capitalism logo . . . these logos were um, 'right click,' 'save file,' 'save image as,' and I had them." Jessie pointed out to me that the "ease in which we can break the law, ah, steal, whatever words you want to use" was one of the problems she was trying to illuminate in her movie. She further wanted to educate others about the "disjoints": "whether or not people know that it's illegal when they do it, whether or not they care, and whether or not we have ethical issues that are surrounding these moves."

In tandem with her movie, an interesting component of her digital portfolio is an "open letter" to copyright holders explaining that while she tried to obtain permission for some of the materials in the movie, she was unable to do so and thus uses under fair use. This open letter evidences her taking responsibility and brings to my attention Jesse's concern for acting ethically and legally when possible. With respect to educators obtaining permission as Jesse tried to do, Hobbs, Jaszi, and Aufderheide's (2007) study reveals that obtaining permissions is not a realistic goal for educators because either permission is refused or the cost is prohibitive. It is also problematic because we do not write linearly, and seeking permission relies on a linear plan supporting the composing process. So Jessie echoes the frustrations held by many educators regarding the impossibility of obtaining permission when she says in her letter, "I have sought—to no avail—permission to use your material(s) in my PowerPoint essay showcasing the ease with which a person can commit 'piracy' and take music, video, images, and text from the Internet these days."

Jessie endlessly reflected about copyright and fair use issues as she constructed her movie and reported being told two opposing viewpoints from two professors in her graduate program. One professor cautioned her about showing the movie at an academic conference because her use was not necessarily fair use, and the other said for the most part just about anything goes at a conference because it is fair use. She agonized over these two competing views for quite some time (months and months). Finally, Jessie proceeded to show the movie at the conference with excellent reception. I viewed the movie numerous times and assess that to show the movie at an academic conference is almost certainly a fair use under Section 107. Jessie's ten-minute movie includes small snippets from multiple sources, remixed materials drawn from others' texts, music, images, and quotes. These materials are synthesized by Jessie, and in addition she added her own analysis and presentation to the final product. As a standalone product, the movie is very likely within fair use as long as Jessie is not selling it for profit, but at an academic conference, it is even more likely so because in that context Jessie folds the movie into a conference presentation; the whole text under consideration at that point is presentation itself, which includes commentary about the ten-minute movie. In that context, the movie is a component of the larger whole, and the movie itself is comprised of many pieces.

Jessie's situation recalls the 2006 Second Circuit case *Bill Graham Archives v. Dorling Kindersley*. In that case, without permission, publisher Dorling Kindersley used seven images of Grateful Dead concert posters or tickets in a history book on the Grateful Dead (see Rife, 2007b). Prior to the book's publication, the publisher unsuccessfully attempted to negotiate permissions with the copyright holder, Bill Graham Archives. Since permission was never granted in terms acceptable to the publisher, the publisher went ahead and used the copyrighted poster images anyway. Out of two thousand images in the book, rights to only seven were held by Graham Archives, and these seven images were incorporated into remixed compositions consisting of collages mixed with graphic art, textual explanations, and commentary. Because the images were synthesized in a larger work, and because they were used for a different purposes than what they were originally intended for (to advertise concerts), the court upheld fair use.

The *Graham* holding aligns with the more recent position taken by the register of copyrights, Marybeth Peters. In her recommendation for the 2010 DMCA exemptions, she pointed to examples of remix writing that are likely fair use. Luminosity's remix video *Women's Work*, a piece taking many clips from the television series *Supernatural*, is cited by Peters as a work likely to be within fair use because only small, minutes-long portions were used out of many hours of the entire series, and because the remixed video was "used for a new and different purpose from the original" (p. 50–51). In contrast, Peters points out that some video remixes might not be fair uses, especially when they use "multiple clips from the same motion picture" and "larger percentages" of a single motion picture (p. 51). Luminosity's *Vogue/300* is one such remix described by Peters as "showing an extensive montage of scenes from the movie *300* mixed with Madonna's sound recording, Vogue" (p. 51, n. 187). Unlike the situation in *Graham*, where bits and pieces of many works are mixed together, *Vogue/300* uses just two works, and so the register indicated this type of use is probably not a fair use.

Currently, Jessie keeps the movie posted to the web and available for the public to view without password protection, and by now the three-year statute of limitations (Title 17, USC, Section 507) on copyright claims has expired, so Jessie should be breathing a sigh of relief (to the extent she is aware of the statute of limitations).[4] As we finished the interview, I asked her if there was anything she wanted the reader to know. She answered that she wanted the reader to know "it's our students that are suffering because the laws, the way the laws are." She reported that when guest lecturing in various courses, she asks students whether they know what LimeWire is and they all know. She then asks them if they know anyone who has gotten into trouble for using LimeWire. "There's always a hand that goes up. Someone in that classroom, knows someone, has a friend, who um, [the university] has taken their lap top, taken away their online privileges, and if it ever happens a second time threatened to expel them from the school." The laws, she said, "are set for print; they are not set for our right clicking world. So, that's it. It's the students who are suffering. They are the ones who are getting in trouble."

Chilled Speech Score (0–2 not chilled; 5–4 very chilled): 2.0
Fair Use/Copyright Knowledge Score: 71%
Level of Certainty Score (1 very certain; 5 not certain at all): 3.1

"Heather"

Heather was a third-year undergraduate in a professional writing program. She was also a student employee, plus she was doing freelance web design work for a faculty member at the university she attended. Her work for the rhetoric and composition faculty member involved creating a conference webpage for a professional organization the faculty member is involved in. As a student employee, she also worked with a faculty member in a different discipline, a science program. Heather is very interested in copyright and fair use (to the extent that she eventually decided to attend and was

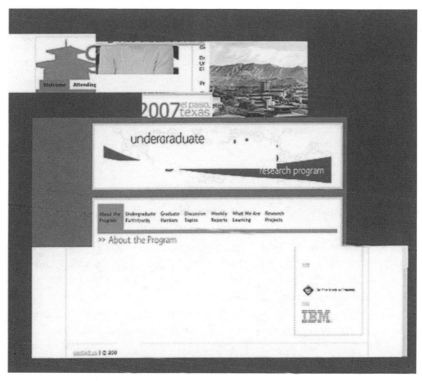

Figure 4.6. Visual vignette of Heather's web writing.

accepted into law school and into a program with an intellectual property concentration). As we proceeded through the interview, she noted how she creates her web designs partially by creating her own materials and partially by using content supplied to her by others (that is, classic remix). Heather's work is represented in the visual vignette in figure 4.6.

In the webtexts Heather shared with me, she is as invisible as was Sarah, in the fashion of a traditional technical communicator. Heather is the expert writer behind the scenes, creating webspace circulating in the "author-light" field, where what's more important is the dissemination rather than the authorship. In order to obtain materials and resources for her web composing, Heather frequents a couple of websites. One website she likes is deviantART.com, She explained this site to me as "a forum for people to put up any images, or even poetry and that sort of thing. You create a profile." She explained deviant art is "sort of like, like Facebook or something like that, but it's not really social networking. It's more like art and creative networking. So you can upload finished products." She went on to explain that visitors can create tools, like Photoshop brushes, that others can use. Heather said she obtained specialized artistic brushes she used to create a background thematic image for one of her for-hire webspaces. "They come in like sets. This set came with I think 3 or 4 other just DNA related brushes, and you have the option of like 'download here,' and then you can install it yourself." She explained where she learned about deviant art, partially from friends and partially from one of her writing teachers. She said she had friends in high school "who were really involved in art, and they all have deviant art pages." She learned about deviant art from those friends as well as the college teacher. The teacher used the web resource in order to teach students how to use the Photoshop brushes. "So that's where I learned about downloading."

Heather felt that it was legally safer to obtain materials from deviant art because people sometimes gave permission. "When people post things they'll have a disclaimer at the bottom, like their own little thing that says like you're free to download it but um sometimes they say that you have to just credit them for it on your website." According to Heather, deviant art users also might ask for a credit in an image, or to friend them in the website. She said she tended to look for downloadable materials that did not require attribution because "it's going to take away from the overall, like image, the product. So I try to find people who say, like just friend me." Like Sarah, Heather tries to locate materials to use that don't require attribution because it may have a negative impact on the design. Heather thinks about ethical issues when others give her materials or when she uses others' materials. On the professional organization conference webpage she wrote, she said she had some concern about where the organizers obtained some images they sent her, but she just wondered and never did anything about it. To make sure she was ethically and legally using others' materials, Heather carefully reads the guidelines for her use of the university logo and tries to follow those to "make sure that I wasn't screwing it up or anything."

In her web writing for a science department faculty, Heather created a science-focused web design. The interface incorporated other students' pictures and reports on an undergraduate research project. She felt confident she acted legally and ethically because she knew students regularly visited the site. Heather knew that the faculty member involved required students to "sign a form at the beginning of the research part, their own program, that was like a photo permission form, and they were all informed of the website." Further, Heather sent the students a link every time "something new was uploaded, so that they knew what was going on."

Heather's own personal digital portfolio was still under construction at the time of the interview, but she had no hesitation about using the materials she created for others as part of her portfolio. She did say that she was not sure who owned copyright in the webspaces she created for others—raising questions about work-for-hire issues. Heather also feels secure about her web design abilities such that she would ask questions of or make suggestions to faculty members if she thought something might be an ethical or copyright issue, as far as materials others gave her. She felt a responsibility to do so in fact, stating that "it's like online and you never know what people are going to put online. I consider this whenever I'm putting things online, and whenever people, especially on like Facebook, where people are putting photos of me online and whatnot." Heather emphasized that she considers permission issues and that she makes sure "someone knows that I don't want this. So whenever I'm doing web work, and there are other people, like their content involved, I always want to make sure that they at least know what's going on and that they don't have any problem with it."

Chilled Speech Score (0–2 not chilled; 5–4 very chilled):   1.0
Fair Use/Copyright Knowledge Score: 50%
Level of Certainty Score (1 very certain; 5 not certain at all):   2.9

"Amanda"

Amanda was a recent graduate with an undergraduate degree in professional writing. At the time of the interview, it was about two years since she had graduated and she was in her second full-time employment position. She was working for a national nonprofit health organization as an online communication specialist, regularly maintaining its website and using the organization's intranet. The visual vignette provided in figure 4.7 contains pieces of Amanda's professional portfolio. She is involved as an alum with her undergraduate program and generally finds it beneficial to stay marketable and keep her web portfolio up to date and reflective of her current position and past experience. Yet her portfolio is forward looking as well since she does participate in various professional activities, some of which are competitive—such as applying for a teaching-abroad opportunity and seeking promotion and raises. Again we have an example of the past, the present, and the future converging in the webspace as commonplace.

Amanda's portfolio is extremely robust, containing samples of every kind of imaginable writing, from memos, to book chapter edits, to original poetry, to web design. In several areas of Amanda's portfolio, she features others' work she edited. In other areas, she features work completed collaboratively. Amanda also keeps a copyright mark on the bottom of each webpage—not to stop people from taking her materials since she thinks anyone who wanted to appropriate her materials could do so and there's really no way she could find out, but because she thinks it looks more professional. Amanda tells me the copyright mark gives "more legitimacy.

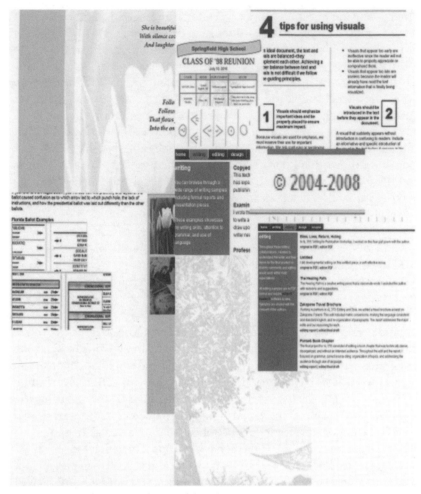

Figure 4.7. Visual vignette of Amanda's web writing.

Basically saying, you know, it's my work. It gives a good idea of when it was started and that I still update it, because the dates are on it."

Amanda's composition incorporates texts, visuals, and designs created by others. She uses stylized proofreading marks in her design, which she obtains on the web and considers a fair use partially because she retrieved these marks from a university website that was used to teach students editing marks. (However the fact that the editing marks were used to teach, on its own, does not necessarily mean others can legally use them without copyright concerns.) She has a knack for incorporating undergraduate course assignments into her portfolio in such a fashion as to make these items look like work completed in for-profit environments. Part of this knack comes from her ability to keep everything clean and professional. Amanda wants to showcase her editing abilities, but when using others' texts she asks permission. She explained some of her materials, telling me that some of the pieces were completed in a class "where everybody was developing their own published work." She explained that her "role in each of these pieces was really to do some kind of editing." And so with the items she edited, she "did ask permission from the people who wrote the original to have their work up there." That way, Amanda could include both the original and the edited version.

Smartly, Amanda also notes throughout her portfolio "used with permission" in order to signal to her audience awareness of the ethical issues that arise when incorporating others' texts into one's own writing. Some of the other materials on Amanda's website are chapters and flyers she's edited. These items are from real companies. She does not include the originals because she does not have permission from the companies. But interestingly, the original chapters and flyers were provided to her by the teacher of an undergraduate course. I asked her, "Did the teacher in any of these courses tell the students, like did any of them address issues of copyright and fair use, or using those kinds of materials in your professional portfolio . . . how did you decide; was it part of the curriculum?" And she replied: "No. No it wasn't discussed." So she independently decided that it would be unethical to use someone else's materials without their permission even in this case of doing it to illustrate her own editing skills acquired at an educational institution. However she did include the original when blended with her edits. She clearly states her concerns are ethical, not legal.

Amanda's design uses lots of white space and not many visuals on each linked interface page of her site. While I thought perhaps this was because she feared copyright liability, she emphasized that she avoids using visuals because of design reasons. "I wanted it to be more clean, and there isn't really a lot of . . . with pictures, it's not necessarily going to be consistent . . . I just wanted to keep it clean and simple." In her portfolio, she wished to emphasize the work she did "with the text" rather than her design skills. So the visuals were less important to her. With respect to the visuals she did use, some of them are very generic and from her early college experience—at times she was the only student in her class doing a webpage for a course assignment. She did not remember where she obtained these generic visuals, although she knew she herself had not made them. As far as copyright, Amanda is not terribly concerned about it.

In her job, the employer provides forms that others must sign to release their rights to donated materials, pictures, and texts. With the advent of user-generated content, such releases are crucial for Amanda to perform her job. She is well aware that she is not the author of material she completes as an employee and also feels a sense of responsibility as a representative of the organization to make sure the organization is presenting a uniform identity and is using others' materials fairly. Speaking for the organization, she said, "We want to make sure that . . . we are presenting the same information that we are presenting everywhere else, to make sure we are pulling all of our statistics from the same place." Amanda pointed out to me the importance of users' ability to validate that the content on the website is indeed from the nationally known health organization. She also emphasized that when interviewing users (as their stories are included and integrated into the webspace), the users are properly attributed and sign consent forms so that "we can use anything that they say, and any images that they supply, or anything like that in whatever way we feel best." She explained to me that the organization has several forms it requires user-contributors to sign including a publicity form. "If it's a kid then the parents have to sign it . . . it has all the same sort of language that like our websites have when people want to share their story, or talk about their experiences." Amanda reminded me that users trust the organization, and so the company must assure that no use is "disrespectful, or judgmental about their character, or anything." She further pointed out that the release forms user-contributors sign is to protect both the organization and "the people who we are getting the stories from." In addition to having the proper forms signed, when Amanda works with users, she also gives "them the option to review it first before I publish it. . . . It's just a courtesy."

As we ended the interview, I gave her an opportunity to tell the reader what she wanted them to know about the importance of copyright in educational contexts, or otherwise. She wished to remind the reader that it is "definitely important to teach it and I know in our program it definitely was, but I don't know if it was in other programs." She is especially concerned about how user-generated content might intersect with copyright issues. She is concerned that the issue of plagiarism with respect to using images on the web isn't being focused on sufficiently in college courses. "I think it's not really clear what you are allowed to use and when you are allowed to use it, and when you have to get permission, stuff like that." She also wished for more education and training with respect to using licensed images (Creative Commons, for example) and materials from the web "because I still don't understand that completely."

Chilled Speech Score (0–2 not chilled; 5–4 very chilled):   2.0
Fair Use/Copyright Knowledge Score: 57%
Level of Certainty Score (1 very certain; 5 not certain at all):   1.5

A Few Observations

I'll end the chapter by summarizing some key observations that came from the interviews, and extending these observations into more detailed analysis in the remaining chapters. As I examined composing processes of digital writers, I learned they drew materials for their webtexts from many sources; materials are cut, pasted, and then synthesized into new web compositions. Some research participants did not recall where each image came from, or where every idea derived from. So the webtexts are both new (novel) and not new (discovered) simultaneously. Miller's (2000) discovery-novelty dichotomy analysis has relevance since it may inform developing definitions of remix in digital composing contexts. And as Perl wrote back in 1979, "Composing always involves some measure of both construction and discovery" (p. 35). In turn, Miller's discussion of discovery and novelty reminds me of Lessig's discussions of remix culture. Remix writing, like that evident in the digital commonplace, relies on the circulation and appropriation of the intellectual creations of those other than the remix writer working at any particular moment in time. Digital writers like those in my study, working in the web's commonplace, bring together and synthesize the familiar, creating something new or unfamiliar. In the process of web composing, writers "hunt" for content, and for reasons to make one choice over another—studying the tracks on the ground; they conjecture and invent in the same rhetorical sense that Carolyn Miller describes in her analysis of the discovery-novelty dichotomy.

During our interviews, the digital writers revealed to me the web composition's seeds, how and where they generated ideas, who did or did not give them materials for the composition, and whose material had or had not been appropriated. Jessie, the master's student about to go on to a doctoral program, surprised me when reporting her inventional process for the digital movie was inspired by her son's animated, multimedia PowerPoint. Jessie took ideas from an amazing variety of sources; she drew from her knowledge of popular culture, music, movies, her son, and Google.com. When I asked her to discuss her composing processes, she revealed to me her ingenious inventional strategies, simultaneously discussing the origins for her ideas as well as the source material she remixed into her own digital writing.

The stories digital writers use to describe their inventional processes are stories tracing the origins of their webtexts, like creation stories. Origin stories (whether pertaining to texts or a people's first entry onto the earth and into history) are author-functions because they work as *activities* that produce authors (the authors of a people, culture, group, community, text). Authors are represented as the originators of texts, artifacts, ideas, and, in

Foucault's words, "fields of discourse." The origin stories of a community permit the persons in that group who tell those stories to be the authors of their own beginnings. But, of course, an examination of authorship necessitates a return to the initiation of a text, and that act of return in itself never stops modifying the point of origin (because that point of origin, the initiating inventional act, is then subject to the continual operation of interpretation). Simultaneously, the operative act of interpretation is required in this context because it is that "operation" that results in the "Author" (Foucault, 1972, p. 24). Unity, Foucault argues, is the result of an "operation," and that operation is "interpretive" (p. 24). The originating point under examination—which must always continue to be under examination because of its nature as the initiating point— becomes its "own void," an ever-changing, ever-receding "secret origin" that can never quite be grasped (Foucault, 1972, p. 25). It follows logically that if the true origins of an initiating act are ever receding, then so is the true authorship of any composition because to be an author is to be the initiator. I explain these ideas more in the next chapter. But for purposes of the vignettes, while I did trace authorship, I certainly did not find the ultimate originating point for each webtext. From a research perspective, if we take seriously Foucault's argument about the originating point as its own void, it would be an impossible task to locate such a point as a fixed place. Instead, as researchers, we can attempt to trace back a line of authorship, or a network, within a specific timeframe. In the case of my study, my timeframe is that defined by the memories of my interviewees.

As far as sole authorship, none of the student webtexts in my study were created by the student-author in a vacuum, emanating solely from the student's own creative genius (although I think all the student writers I interviewed were both genius and creative). Instead texts, artifacts, visuals, and ideas are liberally taken from others. Heather frequents deviant art, Rob goes to flickr, Jessie uses Google.com, and Leslie draws from various web sources that supply gaming images. All of these digital writers took from sources outside themselves, from multiple places, and then mixed those materials with their own ideas, creating something new. Student interviewees in this study produced something new in their writing—new remixes, new ideas, new assemblages (Johnson-Eilola and Selber, 2007). Here I offer you empirical support that rhetorical invention is useful not just to arrange existing information, but also to produce new knowledge as the research participants did in their web writing.

As I discuss more in the next chapter, the category and othering of "student" subjectivity may serve the useful purpose of organizing meaning in the institution, but web writing otherwise seriously challenges the reality and usefulness of this category. Grabill (2007) states he does not believe "in clear classroom-community or university-real world distinctions," reminding us that "the people in our classrooms are citizens as well as students" (p. 121). Grabill argues our students participate in civil society and civic cultures "in ways we could not imagine for them" (p. 121). Proponents of community, informational, digital, and multiple literacies already push against traditional notions of "studentness." DeJoy (2005) addresses the othering problem by arguing that we might bring students in as stewards of the discipline. We might more closely read their writing. The implications for teaching and research are many.

If students are writing in for-profit environments without being paid (that is, doing digital "gift writing") as I discovered in my research—this might reshape our pedagogies and curriculum. Some students, like Sarah, also want to become web-writing entrepreneurs. Have we enabled this? The category of "student writing" certainly changes shape between the three-page paper essay, handed solely to the teacher, and the digital remix, digital portfolio, "letter to copyright holders," and student-created movie challenging our notion of digital theft. New considerations of audience are in order when we consider teaching writing. In my study, the copyright holder and the potential appropriator become members of the student's audience. It doesn't take that much of an imagination to envision a panel of appeals court judges as an anticipated audience, one day evaluating your composition and appropriation of others' materials. Jessie had written an open letter to copyright holders that was posted to her website; Rob had had his content ripped, mixed, and burned by another web composer. Do current writing pedagogies take into account, at minimum, the copyright holder and the potential appropriator as members of the audience? These considerations are important as we move forward, teaching and researching writing in the twenty-first century. I present these vignettes of digital writers to establish a foundation for the discussion following in the next chapter, where I further draw in and synthesize the information gathered from the survey in order to develop a theory of authorship in digital contexts.

5

A Remixed Theory of (Digital) Authorship

> Who is speaking?
>> —Michel Foucault, *The Order of Things*, attributing Nietzsche

> Who is speaking?
>> —Michel Foucault, *The Archeology of Knowledge*

> What does it matter who is speaking?
>> —Michel Foucault, "What Is an Author?" attributing Beckett

As part of the mixed-methods approach, in the next couple of chapters, I integrate and synthesize the data from the surveys and the interviews. First, I discuss a framework, a digital-context, remediated theory of Foucault's "author-function" mixed with ANT, a theory of authorship reaching beyond the traditional "literary author" and deriving in part from my empirical work with "live" digital writers and their texts. Next, because of the changed nature of authors and writing due to digital environments, I map out an understanding of the Commons, which situates common knowledge and other kinds of texts and artifacts we frequently encounter. I end the chapter by discussing how this remixed theory of authorship challenges traditional, fixed understandings of "studentness," further exploring some of the implications of digital authorship.

In "What Is an Author?" Foucault focused part of his discussion on authors as others typically understand them, in the very limited sense of literary figures. Subsequent writers relying on Foucault's ideas about authors tend to work with and theorize around the "literary" author—probably because they are indeed writing about literary works, and that's why Foucault's essay is deemed relevant to their discussion (see, for example, Rose, 1988; Ray and Graeff, 2008; see also Gutting's [2005] chapter on Foucault and "Literature"). Reyman (2010) broadens Foucault's theory a bit by discussing the Foucauldian author as a "construct" in order to emphasize the connection between copyright law and the formal notion of the "modern Western author" (p. 14; see also Woodmansee and Jaszi, 1994). In her study of narratives and metaphors in the peer-to-peer file-sharing debate, Reyman summarizes the digital author as one of the many "unfulfilled promises of the Internet" (due to legal and "code" restrictions). The promise of the "digital author," according to Reyman, encouraged "a type of authorship that allowed for collaborative creation, the social construction of meaning, and dynamic and malleable texts" (p. 17). Reyman's discussion is one to build on and further complicate as we move forward in theorizing and understanding digital authorship. In this chapter, I build upon Foucault's idea of author-function by extending and complicating it with ANT's concepts of radical symmetry and actor networks in order to make "author-function" more relevant to twenty-first-century writing practices. I tend to think of the author as a "node" or "product" because I want to focus on the *materiality* of the author. My hope is to work toward theorizing not only the author as a product or node, but to imagine the kind of work (activities and operations) this author/product engages in upon its emergence, and what networks go into creating the author/product at its inception.

To fill out the picture we have now, I build upon two senses[1] of the word *function* (a word frequently used by Foucault throughout his writings)—one as a noun—where the word "function" is replaced by "activity" (Foucault himself refers to the "activity of the author function"; 1979/1984, p. 117)—in other words—*activities leading up to* and producing authors or activities of the author once he (it/she) emerges. The second sense is of *function* as a verb—to operate or to *perform a duty after* the author emerges. So if an "author" is a "node in a network" (Foucault, 1972, p. 23; Law, 2003, p. 4), the idea of "author function" or author-function as I refer to it, helps us analyze and theorize what occurs both upstream and downstream from the "author." In "What Is an Author?" Foucault focuses on what occurs downstream from the emergence of the author (in this view, the author is "the principle of thrift in the proliferation of meaning" [1979/1984, p. 118]; that is, the author acts as filter and impediment to the circulation of information).—But Foucault does make references to the production of the author as a function of discourse and power ("the author does not precede the works" [p. 119]). In *Discipline and Punish*, when describing the Panopticon in the same way he described the author-function, Foucault wrote, "It is a way of making power relations function in a function, and of making a function function, through these power relations" (1977, pp. 206–7). Throughout his writings, Foucault did discuss what occurs both upstream and downstream from a "node in a network," but he tended to discuss it in a much more convoluted way than the ANT writers do, and throughout his writing career, he revised and clarified his views (Burchell, Gordon, and Miller, 1991).

Perhaps Foucault's writing is difficult because he was trying to "escape from a fixed identity" and used writing to change identities, in the hopes of pushing language to its boundaries by "never really being anyone" (Gutting, 2005, p. 10). I want to make clear that I, of course, can never know what Foucault *really* intended, which is one of the ironies Foucault pointed to in his writings: the "author" provides a mechanism by which to organize meaning and resolve all conflicting meaning across "works." It's easy to see in this book that I clearly use "Foucault" to categorize a set of ideas, but even Foucault himself (ironically) suggested that his theories were consistent. For instance, in the French journal *Esprit*, he asks the reader to allow him to "speak not only of my last book, but also of those which preceded it . . . because together they form a cluster of researches whose themes and chronological reference points are quite adjacent" (1991, p. 53). The political analysis used in *The Archeology of Knowledge* and *Discipline and Punish* can be understood only "by reconstructing certain 'techniques of power'"(Gordon, 1991, p. 3). The techniques of power to be studied are "designed to observe, monitor, shape and control the behavior of individuals within a range of social and economic institutions such as the school, the factory, and the prison" (Gordon, 1991, p. 4). Foucault said the method of analysis he used to study individual humans located in "local institutions" could also be used in other contexts, for example, to address practices of governing between a "political sovereignty over an entire society" (Gordon, 1991, p. 4). My intent here then is to take Foucault's ideas and build upon them to my best ability, finding in them as I can consistency within his work, with the hopes that others, someday, will continue the conversation where I leave off.

The ANT theorists themselves acknowledge clear connections between ANT and Foucault's theories. John Law (2003) categorizes both ANT and the work of Michel Foucault as "post-structuralist semiotics of materiality" (p. 4). Both, he says, have to do with and explore "relationality." According to Law, in both ANT and Foucault "entities, things, [and] people, are not fixed" (p. 4). A researcher's job, according to Law, is to "explore how those relations—and so the entities that they constitute—are brought into being" (p. 4). In ANT, nothing, including people, science, and any "particular node in the network," has significance on its own without being considered in relationship with other nodes (p. 4). Neither people nor science is very special (Law, 2003)—this idea provides the "radical symmetry" component. Using radical symmetry, I can offer evidence that some existing historical scholarship, or even current events, are sometimes discussing activities and operations that function in the same way intellectual property laws and authors do, although such practices are not named "copyright law"—for example, practices around discourses of plagiarism, ethics, discourses within academic disciplines involving the study of great authors (that is, English literary studies), discourses around great inventors or discoverers, decisions around whose version of history (origins) prevails, and even cultural practices involving dress and attire. All support the ideological production named "author."

Like John Law, Foucault emphasizes the importance of hunting for origins by severing the connections that appear so easily in response to our initial inquiries. Urging us to "rid ourselves" of notions that lead to "unity" such as "tradition," "influence," "development," "evolution," and "spirit," Foucault says that the unities that "must be suspended above all are those . . . of the book and the *oeuvre*" (1972, p. 23). The "book" of course is inextricably connected to the "author," those functions that produce and maintain him, and even the disciplinary power of the author as a representative being, a power engendering a whole regime of disciplining technologies (copyright law, plagiarism issues, citation practices, the idea of "great works," fields of discursivity, and so on). Through both Law's and Foucault's lenses then, any "entities, things, people," come out of certain relations, networks, cultural operations, or "author-functions" (activities and operations) that produce them. But in contrast to ANT theorists, Foucault tends to focus on discourse and language, and that can detract from the ability to use his theory to see texts (as well as entities and people) as objects circulating and with agency of their own, independent of humans—and that's why ANT is helpful—because it better articulates a methodology arguing for the likeness, or the symmetry of objects that might otherwise not be apparent. So I move forward with these two senses of a more robust "author-function," as activity and operation, to build upon the conversation Foucault started.

In this project, copyright law figures in addition to the human writers themselves because my argument is that under this extended Foucauldian theory, copyright law is an author-function, an activity leading to the production of authors, and also an operation upon the author, a reconstitution of him once he has emerged. Those (multiple and complex) founders of copyright law, Title 17, additionally are authors in the sense they have initiated a discursive practice (case law, interpretations, writings, research, conference presentations, law school courses, international negotiations) that are heterogeneous to the statutory law itself—while at the same time belonging to the field of "copyright law." Each time the law is modified through interpretation (which is exactly what case law, as well as the briefs, oral arguments, courtroom practices, and evidentiary procedures underlying that case law, do in the U.S.), it gains a new originating point—one not necessarily strictly authored by humans—at some point the law-as-text can become the author of itself—and that's where we can think about the agency of nonhuman authors under this idea of "author-function." This is also where ANT proves useful, because it very clearly authorizes us to consider nonhumans as agents in the operation of power. Like any activity or operation bringing together many heterogeneous bits and pieces of information and organizing them together under a sort of oneness, a unity, copyright law is an author-function in that it classifies and divides by assigning exclusive rights to copy, perform, display, create derivative works from, and distribute to the creator of an original, fixed work. Copyright law allows an artifact to emerge, one that is "fixed" and "original," and at least in theory originates in the hands of a single creator, an individual: an author. Once the author emerges in relationship to his text, copyright strengthens and maintains his rights—one then revisits copyright law in order to reassess one's status as an author. Each revisitation though modifies the law and resets its point of origin from thence forward.

While Foucault provided some very useful lenses through which to examine the law-function and the author-function across his work, there are shortcomings because he never explicitly (and clearly) connected these two theories. In my study, since both issues of authorship and issues of (copyright) law are examined, bridging this gap in Foucault's work is helpful. By closing the gap between Foucault's view of law-function (to grossly simplify: in the upstream, laws are created through human practices in order to discipline humans in the downstream) and author-function (again, over simplification: the author, viewed as a perpetual surging of innovation, is instead an ideological production masking both his real function as impeding the flow of information and masking the complex practices that produce him)—in this gap, then, a new theory of authorship can emerge. This newly informed view of "author" can in turn provide a starting point for the theorization of *authorship in digital contexts*, a remixed theory of authorship. Rather than relying on ANT alone to do this, it's important to keep Foucault's theory central because, taken in its primary form, ANT can flatten actors so much that the humanness in my research participants might completely disappear. Furthermore, Foucault writes about authors explicitly and is probably more familiar to the reader.

Data analysis in this study shows that the intertextuality and relationality of webspace writing provides empirical support for Foucault's theory that the single author is an ideological production. "When a historically given function is represented in a figure that inverts it, one has an ideological production" (Foucault, 1979/1984, p. 119). Foucault (1979/1984) emphasizes the author is viewed as a genius, "so different from all other men . . . as soon as he speaks, meaning begins to . . . proliferate indefinitely" (p. 118), when in fact this representation inverts his true function, which is to *impede* the flow of information. Additionally, the author is represented as a unity when in fact he is produced from operations that are heterogeneous, multiple (such as the diverse trajectories of case law applying U.S. copyright Law, Title 17), and far more unbounded than what is traditionally termed *author*. So as a unity, as a node, the author inverts both the activities upstream from his emergence as well as the operations downstream once he has emerged. If one considers the author a set of relationships, then the author can be seen to switch in and out of position in relationship to human and nonhuman actors.

My data supports the idea that author-producing practices, those practices that produce a figure; an author; a single name, person, idea; packaged neatly and without loose ends; these practices are multiple and heterogeneous rather than unified. The author in his initiating act is not he who writes the digital composition; it is the digital composition that produces the author, and the construction of the digital composition is time-consuming, messy, and complicated. In the act of revisiting, researching the authorship of web compositions, as I did—that author as figure is further constituted, crystallized, within that interpretation—the author-figure functions to organize meaning. The seven vignettes I provide for the reader cannot help but further constitute the web "authors" in this study, while simultaneously subjecting their true "authorship" to inquiry.

We can connect Foucault's broader discussions of law-function, the disciplinary power of the law, and the power of discourse produced through institutions to further inform our understanding of digital authorship. Foucault's analysis of discourse arising from problems with lepers and plague (the law-function) connects to his discussion of the author-function. Foucault argues that authors arise from our fear of "proliferation of meaning." This fear is similar to the motivations that caused dividing and grouping practices arising with respect to leprosy and the plague. In those instances, the fear is the proliferation of disease. Like texts, like scripture and government documents, disease is information

Foucault (1979/1984) writes, "The author allows a limitation of the cancerous and dangerous proliferation of significations within a world" (p. 118). When significations spread, they become ubiquitous just like uncontrolled leprosy or the plague. When viral information spreads, so does the disease. For example, some of the interviewees have visual elements in their web compositions and were not sure where these items were originally obtained. Such visual elements include generic images of flowers, mountains, and sunny skies. Because these items are unoriginal and contain no authorship information, they become ubiquitous on the web. Such cliché visual elements are easily appropriated and in turn proliferate. U.S. copyright law creates a check on this. The law makes authors more likely to exist and sustain and in turn makes any text that might be copyrighted less likely to be ubiquitous. Interviews in this study show that when a remix writer has just some knowledge of copyright law, that knowledge causes a hesitation before using another's materials. One has to assess whether or not a text is copyrighted, if so by whom, whether or not one's use is "fair," or whether permission is needed. If permission is needed but unlikely to be forthcoming, one might weigh the chances of being caught using the others' materials, and whether or not one will then be taken to task on possible copyright infringement.

The thought that an "author" may exist, and that one may be held accountable under copyright law for transgressing his rights, slows down, impedes the flow of information and the construction of new texts. Leslie, whose knowledge score is just 50%, did think about copyright law but weighed the possibility of being held accountable versus the time it would take to design around copyright. She noted in the interview that she did not worry much about possible copyright liability when taking images from flickr because she just cannot imagine someone "coming after" her for that. Carey, whose knowledge score was a high 71%, chose to keep her personal web publishing as barren as possible so that she did not have to consider all the implications of copyright law. This turns out to be a time saver for her. She does not need to hesitate in her web writing because she simply avoids writing at all rather than perfect her compositions with respect to copyright limitations.

Sarah, whose knowledge score is 64%, spent vast amounts of time reflecting on the legality of various uses in her web writing. She worries about bringing liability on groups she writes for; whenever possible she uses web material that is available to be legally licensed; sometimes she seeks permissions. Jessie as well spent many hours trying to make her web composition copyright compliant and even wrote a letter to possible copyright holders documenting her attempt to be legal. All of these copyright considerations slow down the remix composing process and in turn the proliferation of meaning. U.S. copyright law, like the figure of the "author," attempts to impede the "proliferation of significations." Based on the interviews, even those with scores as low as 50% on copyright knowledge still took at least some time making copyright liability determinations as they used others' materials. Copyright law as an author-function, as a heterogeneous means, one that slows down and organizes the proliferation of meaning, creating order as an effect, appears to be somewhat successful in terms of the seven digital writers I interviewed.

According to Foucault, fear of the proliferation of meaning is likely attached to the fear of total chaos. The web and its ability to instantly deliver information contribute to fear of the proliferation of meaning, to potential chaos. In "What Is an Author?" Foucault is unable to imagine texts widely circulating without authors. He says it would "be pure romanticism . . . to imagine a culture" in which fiction would circulate in an "absolutely free state," available to all, and could develop without passing through something like a "constraining figure" (1979/1984, p. 119). And yet he predicts such a future culture. Edwin Hutchins (1995) conducted computer simulations to show what happens if "every conscious being is in continuous high-bandwidth communication with every other" (p. 252). The computer simulations showed that more communication is not necessarily better than less communication. Indeed Hutchins writes: "Under some conditions, increasing the richness of communication may result in undesirable properties at the group level" (p. 252). What Hutchins names "undesirable properties" Foucault refers to as chaos. Unbridled proliferation of meaning across all networks results in chaos. The web, in theory, allows an unprecedented ability for information to travel and be exchanged. Viewing the web this way makes the burgeoning discussions of authorship, copyright, and plagiarism sensible. The inability to tamp down this unprecedented ability for information to travel certainly points to the possible death (and subsequent rebirth) of traditional understandings of "authorship," "copyright law," and all the practices put in place to stop plagiarism. If a text can be created, can be detached from its origins, and can circulate ubiquitously, the author disappears. On the Internet, not only is this detachment and circulation possible, but the chances of its occurrence are actually enhanced. Because fiction indeed now circulates without having to pass through a figure– websites like snopes.com help educate users on urban legends circulating on the web. No wonder that since the advent of the Internet, scholarly focus on plagiarism is more intense; some scholars and educators are even fixated on detecting plagiarism. It is as if we are trying very hard to maintain the ideological production "author"—because to do otherwise potentially signals chaos. The author serves to control the unimpeded proliferation of meaning; this is also what prisons, educational institutions, law, and medical practices do, according to Foucault.

While admitting that additional characteristics of the author-function are probably discoverable, Foucault focuses on four. The first is that the author-function is linked to the ability to transgress certain expectations of the institution. For example, copyright law attempts to maintain the author, as do practices of attribution, discourses on plagiarism, permission seeking, literary analysis, and so on. The subsequent practices these author-functions engender are things like abiding by copyright law, attributing, requesting permission, studying "the canon" and "great authors," all practices that serve certain *institutional expectations that there is an "author" somewhere*. Breaking the law, failing to attribute, plagiarizing, using without permission are all behaviors that might "transgress" institutional expectations. If we all transgress in these ways, the author loses potency. He disappears. Amanda is always careful in her web portfolio to give credit to her collaborators and note that she received permission from others to include their materials on her website. It is expected that she take such measures in her role as web author—to do otherwise is a transgression. By crediting and referring to others, she creates and reinscribes, constitutes herself as author. Practices of requesting permission and attributing others are functions that separate Amanda from other writers and in turn produce her as solitary web author.

The second aspect of the author-function according to Foucault is that it does not affect all discourses in a universal fashion. Copyright law protects "creative" work to a greater extent than it protects "factual" work. The idea of *creativity* connotes greater associations with the importance of texts that have named authors, while the idea of *facts* connotes that they have independence from humans. Facts often circulate without authors—but creative works are usually associated with a person—and when an author is not presented, we often strive to find one (Foucault, 1979/1984). "Facts" circulate through author-functions, in "author-light" fields of discourse—the power then is not as much in the author but is in the "fact" and its ability to circulate widely. A new state constitutional amendment banning affirmative action or legalizing medical marijuana (as recently occurred in Michigan) are such "facts"—appearing without an apparent single and creative "author"—but having great import in dissemination. The same thing is true with judicial opinions like *Napster, Grokster*, and now *LimeWire* (Plambeck, 2010; see also DeVoss and Porter, 2006b; Porter and Rife, 2005). What's important is that we all learn file sharing is illegal—not which judge(s) authored the opinion. One can think of founders of discursivity, like Freud or even Jack Kevorkian, and the ways in which texts, objects, activities, or even institutions can be heterogeneous to what Freud or Kevorkian wrote or did, but still belong to what they seem to have initiated within the field of "psychoanalysis" or "assisted suicide."

In contrast, within an "author-heavy" field, a "return to the origin" requires tracing a network of "tightly knit . . . likeness . . . a sequence so perfect and so linear . . . one could not experience the second as other than 'like' the first" (Foucault, 1970/1994, p. 329). In an English literature course, one can categorize a set of texts as "the work of William Shakespeare"—where what becomes important is the author, and the ability to link between his texts and see some consistency across those texts, to see likeness, in order to validate that they are indeed the work of Shakespeare. (Foucault [1979/1984] says when we see something inconsistent with the "author," we tend to disregard it as not a legitimate part of his "work"). The point is the author-function does not impact all fields of discourse similarly.

When international copyright is examined, differences emerge in how the author-function affects discourse. Some European countries have "moral rights" laws protecting the integrity of an author's work. The U.S. does not. China has stringent copyright laws on the books, but in practice those laws have little import. Ghana's copyright law protects folklore in perpetuity, while the U.S. has no similar protection. During our interview, Rob informed me that when attending school in India, he was not expected to attribute individual human authors to the extent those in the U.S. are attributed because the cultural expectations did not require it. Those expectations instead maintained a constant looking back to the scriptures and to God's word (the Vedas). But when Rob came to the U.S., he quickly learned the importance of lists of works cited and references. When Amanda wrote for her organization, she gave up claims of authorship to the company. But when she wrote on her own time she maintained her author status. This study emphasizes how the author-function in different cultures (workplaces, nations, or educational contexts) does not apply uniformly. Surely the author-function works differently in the workplace than it does in a first-year writing course—in the former, authorship functions as a discourse of the organization, providing stability to organizational practices, as Amanda points out, whereas in the latter, the author-function works in complex ways to teach certain practices of community, to assure us that students are synthesizing meaning, to be used for sorting texts, and to control the unbridled proliferation of meaning.

The third point Foucault makes is that the author function is not simply assigning a name to a text. Instead it functions through a series of specific and complex operations (here we can think of John Law's notion of actor networks as patterned heterogeneous materials whose resistance has been overcome). The statutory provisions (Title 17, USC) of U.S. copyright law fill over three hundred pages and define a multitude of complexities that should be considered when determining if a use of another's copyrighted text is legal or not. In interviewee Amanda's case, she had forms to give clients and policies to obey regarding writing for the organization. Author-functions, those activities and operations that produce the author's shape and location, are in Amanda's case the organizations' work-for-hire policies, the forms and releases contributors sign, and all other company practices that support the arrangement of meaning production such that individual expression disappears into organizational expression. It was not just a simple matter of assigning the company name to one text and her name to another. For her web portfolio, she felt certain responsibilities such as asking permission and attributing. These responsibilities were different when she wrote for the organization. Author-functions in the U.S. are complex and draw upon multiple practices such as attribution as taught at educational institutions, and practices around copyright law and its effect, and all the discussions and practices that surround it (scholarship, research, legislative action, lobbying, and so on).

The final aspect of author-function Foucault points to is that the author it is not necessarily a real individual but can represent or be occupied by multiple subjectivities. In Amanda's case, the organization is the author. As Rob points out, God can be an author through the scriptures. In turn the scriptures are author of the cultural practices in Rob's version of India. An organization can be an author, as can a student, a teacher, a daughter, a mom, and so on. Under the definition Foucault gives, the author-function might be present in cultural activities and operations looking nothing like those that visibly support the solitary literary "author."

In India, according to Rob's interview, it is not that there is no author in the case of Vedas circulating widely without attribution; it's not that the author is dead; it is also not so much that knowledge is "community owned." It is just that God has been assigned the subject role of author, consuming individual authorship. God is permitted to be an author. Individuals are not. Thus when one wants to point to the author, they point to the scriptures, a nonhuman artifact. *The Practical Sanskrit Dictionary* states that according to Hindu tradition, the Vedas are *apauruṣeya* "not of human agency" (Apte, 1965). The text consumes any human author—in a sense, the text becomes the author of itself as it circulates.

The author-function in Rob's Indian culture is comprised of many activities and operations; one is reliance on the scriptures, and another is avoidance of direct, sustained attribution to human authors. These types of practices cause one to continually return to God as author—thus maintaining the scriptures' importance with that particular community of people. But every time one returns to the text, the text is modified. So the author just by nature can never be fixed but is continually modified every time we return to it, to him, to her (so of course even a "single author," like Michel Foucault, will change over time each time he is revisited—as in my writing here, where I have yet again revisited his work). Although continually changing due to the operation of interpretive acts, the values and beliefs in the Vedas then are more likely to maintain potency because they are not diluted by attribution of ideas to individual persons who lived and died subsequent to the existence of the Vedas. These types of author-functions keep agency with the text rather than with the people.

In remediating, extending, and clarifying Foucault's "author-function" (as informed by ANT), I'd like to offer some additional examples of cultural operations or activities to further illustrate a remixed version of authorship. These heterogeneous networks might be sorted into three categories:

1. *Exclusive Rights*: Operations or activities that attempt to give exclusive rights to produce certain kinds of knowledge to certain ordained entities, things, people.
2. *Erasure*: Operations or activities that erase entities, things, people.
3. *Limiting Expression*: Operations or activities that limit expression of certain classes of entities, things, people but not others.

The first type of heterogeneous network I list contains operations and activities that give exclusive rights to produce certain kinds of knowledge to certain ordained individuals or artifacts. U.S. copyright law assigns such exclusive rights, but it is difficult to imagine any human culture without operations and activities that assign "exclusive rights" to produce specified knowledge (that is, "to author") to a specific groups of persons, or specific people, or even institutions (like prisons and educational institutions). For example, in Magna Graecia, the Sybarites gave cooks a statutory, time-limited monopoly on new dishes (Gellar, 2000, p. 212, n. 12). A federal Australian court found analogies to copyright law in aboriginal law (*Bulun Bulun and Anor v. R. and T Textiles Pty Ltd*, 1998). Gellar (2000) notes that tribal art is controlled by "technical virtuosos," artisans instilling it with magical influence. In Africa, artistic know-how is passed on through "kinship, corporate, and other groups" (p. 212, n. 10). A culture that has shamans or supports shamanism has cultural practices wherein author-functions represent certain persons as vested with authority to know or make knowledge or write or tell histories.

In contemporary contexts, the Roman Catholic pope, invested with supreme authority or papal infallibility, is invested as author, in a sense, of the word of God. All the practices that sustain the pope and invest him with authority are author-functions. It can be plausibly argued that sustained deprivation of certain groups (the old, the poor, those in rural areas) in their ability to participate in digital writing, although perhaps seemingly based in economics, emanates from cultural practices that are author-functions. These are activities and operations that respond to our fear of the proliferation of meaning. Regardless of whether they are termed "racism" or the "digital divide," such heterogeneous networks remain practices that give exclusive rights to produce certain kinds of knowledge to certain ordained entities, things, people. Specifically, my examples here are intended to stand as a bit of refutation to the idea that our western version of copyright alone is what produces "authors." That is only true if one sees the author as a solitary genius, a proliferation of meaning, in the "creative" literary fashion.

If certain ordained persons or institutions are exclusively permitted to create certain specified knowledge or artifacts, like doctoral degree holders, the official "word of god," the "prisoner," the "prison guard," then someone who does otherwise will "transgress certain expectations" of the community. And both humans and nonhumans who are assigned such exclusive rights gain power by use of those rights over time, supporting Foucault's idea that the author-function does not impact all in a universal fashion. Institutions like prisons and higher education, as well as websites ranked in a Google search, gain power over time similar to the Vedas described by Rob. The Vedas, and websites ranked by Google, increase their power over time by use. Even contemporary software that tracks and counts the number of times an article is cited, tracks the most downloaded article, creates power in that article over time due to how much it is revisited. The complex operations that create and sustain authorship work in more complex ways than simply assigning a name to a text. Institutions, websites, and an oft-cited peer reviewed journal article constitute their own authority, power, and knowledge over time—supporting the idea the author is not always an individual.

I also provide a vivid example of an interpretive operation (in the form of a judicial opinion) that makes visible practices attempting to give exclusive rights to produce certain kinds of knowledge to certain ordained entities, things, people. Specifically, the practice of a musical performer, a singer-songwriter, attaching his name to a song, a song that becomes ubiquitous such as "My Sweet Lord," certainly implies that the musician is the author, the originator of that song. Until such a unity is challenged, we'd have no reason to suspect otherwise, but in the case of George Harrison and Ronald Mack and the Chiffons, the *Bright Tunes* case, which I discussed earlier, the exclusive rights acquired by Harrison were ultimately lost. The heart of the issue in *Bright Tunes* was whether or not Harrison was the "true" author/originator of a (musical) composition, "My Sweet Lord." After extensive analysis, the court found he was not and awarded proper damages to the plaintiff but also corrected history by stating that Ronald Mack, not George Harrison, had authored the music. By revisiting the point of origin in an interpretive act via the judicial opinion, that point was modified.

I can also provide a historical example where exclusive rights were assigned to a particular class of persons, to be authors—but was then challenged. It's the challenge that makes the assignment of exclusive rights become visible. There was a time in the U.S. when African Americans could not be authors either because they weren't considered capable of writing or because for them to read and write meant they might gain increased understanding and power: "For slaves and their teachers, the exercise of reading and writing was a dangerous and illegal one" ("I will be," 2002). In the days of U.S. government–sanctioned slavery, "the slaves themselves often suffered severe punishment for the crime of literacy, from savage beatings to the amputation of fingers and toes" ("I will be"). This exemplifies, as Foucault would say, disciplinary technologies taken through a "hold on the body." But when those types of bodily supervisions fell out of fashion, other "mind-over-mind" Panopticon-style strategies came into play (1977, pp. 205–7). In some sense, the exclusive rights to be an author at all, at the time, were mainly assigned to white men. When we recall the iconic story of Phillis Wheatley, a young slave arriving on the shores of Boston on July 11, 1761, another illustration of a remediated version of the "author-function" emerges. This version of author-function points directly to practices other than U.S. copyright law as sustenance to our idea of "author."

Phillis Wheatley authored some poems. But because of constraints at that time telling the larger society that a black woman could not possibly write, eventually Wheatley ended up before a jury of eighteen men, important men, the type of men who indeed *could* be authors: Thomas Hutchinson, governor of Massachusetts; Andrew Oliver, lieutenant governor; Reverend Mather Byles, minister of Hollis Street Congregational Church; John Hancock; and Reverend Charles Chauncy, to name a few. To them she was commanded to defend the authenticity of her poems. They affirmed her authorship, but according to Henry Louis Gates Jr. (2003), her authorship has never been recognized among more recent black scholars, who condemn her for being a "pariah," a cheap imitation of Alexander Pope, a poetess well fit to the "Uncle Tom syndrome." Either way, cultural operations and activities in the U.S. have served to stifle what Gates describes as Wheatley's sacrifices, courage, humiliations, and trials and instead delegitimize this black woman as "author." Even today, she isn't fully able to occupy the position of "author"—because that position is a set of relationships whose heterogeneity and resistance have *not* been overcome. The exclusive rights are still functioning to exclude Phillis Wheatley.

The second type of heterogeneous network I list contains activities and operations that erase things, entities, individuals. Such practices might include something as pragmatic as rules of attire, might reach to practices that decide who is featured or erased in a family's photographic history (see Rife, 2005), and might extend all the way to sophisticated text-based laws or policies such as work-for-hire. In this category we might place practices that function to erase one history and permit another to prevail. Take, for example, the case of *Suntrust Bank v. Houghton Mifflin Company* (2001). The litigation concerned a conflict between Suntrust, representing the Mitchell Trust, copyright holder of Margaret Mitchell's 1936 *Gone with the Wind* (GWTW), and African American author Alice Randall, who wrote a book entitled *The Wind Done Gone* (TWDG). TWDG was admittedly based on the characters and plot of Mitchell's novel. In *Suntrust*, while at first it seems the issue is similar to *Bright Tunes* because after all it is a copyright infringement case and so the obvious issue under consideration is whether or not the law has been violated, ultimately the fundamental issue at stake really has more to do with who gets to own history: Whose version of history prevails? Margaret Mitchell's? Alice Randall's?

In *Suntrust*, the lower court opinion enjoining the publication of Randall's book was appealed by Randall's publisher, Houghton Mifflin. According to the judicial opinion, Mitchell's book was a bestseller worldwide, second only to the Bible. Randall claimed "persuasively" her novel was a "critique" of Mitchell's "depiction of slavery and the Civil-War era American South" (p. 3). In a rather unusual move, the U.S. Court of Appeals for the Eleventh Circuit, early in the opinion (kind of setting the tone for the holding) emphasizes that "in the United States copyright has always been used to promote learning by guarding against censorship" (*Suntrust*, 2001, p. 9). The opinion notes the similarity between the two novels stating, "Scarlett O'Hara, Rhett Butler, Bonnie Butler, Melanie Wilkes, Ashley Wilkes, Gerald O'Hara, Ellen O'Hara, Mammy, Pork, Dilcey, Prissy, Belle Watling, Carreen O'Hara, Stuart and Brenton Tarleton, Jeems, Philippe, and Aunt Pittypat, all characters in GWTW, appear in TWDG" (pp. 28–29). While the court found that indeed Randall's work was substantially similar to Mitchell's, after an intricate Section 107 fair use, four-factor analysis, the court found "at this juncture, TWDG is entitled to a fair-use defense" (p. 58), overturning the injunction and remanding the case back to the lower court for a determination consistent with the appeals court's findings.

The opinion states TWDG is a "specific criticism of and rejoinder to the depiction of slavery and the relationships between blacks and whites in GWTW" (*Suntrust*, 2001, p. 35). The history depicted in GWTW asserts that "both blacks and whites" were better off in the days of slavery—at one point Scarlett says emancipation "just ruined the darkies" (as cited in *Suntrust*, 2001, p. 38). In GWTW, emancipated slaves are described as "creatures of small intelligence . . . like monkeys or small children" (as cited in *Suntrust*, 2001, p. 39). In contrast, Randall inverts the portrayals in GWTW and makes "powerful whites" appear "stupid and feckless," generally stripping "the romanticism from Mitchell's specific account of this period of our history" (*Suntrust*, 2001, p. 40). Eventually, the case settled out of court when Houghton Mifflin agreed to make a donation to Morehouse College, a historically African American institution, and in return, Mitchell's estate dropped the litigation. TWDG book cover is also shown to bear a seal labeling it "The Unauthorized Parody." This is a very specific example of the way a version of history (Margaret Mitchell's) might erase other versions of truth (Alice Randall's)—and in turn what happens when such operations are challenged in the legal system in a copyright context.

In a more abstract example of the second heterogeneous network wherein entities, things, and people are erased, figure 5.1 is a simple collage I remixed, depicting cultural practices involving dress that serve the author-function in that they, in a sense, erase the individual. I obtained these images by conducting Google image searches, and all can be found in multiple locations. In the spirit of my interviewees who often did not attribute generic images, nor could recall where the images were obtained, I do not attribute my sources since these images are "common knowledge." From the upper left-hand corner clockwise are two pictures of women from the "Texas polygamist" group, U.S. Army soldiers, women at a university graduation ceremony in Iran, Amish girls, and Hasidic Jewish men. Cultural practices that invite or require certain designated groups (women, soldiers, men) to wear similar clothing all erase individuality permitting someone or something other than the individual (God, sect leader, the U.S. government) to be the "author."[2] The author-function is not simply assigning a name to a text, and as Foucault pointed out, there are at least two modes in which texts and artifacts circulate, the author-heavy mode, where the "author" is more important, and the author-light mode, where what is more important is the relationships, places, and ubiquity of a statement's circulation. The function of uniform dress serves the same

Figure 5.1. Visually symmetrical cultural attire collage.

purposes, in some respects, as does copyright law and operates in the author-light mode—the mode where individuals are not important, but what is important is the networks in which the objects (both the photographs and the people themselves in this case) circulate. That is, the function of dress can be to assign or restrict the right to produce certain kinds of meaning—countering our fear of chaos. These practices of dress organize knowledge production.

The last kind of heterogeneous network I list, and this is not an exhaustive enumeration but a mere start, contains activities and operations that limit expression of certain classes of entities, things, or people but not others. U.S. copyright law accomplishes this in that it limits the ability of a new work to copy or draw from an existing work. Such activities might also be seen in religious or cultural operations that do not allow women to speak in public, or to be religious leaders, priests, or popes. Another copyright-related example is the Creative Commons licensing regime. Pursuant to Creative Commons licensing, a creator can, for example, select a license from many choices, among them the Creative Commons Attribution 3.0 United States License, which permits others to modify the new work and use it for commercial purposes as long as attribution is given. So while others are not prevented from using, their use is limited.

Theorizing the Commons and Common Knowledge

Analysis in this study helps bring forward a small bit the ways we think about the spaces of common knowledge and the commons in relationship to each other. Figure 5.1 is a visual collage drawing upon a visual sort of common knowledge but is only understandable to those who have experienced the web. How might digital composing practices revise our understanding of "common knowledge"? Where might "common knowledge," "commonplace," and our understanding of "the commons" intersect? The commons, like the commonplace, can be a space, a topos—bringing forth a conjectural paradigm (McKeon, 1998; Miller, 2000). The commons can be a discourse, can be drawn upon as a strategy for appropriating culturally contested property (Flessas, 2008). In figure 5.1, what I have characterized as common knowledge—that knowledge so ubiquitous the author is of little importance, arguably knowledge "owned" by all—is just that for *this* audience at *this* moment in time. Common knowledge is time stamped. I have made it clear I did not create the individual images myself—but even that seems overdone since most readers will find the images familiar. Many will correctly assume I did not travel to Texas or to a U.S. Army drill in order to obtain the images directly. Anyone who observes the news will understand what these images represent. The images will probably disappear one day from their current locations, and so any URL provided will become useless and extinct anyway. For us—I cannot see any logical reason to attribute the images that comprise the collage since anyone capable of doing a Google image search can find these images.

But how can we more accurately theorize when citation is needed and when it is not? While this book may bear my name because it is important for books to have authors, at least this type of book (as opposed to a government-authored or religious text), and while I expect others who use my work to cite it, as I myself have cited their work throughout, I used Microsoft Word to write this book—but I didn't include it in the book's reference list. I mainly used a Dell laptop to write this book, but I also navigated between a couple of other computers here and there—I used paper manufactured by Staples Brands Group to print off multiple copies of drafts, and I used a thousand other technologies, people, institutions, and artifacts as well as experiences gleaned from fifty years of living to complete this project—yet none of these "authors" are cited because citation is not expected nor is it perhaps even possible. In these types of discursive fields, what is important is the mode of circulation and the ubiquity, not the individuating citation.

Under Section 107, copyright law gives fair use protection to work drawing upon or incorporating a preexisting copyrighted work if the new work sufficiently transforms the old. But how do we know when, at what point, our new work so transforms the old that it becomes distinct? Foucault wrote that "exactly identical . . . enunciations . . . made up of the same words used with the same meaning" do not necessarily mean the exact same thing (1972, p. 143). At the start of this chapter, I provided two direct quotes from Foucault from two different books. He wrote: "Who is speaking?" (in the first instance he attributed the words to Nietzsche, and in the next he did not).[3] However one need only look at these words in the context of each book to understand that the meaning is not identical—especially considering the level of irony Foucault used in his writing. Even though the words are identical, Foucault transformed their use enough to provide the reader something new—something making each of these two books worth reading. In the *Bill Graham Archives v. Dorling Kindersley* case, the court found a subsequent use of Grateful Dead posters, not used to advertise concerts, but instead used to create a history, was an acceptable fair use under Section 107. In that case, the subsequent use, although incorporating identical posters, identical visual materials compared to the original, did not mean the same thing and so was held to be sufficiently transformed. In figure 5.1, none of the images were originally used to create a visual collage in order to discuss a theory of common knowledge and citation practices. So my position is that my use as well is a fair use under Section 107 because my use is sufficiently transformative.

In the case of figure 5.1, the images used are common knowledge because they did not pass through the constraining filter of the author. The system of constraint for me as composer is only that provided by the technology of the web and user-generated content. The images must have been uploaded by someone or something and be downloadable for me to use them. Legality and ethics seem beside the point. Based on interview data collected here, it is a common practice to take images from the web, mix them together, add interpretations, and eventually forget where they were originally obtained. Rip, mix, burn. Ultimately, I believe my use is just— and I interpret the interviewees' stances similarly. In the commonplace of the web, the images circulate and can be located in multiple sites, calling into question the need for any concern of their authorship. The images of the women from the Texas cult are assumed valid because they have been seen over and over again in multiple places—the power comes in part from circulation. They are common knowledge. In this context, their authorship is not important. What is important is what they represent. Images of the Texas cult women represent certain cultural operations and activities, author-functions, that can be circulated and appropriated by others in a network of relations, as I tried to depict in figure 5.1.

In figure 5.2, I try to bring the conversation forward a bit as far as theorizing the commons. What appears as figure 5.2 is a postmodern map showing a vertical continuum representing Foucault's idea that some texts and artifacts circulate in fields of discourse that tend to be author-heavy (the author is very important) or author-light (the author is less important). The horizontal continuum represents a field ranging from a pure open source commons, where the information is relatively free for the taking with little restraint, to the other extreme, which would be a highly regulated commons. A well-regulated commons with "clearly de-fined boundaries" (Ostrom, 1990) might be all items labeled with Creative Commons licenses. A commons that is much less regulated might be that space containing all works in the public domain. I have the map populated with a few examples. J. K Rowling's work would be, I think, circulating in a field where the author is very important and the commons is highly regulated since Rowling (or her publisher) are known to police derivative works (see "Harry Potter," 2008, for example, but see also Sturcke, 2010). Images of Martin Luther King Jr. also are in a highly regulated commons, which we know because the estate is infamous for policing and control-ling or even eliminating the unauthorized use of photographic images of Martin Luther King Jr., but the photo's author is not necessarily important in these circumstances. Microsoft Word and PowerPoint are also exam-ples of artifacts and technologies circulating where, from a proprietary business perspective, Microsoft will go after others who infringe on their

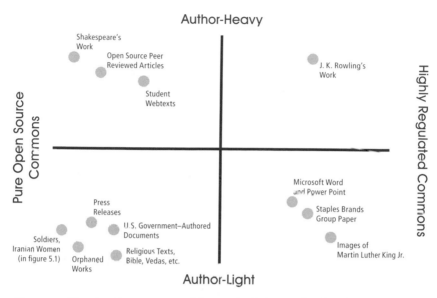

Mapping the Commons

Author-Heavy

Pure Open Source Commons

Highly Regulated Commons

Shakespeare's Work

Open Source Peer Reviewed Articles

J. K. Rowling's Work

Student Webtexts

Microsoft Word and Power Point

Press Releases

Staples Brands Group Paper

Soldiers, Iranian Women (in figure 5.1)

U.S. Government–Authored Documents

Orphaned Works

Religious Texts, Bible, Vedas, etc.

Images of Martin Luther King Jr.

Author-Light

Figure 5.2. Mapping the commons with a remixed theory of authorship.

trademarks, patents, or copyrights, but where Microsoft-as-author of those products during their use is relatively unimportant—I'm not expected to cite Microsoft in my reference list. The same is true with Staples Brands Group paper, which I have used for printing this manuscript throughout the book-writing process. For literary works in the public domain, like Shakespeare's work, the author can be important, but the use of his work is not regulated. Open source peer reviewed journal articles can be used freely, but the authorship of those articles is still important—attribution is expected—the same is fairly true for student webtexts, like the ones I studied. In the quadrant representing work that circulates in an unregulated commons where authorship is not important, I'd place items like press releases, religious texts, orphaned works, the images I incorporated in figure 5.1, documents authored by the U.S. government, even the uniformed people themselves such as the U.S. Soldiers or the Iranian women. It is in this "pure open source," "author-light" quadrant where we'd find "common knowledge." Of course even in the unregulated quadrant there are still those invisible restrictions such as the architecture of the book or the Internet, and various other digital rights management technologies that can get in the way of use.

There is hope that orphaned works will become even more available to users since, as I write this, Senate Bill 2913, the "Shawn Bentley Orphan Works Act of 2008," is under consideration (the legal system moves very slowly, but the law continues to be under consideration; see Samuelson, 2010). It would reduce liability for those who use found images and other materials in the commons if they complete a "diligent effort" searching for the owner of material without success. The law appears to be following the digital composing practices of the writers in this study. The proposed act, if adopted, would make it easier for users to appropriate texts, images, and sounds that have no "owner"—technically they have no creator because their creator cannot be found (Curtis, 2008; Zimmerman, 2009). The concept of "orphan" works acknowledges that things people make can detach from their creators and take on meaning and power that were never anticipated. It acknowledges a commons containing abandoned or lost materials.

Student Writing?

In addition to complicating Foucault's concept of the author-function, and offering some additional methods to understand the commons and common knowledge, the remixed theory of authorship emerging from this study also challenges traditional understandings of students or studentness in the context of digital writing. Web compositions are sites of cultural collision, or commonplaces, where writing students occupy sometimes conflicting positions such that the very notion of "studentness" is inverted. In other words, "student" is nothing more than a representation that emerges from a number of practices that are multiple and heterogeneous. The result of these practices, and a method by which to organize and simplify them, is to create a name: *student*. Simultaneously, after this object—the student—emerges, there are operations that revisit and reinscribe the student category: discourses, operations, and activities around "student writing," "student housing," "student population," "student plagiarism." But upon examination of digital student writing, it became clear in this study that students are much more complicated than the label attached to them implies. This is always important to remember, because when a name emerges from complicated practices that produce it, that name can then circulate independently of its origins, become detached from them, and entirely lose an attachment to the motivations and reasons for that name's existence. The name *author* illustrates this. Pursuant to this study, it became clear to me that authorship is a name assigned to simplify and organize a number of multiple and heterogeneous practices. The simplification that occurs during this meaning-organizing practice of naming can in turn oversimplify our understandings of that term. Because of the web's advent, those interested in writing must revisit exactly what we mean by author and authorship since some of the simpler ideas about those concepts are certainly challenged in digital environments.

The interviews and subsequent data analysis showed that the category of student, as far as an individual doing something like "student writing," really does not withstand scrutiny. What I mean to say is, due to the webspace as commonplace and the remixing that occurs in web writing, I am not sure what "student [web] writing" might look like. All of the interviewees, not just the two who had recently graduated (Amanda and Sarah), were writing for the web in contexts outside school. Rob, an international PhD student, along with Sarah, a recent master's graduate, were regularly doing what I term *gift writing*—writing for the web on behalf of family members and friends. This phenomenon probably comes from the digital divide, in that some individuals who are perfectly capable of putting together a traditional paper flyer or brochure have no clue how to write and publish a webpage. Thus they tap into the generosity of folks around them who can—probably younger family members. Since Rob is an international student who completed some of this "gift writing" while living in India, my observations in this area are not limited to individuals in the U.S. Those individuals we experience as "students" may be active web writers in "for-profit" environments, although they themselves are not getting paid. Rob completed webpages for his father's business as well as the professional dance business of a friend. Sarah created websites for a couple of churches as well as a website to promote a relative's for-profit book sales. Heather, an undergraduate, was doing professional web writing for faculty members and professional organizations. Several students were also working as teachers and marketing themselves as potential employees.

This issue of the digital divide and the pressures it exerts on younger web writers might inform our understanding of digital authorship. We might revisit the days before everyone could write—when the "illiterate" signed an "X" in place of their names on legal documents and hired others to write for them. In an e-mail follow-up to our interview, Amanda summed up the complexities of these issues in the context of her own family. In the e-mail, she explained that at one time when she was checking her "web presence" by Googling herself, she located one of her recent wedding photos on a genealogy site. "The site had my mom listed as the owner of the photo." After investigation, Amanda learned her mother had taken the photo from the wedding photographer's website and "sent it to some distant cousin in Texas" who had control over the website and posted the picture. Of her mother, Amanda said, "She didn't understand the issue of copyright belonging to our photographer." Of course Amanda was concerned because she had signed a contract stating she "wouldn't reprint or publish our professional photographs without our photographer's permission." Furthermore, she was concerned because the picture had been "degraded in the process so it wasn't representative of the photographer's talent." Upon this discovery, Amanda e-mailed the webmaster and asked them to remove the photo, which they did. She then explained to her "mom how fair use and copyright work on the Internet." Amanda found herself in the uneasy predicament of policing her own mother's behavior with respect to wedding pictures. It is difficult to imagine such a seemingly trivial matter between mother and daughter triggering copyright considerations, but it did. In this case, the daughter is more savvy about the issues of web publishing than the mother.

The label of "student" connects to Foucault's discussion of a discipline's ranking and dividing. To recall, Leslie was acting as a graduate student, teacher, and potential employee all at once in a convergence via her gaming-themed webtext: "Discipline is an art of rank. . . . It individualizes bodies by a location that does not give them a fixed position, but distributes them and circulates them in a network of relations" (Foucault, 1977, p. 146). This art of rank is evidenced by categories such as undergraduate, master's student, PhD student, and so on. The art of rank is clearly visible in law school practices where students are literally ranked against each other—switching in and out of placeholders like "the top 5%" semester to semester.

In the survey, there is not a remarkable difference between student and teacher knowledge scores. In the interviews, master's students were a bit more knowledgeable about copyright law than PhD students. The knowledge scores for PhD students Rob and Leslie were 64% and 50% respectively, while master's students Carey and Jessie both scored 71% on the knowledge portion of the survey. The lowest knowledge scores are from PhD student Leslie and undergraduate Heather, both at 50%. Heather was the only undergraduate interviewed and the low score might be expected, but Leslie dashes those expectations because as a PhD student she scored just as low as the undergraduate. Examining the scores of all the interviewees really does not permit any inferences on correlations between education level and copyright knowledge level. In addition to illustrating the inability to pigeonhole student writers into categories with respect to their copyright knowledge levels, the interviews show none of the student digital writers are writing as students *only*. It is possible they are doing more complicated web writing than their teachers as far as navigating and maintaining multiple identities. These students are also employees, business owners, teachers, and family members, and those multiple roles are reflected in their web writing.

Due to my reliance on Foucault and ANT, my focus is not so much on how certain practices repress as on how they produce in the way of judicial opinions, cultural practices, images circulating the web with no author-filter, and so on. It's not that "oppression and the law" are unimportant; in fact, I think some might see a clear alignment between the three heterogeneous networks—the operations and activities I listed earlier and Iris Marion Young's (1990) version of oppression. Young argues the distributive paradigm of justice negates needed focus on oppression and domination. She lists the "five faces of oppression" as exploitation, marginalization, powerlessness, cultural imperialism, and violence. These faces of oppression could be sorted into the three activities and operations I list—activities and operations that organize meaning. Explorations such as those Young suggests are important but provide only -half the picture. Studying how slavery "oppressed" Phillis Wheatley fails to acknowledge how author-functions granted her eighteen male jurors, and later even Gates himself, the power to validate or deny her authorship. In both cases, Wheatley's authorship is turned over to others, and she is not the author of herself, while we examine her "oppression." Such cultural practices thus continue to proliferate.

While many scholars such as Herrington, Hobbs, Jaszi, Aufderheide, Porter, Heins and Beckles, and Westbrook point to how copyright law does or might repress individuals' ability to express themselves; in fact, the existence of such scholarship does illustrate how copyright law in service to the author-function is productive since it has produced an entire discursive formation on copyright, including this book. While copyright law, or fear of it, might repress some, might shape the discourse of others, might slow down a certain type of information exchange, in turn it is productive with respect to all the discourse emanating in order to discuss, parody, or interpret the possible repression of others. That is, copyright law might repress one individual, but in turn a thousand others may speak in some fashion about that repression. As Foucault points out, societal notions of repressed sexuality actually perpetuate the invention of a "wide dispersion of devices" used to discuss sexuality "*ad infinitum*" (Foucault, 1978/1990, pp. 34–35). It takes an entire architecture of law to actually shape what people do—statutes, court opinions, the entire court system, all the texts and messages that bring the law to the people. Copyright law is productive, and the reason is that it is working as a disciplinary power—a device attempting to control and organize meaning. It might organize the production of discourse, but it does not repress all human expression. Whether the way copyright law does repress or impede is just is worth considering.

We do need to examine the ways the law and other author-functions repress, but we also should acknowledge and study their productions—failure to examine this constitutes ignoring what Latour calls the proliferation of monsters. If we ignore the operation of the author-function as a *producer* of knowledge, it will not be possible to amend our practices or take advantage of the ways *we* can rhetorically shape our own disciplinary power such that changes in the law and its implementation are possible. I am offering the notion that based on the history of knowledge production, in the Foucauldian sense, total chaos is not anything we would want to encourage—and so there will need to be some architecture in place to help us organize the production and dissemination of knowledge. I offer that the text-based copyright law in the U.S. is not completely unworkable, is not chilling writers' speech to the extent they cannot express themselves, and really is an acceptable method, at least in theory, to organization knowledge production. The IP Watchlist 2010, published by a2knetwork through Consumers International, "the only independent global campaigning voice for consumers," ranks the U.S. third out of ten as a "best rated country" for access to knowledge (India is first). Chile is first out of ten for being the worst rated. In the U.S. things are not perfect, but when an international organization specifically focusing on access rates the U.S. this high, it is something to take into account in our analyses. This is just something to continue thinking about as we move forward. Especially because of the web's ability to facilitate the unbridled proliferation of meaning, we need some mechanisms to organize the production of knowledge, that is, "author-functions." Rhetoric will prove useful in allowing us more choice in such matters.

Foucault eerily predicted our fundamental understanding of author and the practices that produce this author would change. He wrote that in the "very moment" when society is in the process of changing, "the author function will disappear" such that fiction will continue to circulate but still within "a system of constraint"; that mode of circulation will not be filtered through the "author" (1979/1984, p. 119). Yes, Foucault was correct—our "system of constraint" has changed due to the Internet—the constraints are still there, through digital rights managements, access to the technology itself, Internet filtering, and the open availability or proprietary nature of information on the web itself. These systems of constraint are not based on the literary "author." However the author-function is still at work in the most traditional sense in many fields of discourse, simultaneous to new systems of constraint yet being invented. "Authors" do still matter—for students who must incorporate the proper academic citations, for those of us who are rewarded because of our ability to be authors—of blogs, books, tweets, or in whatever medium we chose. So as far as Foucault's prediction, it was accurate in foreseeing that the systems of constraint would change but didn't foresee that the "author" would still be there, layered into the newer systems of constraint being invented.

Foucault predicted our society would undergo significant change in how information circulates in relationship to traditional notions of the author. Clearly, our society is undergoing a process of change in this area due to communication enabled by the Internet. We even wondered not so long ago whether copyright law had disappeared with respect to web writing (Herrington, 1997). We know things are different, but as Foucault says, we have to "determine" or "experience" this new system of constraint—it connects to James Kinney's (1979) definition of empiricism—empiricism is the method through which we can experience this new system of constraint, "through the senses, through direct, physical experience" (p. 352). Latour (1993) suggests that we conduct empirical work to explore networks—that we "slow down, reorient, and regulate the proliferation of monsters by representing their existence officially" (p. 12). In the future that Foucault (1979/1984) predicts, instead of asking the traditional questions of who really spoke and with what authenticity, we will instead ask, "What difference does it make who is speaking?" (p. 120). Upon examination, digital composing practices bring this future Foucault predicts clearly into view.

6

Toward a Metatheory of Rhetorical Invention in Digital Environments

> In their examination of the rhetorical malaise, they isolated
> the dead art of invention as a major cause of the writing
> problem. . . . Then began the faint call for the reinstatement of
> the lost art of invention—the art of discovering "what to say,"
> of making original judgments on experience, of discovering
> means of communicating this unique insight with a particular
> voice to a particular ear, of deciding between nonsynonymous
> utterances. But a call for invention is not enough. What ars
> inveniendi is needed? The Topics? Has invention remained
> static since its Ramian exile from rhetoric?
> —Janice Lauer, "Heuristics and Composition"

An Inventional Heuristic for Digital Writers

In this chapter I offer an inventional heuristic that takes into account the theory of authorship I developed in chapter 5. The inventional heuristic I offer in this chapter better situates the seven rhetorical topics (probability, copyright, fair use, ethics, design, culture, and employer requirements) I began with. Since a theory of rhetorical invention is an epistemological theory, a metatheory of invention as I try to develop in this chapter might inform our understandings of research methodologies in addition to informing teaching philosophies, pedagogies, and writing curricula. Janice Lauer and Richard Young particularly call for us to extend, test, and explain theories of rhetorical invention. Presently, the trigger for this research, or the crisis, as Young might characterize it, is due to the digital component in our writing environments along with how those digital environments make more transparent the concept of authorship as complex and multiple rather than singular. Digital writing, it is argued, fundamentally changes the nature of writing (DeVoss and Porter, 2006b; Digital Rhetoric Collective, 2006; Grabill and Hicks, 2005; Selber, 2004; WIDE Research Center Collective, 2005; Yancey, 2009).

The composing heuristic I offer in figure 6.1 contains the five qualities I started with—qualities that one looks for in an inventional heuristic: (1) transcendency, (2) flexible direction, (3) generative power, (4) the quality of encouraging probability thinking, and (5) with special topics being tied to special audiences (J. Lauer, 1970; Haller, 2000). However based on my research, I am able to give more shape to this heuristic, better reflecting the hierarchical and embedded nature of its elements. Also I do have two considerations to add to the inventional metatheory. One is a refined definition of "transcendency," and the other is a theory of authorship; a theory of authorship will inform how the heuristic is applied, as invention is going to be anticipated differently depending on whether one is operating with the understanding that authors are single people, or that authorship can be complex and multiple. The mediational heuristic that emerged in this study appears in figure 6.1.

The mediational-digital composing heuristic has transcendency because it can be applied in numerous situations. Mediational means are by definition transcendent—as are tools. Tools can be used in a variety of situations—this is indeed what gives them their "toolness." I'm going to take a

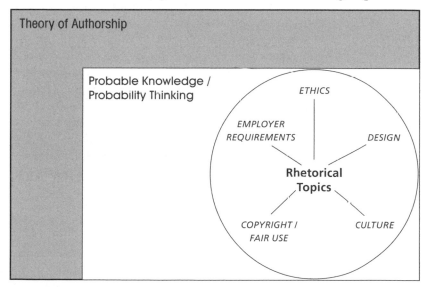

Figure 6.1. The mediational-digital composing heuristic.

Copyright Law as Mediational Means

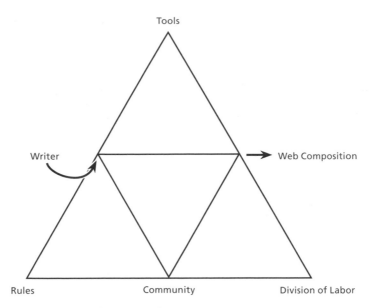

Figure 6.2. An activity theory triangle.

moment here to elaborate on this idea of "toolness" as it relates to AT and copyright law because it will help develop some of the ideas in this chapter. The second-generation AT triangle, as commonly visualized and depicted in figure 6.2, includes placeholders for rules and tools (Engestrom, 1990).

As shown in figure 6.2, in the placeholder for mediational means are tools (like copyright law), but if the writer is unaware of the law, for that actor the doctrine is neither a mediating structure nor part of mediational performance (although it might be a rule). Bracewell and Witte (2003) point out Engestrom's second-generation expanded triangle has no place for examination of the relationship between the different nonmediational positions and each other. Likewise, Engestrom's triangle does not provide a method to examine the relationship between mediational positions and nonmediational positions (that is, the relationships between rules and tools). But for those interested in composing process theory as well as those interested in how copyright law impacts writing behaviors, the differentiation between rules and tools is important.

While interviewees in this study are aware of copyright law as they select content for their web compositions, and weigh and balance the risk of being held accountable for use, they sometimes decide design and ethical considerations trump copyright law. Copyright law is not a "rule" for them. As Haller (2000) points out, arguments facilitated by mediating heuristics (in her study a design heuristic) are erased in the finished text. So when one examines the deliberations that go into composing decisions, instead of analyzing digital writers as controlled by either biological urges/natures or the environment, AT's formulation of mediation allows humans to control their own behavior from the outside "using and creating artifacts. . . . Activity theory has the conceptual and methodological potential to be a pathbreaker in studies that help humans gain control over their own artifacts and thus over their future" (Engestrom, 1999, p. 29). Copyright law is intended to control the actions of others, to be a rule, to discipline individuals into virtuous citizens rather than incorrigibles. But that intent is dashed if as the activity theorists imagine, humans gain control over their own future by leveraging the toolness of copyright law rather than submitting to its ruleness. When digital writers consider copyright law, as well as the other mediational means (ethics, design, and so on), any chance of a linear writing process is confounded.

Another quality of the mediational-digital composing heuristic in figure 6.1 is flexible direction. Flexible direction suggests a series of steps, or considerations as one invents; the rhetorical topics specifically name some considerations digital writers reflect upon as they work. The heuristic has generative power, as in my study it is foundational and provides the basis of arguments and deliberations digital writers engage in when making composing choices, choices that produce their creative webtexts. Figure 6.1 expressly acknowledges the probability thinking that is encouraged when writers must weigh and balance the priority and import of the rhetorical topics under consideration. And finally, the last quality an inventional heuristic should have is that for special topics it is tied to special audiences (Haller, 2000). In this case, we are expressly focusing on digital writing, and even specifically on the mediational role of copyright law in digital composing choices. All of the qualities of an inventional heuristic are thus present in figure 6.1. The sixth quality I add to the inventional metatheory is that it should have a theory of authorship explicitly stated, in order that one know how to proceed as that inventional heuristic is applied for research or teaching.

The rhetorical topics shown in figure 6.1 and at work as mediational means in the minds of the digital writers I interviewed include (1) ethics, or ethical/political considerations including considerations of attribution; (2) design standards, or issues of design/content rather than issues of copyright as influencing composing choices; (3) culture, or reasoning based on one's cultural background; (4) employer demands or requirements, or reasoning based on the demands or requirements of one's employer; and finally (5) copyright/fair use, or using, applying, referencing copyright law such as asking permission, referring to originality, referencing fair use or the four-factor fair use test of Section 107 (fair use elements such as purpose of use, amount used, proportion used, and so on). The rhetorical topics interact together as the writer weighs and balances the import of each one—that is, the probable knowledge factor. Probable knowledge is rhetorical knowledge, that knowledge in between fact and mere opinion, and it requires interaction of all the rhetorical topics. Probable knowledge in figure 6.1 is thus represented as encompassing.

And so, based on my research, two qualities or considerations must be added to the heuristic I started with: (1) a theory of authorship (especially important for the researcher) and, (2) an explicit acknowledgement that inventional heuristics are mediational. The mediational quality of the heuristic, by definition, requires the heuristic have the potential to bring agency or power to the inventor, and the heuristic be tool-like rather than rule-like. That is, an inventional composing heuristic for the digital age should be expressly acknowledged as mediational, should be framed with a theory of authorship, should encourage probability thinking, and should contain at minimum rhetorical topics of ethics, design, culture, employer (or potentially teacher) requirements, and legal concerns. If these considerations are not taken into account when researching, teaching, or doing invention, the perspective is incomplete.

An implied theory of authorship is at work in some of the earlier inventional theories such as tagmemics and the dramatistic pentad, and in the earlier inventional theories of Flower and Hayes, Emig, Perl, and others. Such theories implicitly rely on an author that is a solitary genius, a perpetual surging of innovation. However Foucault's theory, as well as developing theories of remix writing, suppose the author is inherently multiple, and much more complex than a single actor or person. I did take this into account in my research, and my examination of digital writing processes did support the idea that authorship is not singular, and maybe not even always human. But whatever theory of authorship one has as one moves forward in implementing or imagining an inventional heuristic, that theory is no doubt going to shape the outcome. In my research, authorship is found to be extremely complex, with writers pulling from multiple sources, and webtexts taking months if not years to complete. It is not uncommon for a webtext to be written by many people switching in and out of author position consecutively, who take care of that webspace over a period of years. This is certainly a different vision of writing than that focused on by Emig, Perl, and Flower and Hayes. And so one needs some articulated theory of authorship when mapping out or implementing an inventional heuristic for digital writing, whether for teaching, for writing, or for researching.

Ethics Trumps the Law

Among the rhetorical topics under consideration in figure 6.1, I find ethics is more important than legal considerations for these writers. As far as the ranking of the other rhetorical topics listed, in figure 6.1, I offer only tentative placeholders. The rhetorical topics likely circulate in relationship to each other depending on the writing context. My study was not designed to locate a ranking of rhetorical topics but simply to discover or confirm their existence in the composing process. It is possible another study could capture this, but overall it might be a difficult chore since the topics work together complexly. Nonetheless, ethics considerations are pronounced among the writers in my study, trumping legal considerations. This is supported in both the survey and the interviews. The seven interviews certainly support the idea that digital writers are more concerned with attributing and not harming others than they are about legal violations. Sarah, for example, has deep concerns about the implications of using others' content, not with respect to herself, but with respect to the church she writes for. She even contacted someone in Sweden to receive assurances that she did not have to attribute the use of his boilerplate web template on the church's webpage she was creating in order to avoid a lot of questions from church clientele. She said: "The whole thing was just really confusing to me, but because I was getting paid for it, it made me, it wasn't like in school where I didn't really worry about it because it wouldn't really matter, like, I didn't want this to come back to the people I'd done it for."

Amanda's concerns about ethical implications of her writing choices weighed heavily on her as did Sarah's. Even though Amanda completed many of the editing projects featured in her web portfolio in an undergraduate professional writing class, according to her, the teacher never instructed students on the ethical issues of using others' materials to showcase one's own editing skills. Amanda figured out on her own how employ rhetoric to handle the situation ethically, by first asking permission and then noting in her website "used with permission." For a number of interviewees, even though they could use material under fair use without receiving permission, they requested permission anyway, not because of fear, but because it was the "right" thing to do. Not only does this provide evidence of ethics trumping law, because the uses could have taken place under fair use and without permission, but it also provides evidence of possible inadequate instruction on the ethical aspects of using others' materials in one's own digital portfolio. The focus in the course was editing, and for some reason, according to Amanda, the teacher did not see the ethical component or imagine the web portfolio becoming a permanent part of the digital writer's web persona.

The idea that ethics can or should trump the law has some precedent in rhetoric and composition. Porter (1997) argues that if the law is unethical, we can break it. The majority of writers in this community agree with Porter as evidenced in the survey and backed up in the interviews. Logie (2005) replies to Porter's suggestion to avert law, arguing instead that such tactics should be public and organized, which is a valid stance if we think of public advocacy. But only one of the writers I interviewed, Jessie, is involved as a copyright activist by presenting at conferences and writing journal articles. In his 1998 book, Porter states that one of the first steps to developing what he calls a critical rhetorical ethics in cyberspace involves recognizing that web writing has "legal and ethical implications" (p. 145). DeVoss and Porter (2006b) further capitalize on this idea in their Napster piece wherein they argue the digital age begs us to teach a certain ethic of fair use and attribution—to give credit where credit is due. We are there. The three-hundred-plus survey takers are aware of legal and ethical implications of web writing as evidenced by an average score of 63% on the knowledge portion. A significant majority also agree that on occasion it is acceptable to follow your conscience rather than the law. All seven writers I interviewed were aware of legal and ethical implications. Heather tacitly screened photos her employer sent her as web content since she knew of possible negative implications. Leslie used Adobe filters on flickr images in order to protect young game players' identities. Carey kept her social network site content-free in order to protect the institution and its connection to her professional identity. Amanda has the same kind of concerns with her web persona and her institution's identity.

Why did ethics trump the law as a factor in digital composing choices? We know from both survey scores and interviews that digital writers studied have significant understanding and awareness of copyright law, and therefore a total lack of legal awareness cannot be the cause for the emphasis on ethics. While some research shows that with increased education comes the increased willingness to break the law on exceptional occasions, this alone does not offer a complete explanation, and knowing why ethics is more important than law could not just inform pedagogy but could also provide insight into why writers make the choices they do—and in turn, an understanding of the rhetorical appeals to be used if one intends to change or influence others' composing behavior. If we teach digital writers to obey the law, it may be for naught if they instead turn to ethics for their writing decisions. Stakeholders wishing to encourage certain kinds of uses over others might do well to acknowledge that ethical appeals may *work better* than threats of litigation. Ethics may have priority over law because rhetoric and composition already has a literature on and a concern for issues of plagiarism, attribution, and permission.

Probable Knowledge: Probability Thinking

One of the qualities an inventional heuristic should have is the ability to encourage probability thinking as depicted in figure 6.1. This quality also helps ensure its toolness rather than its ruleness by substantiating the element of choice among rhetorical topics under consideration. By using the inventional heuristic I offer, digital writers arrive at some sort of tentative truth defining the situation such that they can make a content decision. But how do digital writers arrive at the "truth," at the final decision to include one piece of content over another, or to create something from scratch? As it appears in the heuristic, this is indeed a complicated process; my representation only makes a start towards our understanding of the digital composing process. But according to my interpretation, to arrive at the "truth," digital writers must rely on probable knowledge. "Probability thinking" in the inventional heuristic derives from data showing that digital writers weigh and balance a number of different rhetorical topics as they make composing choices. Their ultimate decisions are based a rhetorical kind of knowledge. By using rhetorical analyses along with activity theory (and influences of actor network theory) as a research paradigm, we might align the way probable truth, with its accompanying levels of certainty, is constructed at different times and locations, and see these constructions as emanating from author-functions within different cultures. Foucault specifically invites us to test his two assertions regarding what he characterizes as a "regime" of truth. He states, "'Truth' is to be understood as a system of ordered procedures for the production, regulation, distribution, circulation, and operation of statements." He goes on to write: "'Truth' is linked in a circular relation with systems of power which produce and sustain it, and to effects of power which it induces and which extend it" (1979/1984, p. 74). Thinking upon a "regime" of truth, and the ways in which the legitimacy of knowledge is constructed, we might be able to examine how differing heuristics of probable knowledge (inferential statistics; burdens of proof in law; the argument, counterargument, concessions, and rebuttals in classical argumentation; and so on) organize meaning—how such heuristics mediate knowledge within a culture. As Kennedy suggests in his discussions of argument from probability, and as Lauer explicitly states, rhetoric can be a way of knowing the world, an epistemology. Very few claims can really be "scientific and exact" due to the all-too-possible ability to "demonstrate the probability of exact opposites" (Kennedy, 1963, p. 31). Perelman and Olbrechts-Tyteca (1971/2006), in their discussion of argument from probability, point out this rhetorical technique can indeed "modify the concept one has of certain fields . . . the use of certain forms of reasoning cannot help but have a profound effect on the very conception of the data which are their object" (p. 260). Using the technique of argument from probability doubly, one might be able to examine arguments of probability within a field or area like inferential statistics, and compare them to other disciplinary arguments, illustrating how they are rhetorically constructed. This method itself then becomes a meta-level argument from probability.

We could align the regimes of "truth" in statistics ("very highly significant," "highly significant," and so on) and in legal contexts ("beyond a reasonable doubt," "clear and convincing," and so on) and make visible the rhetorical nature of "truth." As J. M. Lauer (2008) points out, Wayne Booth' s 1974 book *Modern Dogma and the Rhetoric of Assent* tells us how rhetoric can be helpful in constructing knowledge in between "fact" and "mere opinion." Similarly, the knowledge produced pursuant to the inventional heuristic I offer in figure 6.1 is the tentative truth digital writers produce somewhere between fact and mere opinion. Certainly, the probable knowledge informing their ultimate composing choices is more than mere opinion, but none of the writers, I dare say, believe that the information they rely on to move forward is hard fact. (If that were true, the survey would have shown significant numbers of participants selecting "very certain" as to certainly in their knowledge and this *did not* occur.) The inventional heuristic I offer, like other mechanisms in other places and times, offers a rhetoric of probable knowledge, a guide to the navigator searching the night sky for clues on how to proceed. The arguments that underlie the final decision of each digital writer sustain the legitimacy of those decisions, the same way numbers in statistics, or evidence in a court of law, sustain the legitimacy of the decisions ultimately reached in those respective contexts.

Probability calculations involve conjecture—hunting for the right choice. As Carolyn Miller (2000) discusses, *metis* is connected to cunning intelligence and the hunt, the conjectural paradigm. According to Detienne and Vernant (1978), all activities involving *metis* involve a "conjectural type of knowledge" (p. 311), and "to conjecture" is "to open up a path for oneself with the aid of guide-marks and to keep one's eyes fixed on the goals of the journey just as the navigators do, placing their trust in the signs of the diviners and the luminous signals in the sky" (p. 310). Probable knowledge is like a "long journey through the desert . . . where there are no visible paths and where one must constantly guess the way, aiming at a point on the distant horizon" (p. 311). When writing for the web in copyright-imbued environments, "one must constantly guess the way." The "guide-marks" are the rhetorical topics we consider as we write. Is the use of this image legal? Ethical? A good design choice? Do the copyright stakeholders have deep pockets? Will they pursue me or leave me alone? Can I "hide" my digital writing from "the law"? Can I disguise the texts I have appropriated by changing their shape, texture, meaning? By synthesizing? These are all guide-marks, or part of the mediational heuristic considered by interviewees as they constantly guessed their way in the digital composing process.

Heather, the undergraduate professional writer working for faculty conference organizers, drew on probable knowledge by staying quiet about questions she had on the origins of certain content given to her during the composing process. During our interview, Heather stated she didn't really worry about copyright and none of the faculty she was working with seemed concerned either. However after she was given photos to use in conference website construction, she said, "I did wonder like where the photos from the front page came from, but I didn't really do anything about, like that curiosity, but, um I did think about it." She became concerned because she was constructing an informational webpage regarding the guest speaker and the conference organizers sent her several photos of the speaker to choose from. But "they seemed to be from different time periods, like one was when he was younger, like he didn't have so quite a gray beard, and um, I was just wondering like did they get them from his website?" So while she had concerns based on clues received during the composing process, she never felt the need to follow up with anyone since the conference organizers seemed responsible for supplying the content.

Although vigilant, Heather decided each time to defer to the faculty members, trust their judgment, and stay quiet about any of her questions. Considering Heather's position as a for-hire writer and a young undergraduate, it was probably strategic for her to remain quiet. She was not really in a position of authority to question, and ultimately, she was not responsible for the content in the way that faculty members were. However when inserting images of students in a webpage that supported a grant, she did say she screened the photos to make sure no one was pictured in a way that might be misinterpreted. She explained that faculty might not notice such things since "the professors and the directors are really concentrated on just making sure that the text is right, and the, and that they are getting funding and that sort of thing." Heather never voiced any concern to her employers, but said she did screen the photos provided to her "especially if there's someone like drinking beer in a photo or something like that, I would you know, just try to casually mention, you know, is this person OK with this, do they know that we are putting it on the website, that sort of thing." Heather, whose contemplative thoughts during the composing process will never be known to her employer, used probable knowledge to perform her role as undergraduate "student" employee and invisible writer.

Rules or Tools? The Agency of the Law in Invention

The ability for an inventional heuristic like the one in figure 6.1 to provoke probability thinking is important and is related to its toolness and flexibility in use. Copyright law is one of the rhetorical topics writers consider as they compose, but it is not the only topic under consideration, weighed and balanced by writers. However copyright law certainly has some influence and some power among digital writers. Its presence did seem to relate to knowledge levels, as did its power to chill speech. It appears that the more writers know and understand about copyright law, the more easily they can move within their own writing—the more freedom they have in choices they make because their decisions are more informed than those with less knowledge.

More knowledge about copyright law among participants seemed related to increased mediational power, or toolness of the law. Copyright law had less presence in the web compositions of Leslie and Heather, both of whom scored 50% on the survey's knowledge portion—lending credence to the idea that with increased knowledge of an artifact comes the artifact's increased mediational power. Although both Leslie and Heather have some concern about copyright law's implications in their writing, prudent Leslie abides only if it is easy to do so. Leslie makes most composing decisions for ethical or design reasons. The same is true with Heather. Neither Leslie nor Heather use copyright symbols or terms of use in their web writing. Jessie and Carey have the highest scores on knowledge. Jessie's work definitely has the greatest presence of copyright law since she uses fair use and copyright as themes in her digital compositions. Carey did not share a web portfolio with me, but there is a huge presence of rights management on the teacher database exchange she manages. She is very reflective about these issues and constantly evaluates the copyright related practices of users. On her social network site, she did not supply a lot of web content, but the main reason is she did not want colleagues to perceive any code errors. She also knows she is representing the institution and thus knows any use she made of others' materials might possibly be evaluated for copyright violations—therefore she decides to take the most conservative route. Copyright law's presence in her social network site was actually evidenced by the absence of content.

The certainty scores for the entire group of 334 is relatively stable around 2.3, somewhere between "somewhat certain" and "not too certain." The interviewees' certainty scores range from fairly high certainty—by Amanda at 1.5, to lower certainty by Jessie at 3.1. Jessie and Carey, who had the highest knowledge scores, had the lowest certainty scores. The two participants actually show the opposite of my original hypothesis, that with increased knowledge comes increased certainty. As someone who works with copyright law on a regular basis, I think this might make sense. The more one understands copyright law, fair use, and the individually determined, context-based court interpretations, the less certain one becomes about outcomes. The more knowledge of the law, the more possibilities, variables, and probabilities come into view. The more tool-like copyright law becomes, as opposed to rule-like, the more a user might feel able to push and pull on that tool.

Engestrom (1990) states that rules are restrictive while tools are malleable, transformable. Rules, being more definite, may provide more certainty rather than less. In the case of fair use determinations, being *less* certain might be a logical outcome of having *more* knowledge. That is, the more tool-like copyright law becomes to the user, the less certain the user becomes. The more tool-like, the more mediational—in Engestrom's triangle, rules are not mediational. Rules occupy a position on the triangle that Vygotsky might describe as promoting "unmediated" memory— simple stimulus-response behavior. But, overall, I would enjoy seeing higher knowledge and certainty scores across the board. To have higher scores might facilitate probability thinking and the construction of probable knowledge rather than rule-based knowledge. Higher scores might facilitate more rhetorical knowledge, that knowledge between fact and mere opinion.

In his research, Vygotsky focuses on how human participants form complex intellectual structures (heuristics) through the use of signs or external systems. But he did not look so much at how the sign itself changed. Engestrom, on the other hand, points out that as mediation occurs both the object (in this case the webpage) and the tool (in this case copyright law) change, producing a kind of duality in the mediational placeholder on the AT triangle. The placeholder is both the artifact (copyright law) and the understanding of that artifact (knowledge and understanding of copyright law). Engestrom (1990) did not explain how something goes from being a rule to a tool on his triangle, but he did say that an artifact can be both. His example is medical records, which he says are a tool if they are perceived to be so, in use, by the participants he interviewed. I do not find Engestrom's discussion of tools and rules and their relationship to each other very satisfying. In Engestrom's research, if the participants (doctors and assistants) thought the records were just for storage, or prescriptive rules from above, then in Engestrom's view those records occupy the rule placeholder on the triangle. He also notes people often get confused about whether something is a rule or a tool. Rather than looking at tacit understanding the way I did, he simply asks his participants outright "is this a tool"? Their answer thus depends on however they personally define tool (not having been apprised of the AT definition of mediation and the idea that tools are transformable while rules are not, and so forth).

Distinguishing between rules and tools as far as inventional heuristics might be helpful in furthering our theories of invention and informing curricular and pedagogical decisions. But AT on its own proves unsatisfying for analyzing the relationship between tools and rules, and for analyzing how law functions, what it does to people, how it flows through people, and what people do to it because in AT the focus stays on the individuals' interpretation of the heuristic structure mediating their behavior. Actor network theory (ANT) on the other hand, provides a perspective where not just people, but also artifacts and other entities can have agency, that is, be empowered. To change the research focus with ANT provides a method by which to see not just the people, but also the law change. The digital writers change the law through their understandings and subsequently their changed version of the law appears in their web compositions, but in turn, the law mediates the behavior of the writers. Among writers, motivations and understandings of the law differ. Ethics and other considerations like design best practices, flow through people and collide in webspace. So if we imagine the possibility that what is mediational (tool-like) at one moment on Engestrom's activity theory triangle might be nonmediational (rule-like) at another moment, ANT provides a mechanism to do this because ANT is a useful tool for examining the relationships between things. AT does not have a clear method to do this, and while Foucault acknowledges things are as they are due to their relationships with others, he does not focus on the agency of nonhumans in the same sense that ANT does. The use of ANT here fills the gaps left by Foucault as well as AT.

ANT provides the ability to examine mediational and other artifacts, privilege them in research, and trace their origins. While Engestrom asserts the importance of taking the system and the personal view in research, ANT permits the researcher to take the human and artifact view instead. In my research, *human* writing activity is studied. But with ANT, the activity of the law can likewise be placed in a central position. The inquiry then focuses on what the world would look like to the law. (At the point you are reading this, for you I am a text not a human—which makes more complex the irony that as a human writing this, I maintain I am capable of taking the perspective of the artifact; you see, I can be both a human and an artifact—therefore I am equally capable of taking either perspective; fiction writers do this all the time.) It is just that we are not familiar with using these types of strategies in research.

A changed understanding of authorship, one that sees authorship as complex and multiple rather than singular, connects to growing theories of remix writing in the digital age. Remix writing contains an anticipation element where the remixed text anticipates being appropriated by others at some future time (Ridolfo and Rife, 2011). In order to anticipate a later appropriation, one must assume the text's viewpoint and how it might or could not be appropriated. Because I traced authorship with my questions, the research methods here were ANT-like in that they traced certain networks, or initiated the tracing of certain author-networks. And according to Foucault, competencies of nonhuman artifacts, like laws, are folded into humans; in reverse, ANT permits focus on how human competencies are folded into nonhuman artifacts in the Latourian (1988, 1992) sense. If law has agency in the ANT sense, then one might be able to suppose that like the human participants in Vygotsky's experiments, the law can "learn" and change over time (and in fact it does)—that there might be something like the actual, text-based law, Title 17, and the proximate law—the proximate law being what the law is in people's minds and behaviors. The idea of the "proximate law" and the "actual law" draws upon Vygotsky's theory of learning: actual development and proximate development. Actual development is what individuals accomplish on their own, and proximate development is what they accomplish in collaboration with others. Using ANT, an analogy can be drawn between this kind of learning in humans and the same kind of learning in a nonhuman. That is, like human learners, the law's proximate abilities follow its actual abilities, and the law grows into, or transforms into how the law is actually being applied and understood. Every time a law is changed then, it is always already behind where it should be and is never able to quite catch up to its proximate self.

In a dramatic view of this perspective, Emile Cloatre (2008) of the University of Nottingham, UK, published research using ANT where she examined the presence or agency of patent law in Djibouti. She found a total disconnect between written law and practice. In this case, patented (as opposed to generic) pharmaceutics are widely and exclusively prescribed in Djibouti even though no written law exists mandating this practice. The reason is primarily, she found, that French pharmacists have a huge presence in Djibouti, and in France pharmacists rely almost exclusively on patented pharmaceuticals rather than generic. What Cloatre found is rather stunning; according to her research, it cannot be assumed a written law has anything at all to do with social practice even though as she states, and I can attest to, in legal discussions it is always presumed the law has huge agencies and will change people's behaviors upon enactment. At the law school, it is assumed laws are the ultimate motivators of human behavior. Cloatre's research confirms my sense of a mismatch between how the legal community envisions the agency of its intellectual property laws and the actual agency those laws exert when people actually make decisions—in my case, my experiences at the law school and in the legal profession contrast starkly with my experiences as a teacher and researcher of writing;

when digital writers actually make composing decisions, copyright law can have questionable agency.

Under the Vygotskian view as well as pursuant to Cloatre's findings, the actual written law is almost beside the point. It simply serves as a backdrop to what we are already doing. A follow-up study to mine might explore where writers get their copyright knowledge (see Nguyen, 2011). There might be no connection to Title 17, U.S. copyright law. We can only speculate a connection until we know for sure. I know few nonlawyers who have read the text of Title 17 itself, and Hobbs, Jaszi, and Aufderheide's (2007) study found copyright/fair use misinformation is likely perpetuated from teachers to students (rather than from Title 17 to students). But they assume students get their copyright knowledge from teachers. We do not know this for sure. Teacher-researcher Lisa Dush (2009) examined pre-existing knowledge among students in her own "elective writing course" classroom and found those nineteen-to-twenty-four-year-old students "are not blank slates; they have already had experiences with, appropriated discourses about, and adopted stances toward copyright" (p. 116). This finding arose from data collected from Dush's single classroom. How and whether this might be true for other student populations remains unexplored. I explore this only slightly in the current study. Students could be getting their information from YouTube for all we know. Heather, for example, learned about deviantART.com from high school friends first rather than a teacher. Jessie was told two different things from two different teachers in the same professional writing program and thus did research and made copyright decisions on her own.

To return to my earlier discussion of authorship, Foucault coupled with ANT provides theory on how to invert the focus in the typical AT study onto the perspective of the texts rather than of the humans. Using ANT to imagine copyright law's agency, and how copyright law might flow through writers and change the webtexts they create, might appear as in figure 6.3. One of the difficulties with the various generations of activity theory triangles is that a figure by nature is fixed, and yet I am trying to represent movement. To further this effort, I draw upon the work of Edwin Hutchins (1995) and his discussions of shifting perspectives that surfaced when he studied distributed cognition in the context of ship navigation. Figure 6.3 is based on his diagram of the shifting relationships between a moving boat and the stars, in relationship with an island. In my diagram, at the tip of each arrow one might image a webtext. As the writer's understanding of copyright law varies, so does the impact the law has on the writer's webtext. As the understanding of copyright law shifts, so does the web composition that is produced under its mediational powers. Figure 6.3 also represents Foucault's idea of power flowing through the individual. Finally, figure 6.3

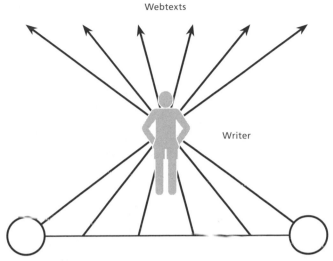

Figure 6.3. Relationship of copyright understanding to a webtext. At the tip of each arrow one might imagine a webtext. As the writer's understanding of copyright law varies, so does the impact the law has on the writer's webtext. The idea of this diagram is taken from Hutchins (1995), except where I have the copyright law, he has a canoe. Where I have the writer, he has an island. Where I have the webtext, he has stars. So as the canoe travels, the position of the stars changes in relation. In western navigation, the island is mapped as fixed.

tries to represent both the ANT and Foucauldian perspective that actors shift in and out of positions in relation to one another. Using Hutchins's (1995) method of mapping here provides a useful way of seeing the shifting relationships between actors, both human and nonhuman. Copyright law as a node is an actor into which human competencies have been folded (Latour, 1988, 1992). Like speed bumps intended to stand in for a traffic cop (Witte, 2005), copyright law stands in for the copyright police, hoping to control individuals economically in the Foucauldian sense. Based on key misunderstandings located in the survey, the proximate law, the law as imagined by research participants (for example, a law that does not privilege creative over factual work; a law where government documents are less ubiquitous; a law where the ethic of antiplagiarism has the force of law) might be more beneficial for these writers than the actual law.[1] We cannot know of course whether the actual law will eventually morph into the proximate law in every instance, but it is certainly worth pondering. It is one way to explain changes in the actual law when they do occur.

The 2010 DMCA exemption for vidders, a positive and substantial change in the law, was based in part upon evidence that the DMCA was being violated by thousands of composers each day. EFF (Electronic Frontier Foundation), proponent of the noncommercial vidder exemption, presented evidence at the hearing from Michael Wesch indicating that each day as many as fifteen thousand videos are uploaded to YouTube that are "remixes of preexisting motion pictures taken from DVDs" (Peters, 2010, p. 39). Wesch had concluded that 7.5% of a random sample of 240 videos uploaded on YouTube were remixes containing DVD movies, and by inference, it was successfully argued that 7.5% of all videos uploaded daily to YouTube would contain the same representative qualities. In other words, the register of copyrights and her panel found it very persuasive that the law was being broken by thousands of composers each day—this, I argue, is the proximate law—the law as it should be, and as it is being enacted through human behavior, and when the register issued her recommendation granting the exemption, she pushed the actual law towards the proximate law. It was the proximate law—basically illegal behavior—that in part spurred this change. Yet while it was illegal behavior, it was also reasonable behavior because the use ultimately made was usually a fair use as illustrated in the numerous examples presented to the register. In these examples, copyright law was visible as an ignored law—the fact that the remixes existed evidenced the actual law's impotence.

As seen in the interviews, sometimes copyright has a visible presence in writers' webtexts, and sometimes it does not. People, things, and entities that are not understood are often ignored. Copyright law as written certainly is not designed to be understood. Imagine if Title 17, a 350-page document, were usability tested. If users were faced with a simple task of selecting an image found on the web and placing it in their own text, legally per Title 17—not only would they have to study Title 17, not an easy task since it is written in legalese, but they would also have to research the origins and ownership of the image to decide the likeliness of a copyright holder challenging their "fair use." If a writer solely relied on Title 17, they might make a wrong choice because Title 17 does not directly refer to all the cases that interpret it. My guess is that Title 17 would be deemed entirely unusable to anyone but copyright specialists—highly paid attorneys. It could be redesigned though. Perhaps this is something worth examining— a usability study of copyright law and development of recommendations. But such a study might be blocked or ignored due to the fact that if the law could be understood and applied by everyday citizens, lawyers would be out of work. But we would be closer to achieving justice in the U.S. if laws could actually be understood by the people they apply to.

And so it appears the agency of U.S. written law in the inventional processes of digital writers is called into question for three main reasons. One reason copyright law has less agency, or power, than one might expect in digital compositions is that copyright law has a certain irrelevance in web-texts due to the physical shape of the browser window, which lends itself to readymade fair use (thumbnails, low pixels, short quotes). A second reason is that copyright law is not the only rhetorical topic under consideration when writers make content decisions. A third reason copyright law is less important than it might be is that people are incredibly imaginative in their understandings of it. It is a tool to them (like most artifacts—I think very few artifacts are actually rules). Tools transform.

Vygotsky (1997) provides a good example of how a tool can be intellectually transformed by an individual, and used for something other than what was intended. In his experiments, he gave participants cards featuring pictures and then asked them to complete some type of memory task. In one of his examples, he used a picture of a crab. Participants usually selected a picture that actually represented the item they were to remember. If they were to remember a crab, they picked a picture of a crab. Such a direct prompt evidences "unmediated memory" in Vygotsky's view—a rule-based intellectual activity rather than a mediational one. He was not very interested in this simple association. What intrigues Vygotsky is what happened when research participants were given cards not corresponding to what they should remember. In his example, the crab card was used to remember something like "theater." So what happened was the research subject made up a story relating the crab to theater. As Vygotsky (1997) describes, the participant explained the crab was looking into the ocean at some shells, which for the crab were as entertaining as watching something in a theater. The research subject's understanding of the crab derives from a heuristic formed by the human subject and is based on a story that connects everything together—not a simple one-on-one association, but a complex structure, a story.

In a more recent example, my colleague just published his fifth book of poetry, and I attended the publication party, where he read several selections. One of the poems he read focused on his now-deceased mother's open-heart surgery. A thematic image used throughout the poem is one of forceps and clothespins. Before reading this poem, he informed the audience the poem's core idea came out of a poetry group suggestion. In this group, he was handed a bag of clothespins and directed to use these artifacts to generate his prose. He said it was difficult to come up with an idea at first, but ultimately he decided to relate the clothespins to the forceps—so he made a story in his poem from the clothespins, which transformed into something very different than what the clothespins, as "tools," were intended for. The clothespins, for my poet colleague and his audience, transformed into forceps. They were mediational. They became part of a story.

In the theater-crab Vygotsky example I offer, Vygotsky did not discuss that the crab in his example actually changed into a theater. Over time, I posit, the story linking crab to theater becomes so internalized it is forgotten by the human subject. The same is true with the clothespins and their relationship to forceps, except in the latter case the poet reminds himself of the origins each time he introduces the poem this way to his audience. Certainly, for the reader of the poem, that originating link between the clothespins and forceps by way of the problem and challenge originally presented to the poet in his writers' group is hidden forever in the finished text—unless the reader has a direct line to the poet as I did in my example. During my research, I tried to retrieve these hidden stories by using the discourse-based interview. When Vygotsky's participant looked at the crab, he did not see a crab, he saw a theater. Likewise, when the writer-participants "see" copyright law, they do not see the law-as-written, they see something else: their story of the law. Their stories are their "misunderstandings" of copyright law. These stories of the law derive from complex structures or intellectually maintained, mediational, and inventional heuristics digital writers create in order to make sense of the composing environment. When writer-participants see their webtexts, the mediational means—the rhetorical topics that lend truth to their decisions—may no longer be visible. This is the reason I used discourse-based interviews, and in turn, the composing heuristic featured in figure 6.1 offers a starting point, a set of guide-marks, for exploring motivating factors in invention.

Misunderstanding and confusion are productive. Misunderstanding is more than just "being wrong." This might explain why Vygotsky leveraged confusion in his research techniques by disrupting routines, providing more than one route to solve a problem, and posing tasks for subjects exceeding their knowledge and abilities. Copyright law in all its complexities, and as an interjector in the composing process, likewise begs for misunderstanding and confusion. And to overcome this, participants create stories of the law. Among the interviewees, the proximate law is their story of the law and not really the actual law; it is a story of the law that makes sense to the writer. "Actors incessantly engage in the most abstruse metaphysical constructions by redefining all the elements of the world" (Latour, 2005, p. 51). So for Rob, his understanding is that flickr.com images are always safe—he thought he learned this in school from a reliable source—and he operates with that understanding even though he is not correct. Amanda thinks that if materials come from an educational source and are previously used to teach others, they are automatically "fair use"—again, not correct. It is clear interviewees twist and shape the law into something making sense for them, into their own "truth," regardless of the literal accuracy of their understanding. So the law did not have as much agency as it might have liked; it did not just pass through people uninterrupted and show up in their web compositions. It shifts and changes due to the writers' knowledge and understanding and, based on that, has a presence or lack thereof in the final webtext.

So copyright law is much more tool-like than rule-like for the research participants in this study. The tools and rules dichotomy Engestrom mapped out is not emphasized by Vygotsky. But Engestrom's mapping of tools and rules surfaces in Vygotsky's differentiation between mediated and unmediated memory. Latour develops these ideas more in his discussion of "mediators" (similar to Engestrom's "tools") and "intermediaries" (similar to Engestrom's "rules"). According to Latour, intermediaries are very rare—they are one thing or even nothing because they can be easily forgotten, like the medical records in Engestrom's (1990) study. Western versions of copyright law in China and TRIPS (Agreement on Trade Related Aspects of Intellectual Property) in Djibouti are forgotten by the people. In China, copyright law is unable to produce anything to keep itself alive, unable to circulate, unable to overcome existing networks that already serve the author-function, that already organize meaning—and so in China, copyright law is an intermediary. Mediators, in contrast, are plural, transforming, potentially infinite. "They might be counted as one, for nothing, for several, or for infinity. Their input is never a good predictor of their output; their specificity has to be taken into account every time" (Latour, 2005, p. 39)—like U.S. copyright law and its mediational effect on interviewees' webtexts.

Copyright law functions as a tool. Human competencies are folded into it. ANT permits the artifact perspective—and from that perspective copyright law can learn the same way amazon.com seems to know which books I want to read next. Copyright law changes and takes different forms for each of the writers in my study. Copyright law can also be inventional. Just like the people in this study, Title 17 has exercised wily intelligence (it is after all a text into which human competencies have been folded). Title 17 has been exceedingly inventive, productive, vigilant, and *efficient*. Figure 6.4 shows some things Title 17 might have associated "in a legal way" due to its "circulation throughout the landscape" (Latour, 2005, p. 239). I offer figure 6.4 as an idea in its infancy stage. The possible networks illustrated in figure 6.4 would have to be explored and verified. Bruno Latour (2010) has recently published an ethnographic study where he did trace the networks in the deliberations of the French supreme court—using ANT to unpack how truth and law are produced. His work provides an excellent example of how we might move forward in copyright contexts to examine similar productions.

From my study now, we do know that overall, copyright law is productive. On a copyright listserve I participate in, along with artists, librarians, professors, and lawyers, during a five-day period in late 2008, fifty-five

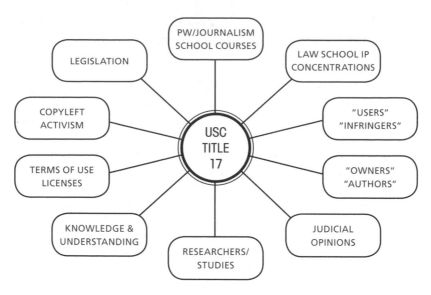

Figure 6.4. Legal associations produced by Title 17.

posts circulated debating the merits of the Orphan Works Act of 2008 currently under consideration (Curtis, 2008). The concept of "orphan" works might indicate the law becoming more ANT-like, and also growing into its proximate self, in that it is trying to recognize what we already know—that things people make detach from their creators and take on meaning and power never anticipated. The Orphan Works Act makes it easier for users to appropriate texts, images, and sounds that have no "owner"—they have no creator because their creator cannot be found. Such texts are construed as "orphans." The fifty-five posts remind me of the law's productiveness—Title 17, and its revisions, continue proliferating.

What would a theory of rhetorical invention for things and entities look like? Grabill (2007) gives us a start with his idea that institutions can be *metis* friendly. I also think that diseases and viruses are "things" that use *metis*, but like the plague, they exercise it without justice. If we think of entities and things as being inventional and productive, of exercising wily intelligence, all kinds of research trajectories open up. Assembling the theories of Janice Lauer, Cynthia Haller, Carolyn Miller, Michel Foucault, Lev Vygotsky, John Law, and Bruno Latour, a small start to defining "rhetorical invention for people, things, and entities" might be: *Rhetorical invention is when people, things, entities create heuristics formed of interlocking stories, stories about situations, and then use those stories as a basis to maintain, act upon, resist, or transcend those situations.*

7

Implications for the Future

> Most teachers know that rhetoric has always lost life and
> respect to the degree that invention has not had a significant
> and meaningful role.
> —Janice Lauer, "Heuristics and Composition"

A theory of rhetorical invention is important to have when conducting research, teaching, or even trying to change the law. In this chapter, I'm going to try to outline ways that this study and its accompanying ideas can be useful as we move forward. First, I examine implications for future research. I next discuss curriculum issues and implications, outlining ways to use Section E of the survey as a portable teaching tool—including some specific examples. I conclude the chapter by discussing how this study might influence the way we think about changing the law.

Research Implications

Implications for research fall into three main categories: (1) research strategies, (2) what I call "research presence," and (3) research trajectories, including further refining our theories of invention by drawing on the concept of *metis*, thinking more about the whole issue of chilled speech, more deeply theorizing copyright law as a disciplinary power, further examining the connection between IP law and classical invention, and considering justice as an overriding framework for digital writing. Issues arising in this study regarding research strategies include ideas on how to research invention. Some methods and techniques to consider when researching invention are: (1) including the use of the discourse-based interview and its limitations, (2) the possible use of an inventional heuristic in order to conduct such research, (3) the utility of mixed methods, and (4) implications for conducting composing research framed in one theory of authorship versus another.

While we do have theorists who have worked in the area of "rhetorical invention," scholars such as Janice Lauer, Kenneth Pike, Lee Odell, Stephen Witte, Cynthia Haller, Gordon Rohman, and more recently Tiffany Portewig (2008), and James Melton (2009), none have clearly articulated a metatheory or research strategy applicable for the very specialized area of *researching invention* in composing processes. But there actually are some interesting commonalities between Vygotsky's research and the research of those who study and theorize invention. Lauer's (1970, 1972, 1979, 2004), Miller's (2000), and Haller's (2000) discussions of rhetorical invention as epistemic and Vygotsky's theory on the activity of higher intellectual processes share some features. The rhetoric-based theories of invention described by Lauer, Miller, and Haller include the very Vygotskian notions of problem solving, creativity, the weighing and balancing of differing options, and even concepts similar to Vygotsky's theories of internalization and mediation. What Lauer calls creativity and problem solving, Vygotsky calls "higher mental functioning." Haller explicitly discusses heuristics as mediational, while Lauer implies heuristics structure writers' abilities to generate new ideas or think creatively, similar to Vygotsky's notion of a mediating structure. Vygotsky (1997) states that his research has "heuristic significance" because it supports the idea of "the correctness of the structural law of memory in contrast to the law of association" (p. 181). Vygotsky himself acknowledges that although it appears he studies memory, what he really studied was "the active creation of structures" (p. 182). Heuristics are structures.

Historically Vygotsky's work has been relied upon in composition studies when discussing composition theory, and although some writers have come very close, a clear connection between theories of invention and AT have not yet been drawn. For example, James Britton (1982/2003), when referring to what many would deem the "inventional" writing activities of small children, references Vygotsky's theory. Hinting at the possibility of relying on Vygotsky to theorize rhetorical invention, J. Lauer (1970) encourages us to develop a transcendent, generative theory of rhetorical invention and suggests that an especially appropriate field to examine in order to develop our metatheory of rhetorical invention might be psychology. She supplied almost two hundred bibliography entries from psychology scholarship especially with respect to creativity and heuristics. Among these bibliography entries are articles between the dates of 1931 and 1968. None of them are attributable to Vygotsky although he died in 1934. However "many of his publication dates both in Russian and in English, are contemporary" (Glick, 1997, p. v). *Mind in Society* was not published until 1978. Therefore he was unlikely to be expressly referenced in Lauer's bibliography because she would not have had access to his work at the time she wrote her 1967 dissertation or the *CCC* article "Heuristics and Composition" (1970).

It has taken many years for the field of composition and rhetoric to discover Vygotsky's work and find its relevance. But now that Lauer's writings on invention; Emig's, Perl's, and Flower and Hayes's writings on composing process; and Vygotsky's work on the activity of human development are before us, we can truly appreciate that "evidence of this kind is often ignored, and it takes a Vygotsky, speaking across the decades since his death" (Britton, 1982, p. 163) to reveal to us the nature of writing, the nature of the intellectual work that goes into writing (see Vygotsky, 1978, p. 117). I think that further exploration of the ways Vygotsky's theory and research methods might help those of us wanting to study invention in composing is certainly merited.

Research Strategies

When Vygotsky studied what he called the "the active creation of structures" (1997, p. 182), what I call "invention," he used three strategies (disrupting participants' routine methods, providing more than one route to solve problems, and posing tasks exceeding participants' knowledge and abilities). Because copyright law issues as well as, I learned, rhetorical topics around design, employer requirements, ethics, and so on, interrupt a writers' composing process, copyright law's mediational influence in the composing process provides a research scene where the three strategies Vygotsky used are already available. I found Vygotsky's research mechanisms helpful in permitting me to "see" invention. When we question research participants about their composing choices in light of copyright law, the law's existence and potential imposition in the composing process provides a method to test participants' problem-solving strategies. Like one of Vygotsky's key methods, writers' copyright law considerations disrupt routine methods of problem solving. Instead of only considering design heuristics when composing, writers also found themselves considering copyright law separately from design. Examining writers' thinking here provides a view into rhetorical inventive processes. Because probability calculations are usually made when considering the application of copyright law or the chances of being held accountable for its violation, the law's imposition into the composing process also provides a variety of methods or routes to solve a single problem. This problem of choice provides a view into the use of probability considerations by digital writers. For example, Leslie password-protected copyrighted materials only if it was easy—a logical decision based on perceptions of low chances of getting caught. Since writers' knowledge and certainty of knowledge regarding copyright law in the context of digital composing was examined, I learned what occurs when a writer needs to accomplish a task that exceeds that writer's knowledge and abilities. The research methods I used to make invention visible fit neatly into Vygotsky's methods of measuring and observing mediated activity and are informative to theories of researching rhetorical invention as well as our understandings of how heuristics function. In other words, I offer up the idea that like Vygotsky, if a writing researcher wants to study invention, she should find a research scene where research subjects have their routines disrupted, have more than one route to solve a problem, and where a task is imposed upon them that exceeds their knowledge and abilities. A researcher wishing to study invention in composing might wish to locate or even prompt a research scene where some of these strategies are in place—strategies that appear to invoke invention or make it more visible to the researcher.

More generally, as far as the utility of research designs, we could further explore and test AT to study writing. The use of AT has proved especially fruitful in this study, supporting the stances of its proponents Hart-Davidson (2007) and Geisler and Slattery (2007). By separating knowledge and understanding of copyright law as a potential mediator in the writing activity of digital writers, the mediational means actually located (as evidenced in figure 6.1) ended up much more complex than originally imagined. In contrast to Vygotsky's research, my study did not take place in a lab but among mature writers who had been exposed to cultural signs over their entire lives. Unlike Vygotsky, I did not isolate a set of signs (he used cards with pictures for example), and then watch while participants internalized those signs. Instead I used the discourse-based interviews to draw out internalized or tacit knowledge that participants previously absorbed. Thus it is not surprising that copyright law was woven together with a number of other rhetorical topics, creating a heuristical structure that writers drew upon in their work. The discourse-based interview method provided a unique opportunity to examine writers' tacit knowledge. Although I limited the interviews to seven, it still provided me ample data from which to draw (almost one hundred pages after transcription). I felt this sampling gave me a very good view into the writing process of the digital writers in the context of my research questions.

While I could have used observations or the talk-aloud protocol, I instead opted to use retrospective accounts in order to apply discourse-based strategies. Retrospective accounts of writing have limitations in that they rely on people's memories. Prior (2004) reports that people may forget the moment-to-moment details that went into their writing decisions. He states that the farther between the act of composing and the account, the greater the chance details will drop out and new details added to suit the "social situation and time in which they are produced" (p. 185). But observation and talk-aloud protocols, as well as screen capturing and diary studies have their limitations too, especially with respect to time and data-overload (sheer amount of data on one's hard drive). Jessie reported having at least 150 production hours in one of her compositions, not including all the times she had presented and further revised this particular piece. As my interviewees noted and as Prior (2004) argues, texts often contain a multiplicity of authorship not observable by watching a single writer in a single context. It was common for the interviewees to have pieces that were previously authored by unknown persons, and then taken over by them at a given time (organizational webpages lend themselves to this). It was common for the interviewees to present for consideration in this study web writings that had been revised over a period of years, and had transformed in purpose. Leslie, for example, created a digital-visual composition for a graduate course that was later integrated into a first-year writing course she taught. Jessie, soon to be a PhD student, created a digitally remixed movie for a course assignment that ended up being a showcase piece for her digital portfolio and the center of many conference presentations as well as a journal article. It was not uncommon for interviewees to be at least partially supplied with content by others, and to complete only the arrangement and style aspects of authorship. Heather, an undergraduate student working across the university in different fields, was always supplied with content by others for her organizational web writing. Amanda, a recent four-year graduate working for a national health organization as an online communication specialist, was supplied by her organization and its constituents with content for web compositions.

One special strength I found when using the retrospective account was the ability to learn when web authors had forgotten where they had obtained materials that appeared in their own web compositions. These interviewees, such as Leslie and Amanda, knew they had not created certain visuals in their own digital texts but could not remember where these items had been obtained. The fact that this phenomena occurred is noteworthy since it challenges attribution traditions as we understand them in alphabetic text contexts, and *would not have been discovered without use of a retrospective account.* Such composing practices inform our understanding of "common knowledge." We often do not take into account the visual in our discussion of "common knowledge." Common knowledge is usually something discussed with students in their first two years of college in the context of documentation and citation practices. Usually we are referring to ideas and facts as common knowledge or not. But now that our culture has become so visual with the advent of the Internet, our discussion about common knowledge and the visual may need to be expanded and complicated.

In further defense of retrospective accounts, in other discourse communities, particularly the legal community, retrospective accounts like confessions, testimony, and accounts via deposition are all considered legitimate in even the most high-stakes situations of life and death. Taken literally, the whole notion of the retrospective account kind of encapsulates all accounts, even those provided through the talk-aloud protocol because even in that case the researched individual needs a split second in order to process and communicate his or her own contemporaneous actions. A researcher conducting observations and recording the screen of digital writers might avoid a distanced retrospective account of the research subject, but ultimately that researcher will have to provide an account to the audience, and his or her narrative and interpretation will in fact be retrospective.

Another implication raised by this study with respect to researching invention is the utility of leveraging an inventional heuristic to frame research, such as the one I offer in figure 6.1, the "mediational-digital composing heuristic." Since it is a visualization of how writers in my study actually composed, it might be a useful starting point for further research in this area. I certainly invite others to pursue additional research on digital composing processes—research that might further test, expand on, and explain what I located in this study. Also a researcher beginning such a study might want to first reflect on his or her theory of authorship because that theory—basically a difference between an understanding of sole authorship or something more complex and multiple—that theory will likely shape the outcome as well as the research design. The wide array of digital compositions collected from interviewees in this study certainly called into question understandings of "studentness," "composition," "authorship," and "originality," as well as ideas about "beginnings" and "ends" to writing projects. Of course a study directly examining and tracing authorship in both digital and more traditional "paper" texts is certainly welcome and would surely be informative both to existing inventional theories and to curriculum design. I do want to point out though that the affordances of digital writing (word processing, cutting and pasting, online/database research, file sharing and collaborative writing, and file naming) have now become so ubiquitous it might be all but impossible to locate a natural research scene that still remains virginal as to elements of digital writing.

The use of mixed-methods designs might also add to the utility of using the "mediational-digital composing heuristic" because such methods allow an organized but broad array of research methods—for example, survey, interview, observation, and so on. For myself, I believe using mixed methods permitted me to see a breadth of data otherwise unavailable. The interviews added so many crucial details to my understanding of invention in copyright contexts, but without the survey I could not know how much certain phenomena were actually applicable to larger populations (the willingness to break the law for ethics' sake, for example). However there are some limitations to using the mixed-methods approach. It creates an additional burden for the researcher, who must know a number of research methods rather than specialize in a single method. Mixed-methods research also has limitations due to time constraints; data analysis may potentially not go as deeply into one area or another as might be true with a study design that features only a survey, only interviews, only textual analysis, and so on. Yet a mixed-methods researcher may potentially locate a broader and even deeper view of the situation or problem under examination.

Research Presence

Another issue arising with respect to research is the issue of what I term "research presence." I believe fields including journalism, which have embraced quantitative methods and social science research techniques such as "random selection," tend to make such methods easier to implement. It was difficult for me to piece together a membership list of writing programs that actually reflected reality because there is not one definitive list. Making my own list independent of preexisting membership lists would have inserted into the research more of my own subjective worldview than I cared to insert. As of late 2007, the membership lists that did exist, such as those kept by ATTW, STC, and NCTE, also relied on programs' self-inputting the required "list" information. This automatically excludes more marginalized programs—like those at two-year institutions.

To add to this problem, since completing the study I notice that the NCTE writing major list now includes only four-year writing programs. Their most current list states at the top: "This list does not currently include creative writing majors as such, programs at associate or graduate levels, nor does it include certificate-only programs" (Committee, 2009). An explanation is not given. This is true even though the writing major committee's first charge is to "document the variety of majors in composition and rhetoric across the country and in diverse institutional types and in diverse units" (Committee, 2009). I know when I created my master list of writing programs back in 2007, there was representation on the NCTE writing major list of two-year colleges and certificate programs. My point is that for researchers conducting large-scale quantitative research, the underrepresentation of all the diverse writing programs that actually exist in the U.S. (or elsewhere) means those populations are effectively erased from any research as well as subsequent research recommendations or implications. I recommend that rhetoric and composition as a field, together with technical and professional writing programs, create a single defining list that includes not just self-inputted information, but also purposely recruited information, on *all* the types of writing programs available in the U.S. If such a list also included international writing programs, that would be so much the better.

Research Trajectories

The study raises some interesting issues of invention in composing that might be pursued in more formal workplace environments by those researching in the area of technical and professional writing. Work-for-hire issues as they intersect with digital composing processes and how those issues might further inform our understanding of authorship would be a fascinating area to explore. As far as researching rhetorical invention in the workplace, Portewig (2008) and Melton (2009) have made a start here that could be expanded upon. In addition to suggesting a research trajectory continuing my research into the workplace, I also think further research on invention in digital composing could further test, explain, and refine our existing theories on the use of *metis* in composing, ideas on the nature of "chilled speech," rhetorical theories of intellectual property, and theories on justice's intersection with writing. I discuss these ideas next.

A Theory of Metis in Invention

Carolyn Miller (2000) describes *metis* in her discussion of classical rhetoric. She connects invention and the hunt to a conjectural worldview and the quality of *metis*, "craftiness and cunning" (p. 138). I think the special kind of probability thinking that writers in my study used in order to calculate their decisions in light of the law's power does give a researcher some initial thoughts on how the concept of *metis* might be further explored in the context of digital writing in copyright-saturated—or law-saturated, power-saturated environments.

A theory of *metis* is something for researchers interested in technology studies to develop because one of the qualities of *metis* is its ability to adapt, and technology changes and invokes change. Because writing is an activity, one that responds in context to moment-by-moment rhetorical decisions (Hart-Davidson, 2007), it is almost inevitable for those in rhetoric studies to raise up the concept of *metis* as one that might help researchers understand the inventional qualities needed to make composing choices in digital environments. Detienne and Vernant (1978) say *metis* applies to "the world of movement," those locations that are "fluid" and "constantly changing" (p. 20). More recently, Janet Atwill (1998) and Robert R. Johnson (1998) discuss *metis*, and Jeff Grabill (2007) also discusses the concept; Grabill argues that in the context of community literacies, institutions should support a special kind of invention relying on *metis*.

Metis is actually a figure in Greek mythology. She was the first wife of Zeus, but right before she gave birth to their daughter Athena, Zeus swallowed her so he could capture her cunning intelligence for himself. Detienne and Vernant (1978) describe *metis* as "a type of intelligence and of thought, a way of knowing" (p. 3). *Metis* combines "flair, wisdom, forethought, subtlety of mind, deception, resourcefulness, vigilance, opportunism, various skills, and experience acquired over the years" (p. 3). Trickster rhetorics (Powell, 1999; Terrill, 2004), performance based pedagogies (Lindquist, 2004), as well as Haraway's "cyborg" identity are very similar to *metis*. Powell writes, "Ambivalent, androgynous, anti-definitional, the trickster is slippery and constantly mutable" (1999, p. 9). Haraway writes, "Cyborg writing is about the power to survive . . . on the basis of seizing the tools" (2004, p. 33). Haraway invokes the cyborg in order to imagine a world without gender, a subject that no longer attempts to "heal the terrible cleavages of gender" (Rife, 2005, p. 18). The cyborg is a being that no longer depends on "the plot of original unity out of which difference must be produced" (Haraway, 2004, p. 9).

Haraway's discussion is important because in the ancient derivation, Metis *transcended* opposition, which is different than fighting against or opposing opposition. The idea of using invention to transcend, rather than oppose, I think, is worth pondering, especially in light of invention's productive power. Back in 1997, Porter wrote, "the realm of hyperreality can become a realm of domination, unless writers are willing to adopt the role of 'cyborgs'" (p. 63). Transcending concrete systems of power by being productive (rather than always resisting and opposing) seems a possible intelligent choice—but not always the most obvious. Jessie transcended copyright law by fully embracing it with her journal article, conference presentations, open letter to copyright holders, and piracy movie. Thus far, she is experiencing success and I expect that trend to continue.

Haraway's description of the cyborg could have been lifted right from the pages of Detienne and Vernant. Metis, for the Greeks, was a feminine noun, but like Haraway's cyborg, Metis for the Orphics was "an androgynous god with a twofold nature" (Detienne and Vernant, 1978, p. 134) implying that *metis* transcends the opposition between male and female. Metis is likened to water slipping through the enemy's hands, like fire, which can lightly toast or annihilate, polymorphic, like a trap in that it is "the opposite of what it seems to be," like Homer's Odysseus, "an octopus," whose "strings of words . . . unfold like the coils of the snake, speeches which enmesh their enemies like the supple arms of the octopus" (pp. 44, 39). According to Detienne and Vernant, for Aristotle, the *panourgotatos*, octopus, or cuttlefish, was the "most cunning of fish" (p. 159). They point out after Zeus swallowed Metis, cunning was assigned to the gods in an ordered fashion.

Not all gods had it. And it is clear in Greek myth that having *metis* did not necessarily bring happiness and joy—*metis* threatens established order.

The quality of *metis* is relevant to digital composing in light of copyright law's imposition in webspace. The law tries to establish order. The digital writers I interviewed certainly constitute a threat to copyright law. In many instances they rendered copyright law impotent. One thing to point out about *metis* is that having and showing it can be a liability. According to Greek myth, one might try to hide their cunning wit or suffer the fate of Metis who remains locked and hidden forever in Zeus's entrails. Organizational work-for-hire policies, on a much less dramatic level, consume and conceal the *metis* of their employees—that is, they stand as author and supersede individual employees' authorship. Such was the case with Amanda and Heather. Work-for-hire policies though do create order. It would be very difficult to manage an organization's identity with two thousand individuated authors of it.

In Greek myth, not all gods had *metis*; some instead had practical knowledge, prudence, or *phronesis*. Detienne and Vernant (1978) liken *phronesis* to "forewarned prudence", " (p. 138; see also Burns, 2009). *Phronesis* is the kind of inventional quality Leslie had because she was practical in her approach to copyright. *Phronesis* is often associated with politicians. Aristotle made a distinction between prudence and cleverness (Detienne and Vernant, 1978, p. 316), but I see no reason to think that both are not inventive qualities. Leslie's score on copyright knowledge was only 50%. She was aware that she did not have a great deal of knowledge in this area, which is one reason why she did not focus on it in the first-year writing course she taught. Instead she exercised prudence—she password protected things if it was easy to do so—she basically knew that her chances of being held liable for copyright infringement were small. As Chaim Perelman states, legal reasoning is an elaborated individual case of practical reasoning. Practical reasoning is prudence, like Leslie had. Practical reasoning elaborated upon, with a cunning edge, is *metis*. Legal reasoning at its best draws upon *metis*. But even though Leslie was prudent rather than perhaps "cunning" with respect to copyright, she was still inventive.

I think writer-interviewees did exhibit *metis*, although not in a fashion that I can concretely quantify without an additional study. But based on my research, the following qualities might serve as a start to defining *metis* in digital writing contexts:

1. *Kairos*—timing, especially when to keep one's cunning wit hidden or knowing when to stay under the radar of copyright holders. Patience is an element of kairos—when Odysseus and his men were trapped in the Cyclops's cave, Odysseus waited patiently, observing Cyclops's habits, and then waited longer for him to fall into a drunken stupor in order to make

the move that allowed Odysseus and his men who'd not yet been eaten to escape. Odysseus's vigilance included the willingness to sacrifice and suffer; as he waited, several additional men served as Cyclops's evening meal.

2. *Research abilities (research and appropriation or hunting and gathering)*— having foresight, meaning one must have knowledge or know where to get the knowledge one needs. One must also know when a check with the guide-marks is in order. (You need to know what questions to ask, when, and of whom.) We might revisit *stasis* theory and issue spotting to develop research abilities in the context of *metis*. Research abilities encompass the ability to hunt with foresight, to plan, to conjecture in a cunning fashion. Research abilities also include the know-how to gather or appropriate what one needs. One needs to be able to smartly pick and choose.

3. *Subject area knowledge*—cannot be underestimated. In order to make a fair use determination or understand one's potential liability under copyright law, one must study the law and know a lot. Clearly in the survey and interviews, digital writers want to know more about copyright law as well as other laws impacting digital writing. Sarah, for example, wanted to know how to negotiate contracts with clients and how to draft and use permission and release forms.

4. *Flexibility*—readiness to change paths on a moments' notice; have backup plans. Many interviewees made a fair use determination of their use, but were ready to take materials down if asked—had various arguments in place they could use if called to task.

5. *Stakeholder Status*—presence of something serious or very important to the writer. In Greek myths, it was often the person's life or the life of a loved one. For digital writers, it could be their ethos, the ethos of their organization, ethics, religion, or an ingrained sense of justice and fairness. *Metis* usually happens where pressure is exerted.

6. *Success*—whether you are accomplishing your goal—in the case of copyright not getting sued or asked to take something down, it might be an indicator of the presence of *metis*. At this writing, I report that Amanda obtained the international teaching opportunity she applied for, and Leslie took a position at her first choice of employers.

Since it is clear *metis* can involve trickery, deceit, seduction, we have to decide what to do about that problem. As George Kennedy (1963) reminds us, rhetoric (like *metis*) has always been seductive. But Powell (1999) asserts "the trickster doesn't play malicious tricks" (p. 9). In Greek myth, justice is sometimes served through the use of *metis* (although I cannot say it is accomplished without harming anyone, one of the three precepts of Roman justice discussed below). Since all seven digital writers interviewed were trying to act justly and fairly—perhaps why ethics was so important to them, justice might serve as a tempering framework enclosing the use of *metis* by digital writers. Aristotle and other philosophers believed that justice was the virtue that encompassed all others. Jim Porter writes (1998): "To be an effective rhetor, you have to know what is good, be able to move toward it yourself, and be able to have the persuasive capacity to move others toward it as well" (p. 37).

I think all of the digital writers I interviewed used *metis*, a kind of cunningness and craftiness, or the ability to transform one's subject position with respect to authorship. It informed their probability thinking—the "probability thinking" element in figure 6.1. A really good example of *metis* is illustrated in the strategy Rob used, recommended by the Indian outsourcing company where he previously worked. The web writing Rob did for that company involved the creation of promotional pages that would entice people to go to the company's actual website. Rob explained that due to time constraints, the workers didn't have "the capacity to be very creative, we just had to have the work done." Because it was not "humanly possible" to write as much content as was required, the workers were "allowed" to take web content from others' existing websites as long as they "jumbled up the words." So the company had its employees use existing content from the web and jumble up the words, "put in our own spices," upload the pages on the web and then check the URL at copyscape.com, a website that permits individuals to check if someone is copying their digital materials or websites. Instead of using copyscape for that reason, Rob used it to make sure the websites he created did not "copy" another website too much, even though the content was taken wholesale from preexisting websites.

Thinking Further about "Chilled Speech"

Another research trajectory that could use further exploration is the one involving the whole concept of chilled speech. I want to momentarily emphasize how copyright law, in a sense, actually facilitated the production of speech rather than the repression of it. There's a certain tension between the idea that writers' speech is chilled—at least with respect to some specific areas (felt they could have had a more "aesthetically pleasing" web composition if they could have used others' copyrighted materials without fear; had taken things down from the web because of fear of copyright liability even though they had not been asked to; had not posted something to the web to begin with because of fear of copyright liability), and the idea that copyright law as a system of invention organized by rhetoric, *produces* knowledge.

Of course there are areas where speech was chilled or at least impeded because of copyright law. Survey takers acknowledged that their web creations may have been more aesthetically pleasing if they did not have to worry about copyright. The writer-interviewees, particularly Sarah and

Jessie, who had relatively high knowledge scores (64% and 71% respectively), noted how time consuming it was to consider copyright law. Jessie spent hours and weeks trying to obtain permission for the use of some materials in her web movie but with no success. Sarah, who composed websites for churches and nonprofits, likewise spent a great deal of time reading licenses and navigating the legality of using others' web design resources. Sarah spent time talking over her ideas with her husband. Jessie spent time discussing copyright issues with faculty in her master's program. Ultimately though neither of these web writers had "very chilled" speech (Sarah's chilled speech score was 3 and Jessie's was 2 on a 6 point scale with a score of 0–2 being "not chilled"; 5–6 being "very chilled"). So their speech was chilled, but not necessarily *extremely* so. Since neither Sarah nor Jessie received 100% on the knowledge test, maybe their speech was not as chilled as one might expect because they were not fully aware of some legal risks they were taking. Yet, in reviewing their web compositions with them, I was unable to locate anything in their writing that could not plausibly be argued as fair use. The shape of the webspace itself always already lends itself to fair use. Webspace encourages remix, a little bit of this and a little bit of that in a very small visual area. To do other wise risks losing the audience. I do not think that the reason the writers' speech is not "very chilled" is their ignorance of the law. I think it is that they found work-arounds, relying on invention informed by *metis*. They transcended the law.

While copyright law *mediated* digital expression, and it did chill speech to some extent, it also *produced* digital speech. For example, copyright law compelled Jessie to write her open letter to copyright holders, and create her digital movie on Internet piracy. Copyright law suggested Amanda include the copyright symbol on her webpages, not to protect her work but to show the reader that she was aware of such issues. On the national teacher exchange database that Carey managed, copyright law caused users to experience more discourse—the database had to produce more texts explaining the legality of uses, and provide users with means to choose how much to lock down their donated content. Copyright law shaped the digital writing of Sarah, Carey, Rob, and Heather. It caused them to spend more time composing, to engage in conversations with others, to read licenses, to do special searches for copyright-safe materials. All of the licenses they read, texts and words and information, existed because of the power of copyright law. Sarah and Heather purposely searched for online visuals and resources that did not require attribution since attribution would either confuse their clients or make their web designs less appealing. Copyright law necessitated the production of lots and lots of texts, lots and lots of discourse.

Copyright Law and Power

Another research trajectory meriting further exploration is one exploring copyright law as a disciplinary power having impact on digital writers. Copyright law as a mediating power imposes on digital writers the threat of legal penalty for failure to heed the law. Foucault notes the nature of using the law to penalize requires that the penalty be impermanent—while "incorrigibles" can be (permanently) eliminated, the convict must ordinarily have space to "become virtuous once more" (1977, p. 107). Foucault theorized the economics of laws (the law-function)—how law and ethics flow through individuals as measures of efficient control. Foucault might have agreed with Perelman and Olbrechts-Tyteca that argumentation (discursive practice) is a substitute for violence (that traditional hold on the body). Foucault's view connects to Vygotsky's *internalization* as well, with the difference that Foucault discusses the internalization of strategies of power, usually as they pass through individuals, and usually with a negative connotation, where Vygotsky discusses the internalization of knowledge and usually with a positive connotation. Kenneth Bruffee (1984) conceptualizes this internalization as one of an externalized conversation that then reexternalizes itself in the written product. So by mapping Bruffee onto Foucault we might say that as power flows through individuals, one of its products might be writing.

Foucault (1977) very explicitly discusses how, after torture-as-discipline-and-punishment became viewed as an atrocity (drawing and quartering is his initial example), certain legal discourses developed to control individuals' behavior from the outside-in, eventually completely from the inside. Ethics can exercise the same kind of control law might. The same is true with cultural expectations, or for digital writers with their ethos at stake, design "best practices" or guidelines can have the kind of disciplinary force as an ethic, law, or culture. Hutchins (1995) points to the same phenomena when he defines "constraints" during navigation, while Law (2003) might call this control from the inside overcoming resistance of heterogeneous materials. (All three men, Foucault, Hutchins, Law, put different spins on this.)

What I assert then, is that my digital writing heuristic, the "mediational-digital composing heuristic" pictured in figure 6.1, is not weightless. It is not floating in space, not floating at the tip of the AT triangle as is commonly the visual representation of mediational means, or tools, in Engestrom's AT diagrams. This digital writing heuristic has weight. It has power—and to the extent it has power, it has an agency independent of the writer. This fact might inform the use of inventional heuristics in composition pedagogy because I think much of the problem in motivating students to think of ideas is that there is not much at stake, relatively speaking. There is always the grade, the due date, and the pressure of working in the space of 14 to 16 weeks, but for some groups of students such as those I have worked with at the community college, high grades are not a priority.

In addition to addressing and providing a curriculum for the "employer requirements" rhetorical topic on the "mediational-digital composing heuristic," service-learning and public rhetorics probably help create a set of heuristics with force or power since student writing is then tied to other concrete systems of power. Perhaps one of the reasons public rhetorics, real civil engagement, internships or co-ops work in writing curriculum is that such pedagogical strategies exert pressure or force on the student to be inventive. Service-learning presents the student and teacher a readymade inventional strategy comprised of a set of heuristics that may or may not ever become part of anyone's meta-awareness. Heuristics often operate at the tacit level. Some students who already have a highly developed sense of citizenship or justice may already be operating under a set of heuristics that motivates them to complete the assigned task. They may feel the pressure of morals or ethics. The connection between invention and power is worth further exploration.

I have heard more than one famous speaker-teacher in composition studies openly disclaim their teacherly power, or state they do not want the power they have as teachers in the classroom. Based on my research, this view evidences misunderstanding of the vast benefits of the ability to gain power and leverage it to facilitate the success of others. We all hope that teachers facilitate the success of their students. But you cannot help other people be successful if you lack power or the ability to use that power appropriately. Based on my research and the outcome that inventional heuristics exert power on the writer, the best teacher or scholar it follows, is one who knows how to gain power and use it to benefit others and make others successful. The digital writing heuristic I discovered in my research can possibly be used by writing teachers to motivate students because knowledge of the heuristic is empowering. Similarly, writers who gain awareness of how this type of mediational heuristic acts as a tool or rule in their composing decisions also are empowered to have better control over their writing choices.

In order to visualize copyright as both power and mediational means, I offer figure 7.1, reflecting a modified activity theory triangle showing the complexity of what I actually see in the data. Copyright law, like other systems of knowledge production, is a system of invention organized by rhetoric. Law is also a concrete system of power. Viewed through a Foucaldian lens, power produces knowledge. Foucault reminds us that penalties are not simply to punish, and that *we must abandon traditional notions that knowledge production can only exist where power is suspended.* Instead looking at copyright law as a mediational concrete system of power, a

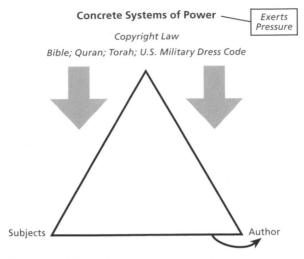

Figure 7.1. Cultural activity system organizing meaning.

system of punishment, means that copyright law is able to *produce* invention, creativity, expression, even the need to rely on *metis*. Different texts or practices in different cultures, while not called copyright law, serve the same function, the author-function. Metrics for truth do function as disciplinary powers and are constructed by rhetoric—when more closely examined such metrics provide guidelines for the production and organization of probable knowledge, thus countering our fear of chaos. The role of power (in this case copyright law) in invention (in this case digital composing choices) is ripe for further exploration.

Connections between Intellectual Property Law and Classical Invention

Another research trajectory that seems promising is one involving an exploration of the connections between rhetoric and intellectual property law—the law concerned specifically with invention. Invention, like the hunt, is discovery in context. Similarly, U.S. intellectual property law, a text constructed in order to incentivize invention, has its origins in topos and contains both the "discovery" and "novelty" senses of invention through copyright and patent. By unpacking these ideas, we can see how a concrete system of power like U.S. copyright law, a system created and maintained through writing, shares similar rhetorical origins as the concept of invention. U.S. copyright law, like the concept of rhetorical invention, contains (and tries to organize) both the discovery and novelty senses of invention. U.S. patent law explicitly requires novelty for an item to be patentable, while copyright law requires novelty only implicitly—but both are concerned with originality. In order for an invention to be patentable it must be novel, not obvious, and useful (Title 35, U.S. Code). Wyatt (1986), writing on patent law, emphasizes the invention sense of "invention" rather than the "discovery" sense: "An invention is an addition to the stock of factual knowledge. . . . Invention is construed as anything that adds to the set of known technological possibilities . . . it is clear therefore that the output from inventive activity . . . is not easily defined, let alone measured" (pp. 3, 19). Likewise, in order for a work to be copyright protected, it must be original (*Darrell*, 1940; Title 17, U.S. Code). The novelty-invention sense of "invention" actually exists in both copyright and patent law.

The rhetorically constructed nature of U.S. patent and copyright law can also be seen from tracing its historical development. Novelty is not always valued (in the "author-light" field of discourse, for example) and as Foucault mentions in "What Is an Author?" texts were once circulated and valorized without an author. Early English patents did not objectively protect all new inventions, but instead were monopolies granted by Royal Prerogative (Feather, 1994; Mandich, 1948). Kaufer (1989) writes that political clashes between Parliament and the Crown developed because under the reign of Queen Elizabeth I in England, patent grants were used to favor royal friends and implement mercantilist policy (p. 6). It was not until the relatively late date of 1624, when the Statute of Monopolies passed, that the friction between the Crown and Parliament was addressed; the Statute of Monopolies abolished most aspects of privilege and established some kind of objective standard. "Thus it appears, according to prevailing doctrine, that England is the first to protect the inventor by a law, even if she is not historically the first to grant patents" (Mandich, 1948, p. 168). Mandich (1948) notes that the Republic of Venice is usually credited as the first to give patent protection to inventors in the form of pure privilege (John Speyer is always the key example). Feather (1994) describes the 1469 patent granted to John Speyer as a "privilege," which gave Speyer the "exclusive right to print books in all Venetian territories" (p. 11). Speyer's protection was not dependent on his inventiveness, or originality, but rather on his industriousness. Early on, intellectual property protection was more concerned with the discovery aspect of invention than the novelty aspect. Over time this changed. But intellectual property law, like rhetorical invention, holds both the discovery and novelty senses of invention and was originally tied to place.

Although histories frequently tie the printing press to the beginnings of copyright law, intellectual property law was early connected to real property. Venetian mineral patents were issued as early as 1409 and paralleled early non-print-related invention patents in their protection of monopolies (Mandich, 1948). Mineral patents involve the protection of mining, and mining involves the hunt for valuable minerals. Like the use of hunting imagery in the Renaissance vocabulary of invention and the quality of *metis*, early patent laws protected the seeking of minerals. What was protected in these early mineral patents was the ability to hunt, or to discover. The hunt informed by *metis* produces a special kind of invention, similar to the inventive strategies employed by the digital writers in my study.

Current U.S. intellectual property laws also protect the ability to hunt and discover. Fair use allows reasonable remixing with a guarantee of some protection for original fixed work. Patent law promises a limited reward for innovation. To the extent intellectual property law presents problems to potential authors, it still is productive as authors become creative in order to work within the law, write articles trying to figure out or change the law, or simply stay under the radar and do as they please regardless of the law. The quality of *metis* as Miller (2000) describes it in relevance to the hunt arises as well in the context of composing for the web in copyright-imbued environments (see also *Treatises on Fishing* and *Treatise on Hunting* by Oppian, second century A.D., cited by Detienne and Vernant, 1978, p. 30). I determined in my analysis that intellectual property law, copyright and patent, are rhetorically constructed systems of invention that also serve as concrete systems of power. *Metis* is used in contexts where the less powerful outwit the more powerful. The use of this cunning intelligence in the face of power produces texts. It is the power, force, or pressure component of the system that makes it productive.

A Frame of Justice in Digital Writing

Another research trajectory that might be further explored is the connection, or possible connection, between justice and digital writing processes and procedures. U.S. copyright law as a concrete system of power purports to sustain justice. We see that by its authorization in the U.S. Constitution and the Constitution's overriding purpose to promote justice. Many scholars such as Thomas Hobbes, David Hume, Adam Smith, J. S. Mill, John Rawls, and Chaim Perelman among others (see Raphael, 2001 for a summary of their stances) attempted to improve ancient definitions of justice (such as those espoused by Aristotle and Plato). Yet every version of justice loosely fits into the three precepts of Roman law: *neminem laedere* (to harm no one); *suum cuique tribuere* (to render each person what is his); *honeste vivere* (to live uprightly) (see Raphael, 2001, p. 86). U.S. copyright law, like *some* of the other productive, concrete author-producing systems of power, is proposed to exist in order to create or maintain justice. By regulating how a writer might use others' materials (not impair their future markets), copyright law attempts to make a subsequent use of one's materials not harmful. Since copyright law and its fair use provision sort rights, it tries to assign or render to each person what is his or hers. Because copyright law is a law in the U.S., and thus presupposes an individual who can abide by that law, it provides a means for one to live uprightly, virtuously, rather than as an incorrigible. It gives us guidelines to live uprightly. The ideals of justice umbrella the decisions of digital writers in my study. A future researcher might ask: "What is the role of justice in the digital composing choices of writers?" The group of writers I studied were all trying to act justly even if that meant circumventing, ignoring, or reinterpreting the law.

In another research trajectory, we might focus on the larger goal of justice rather than ethics since that is what we are all hopefully working towards. Justice is a value-laden concept, a concept that has agency and that exercises its own kind of *metis*—justice is polymorphic, able to change shape on a moment's notice, like water flowing through hands, one of those concepts we will probably never pin down. A frame of "justice" encourages the weighing and balancing of considerations as far as what is good for the whole, the community, the union, versus what is good for the individual. Perhaps Leslie acted prudently with respect to copyright because she managed her time the best she could in order to benefit the learning of her students. Perhaps Amanda willingly conceded her own authorship to the national health organization that employed her because she knew overall, the health organization was doing good things for people across the nation. Giving up her personal authorship in this context serves justice. I have far fewer answers here than I like, but think this is an interesting area for further research. What is the connection between digital authorship, the law, and justice?

Curriculum Issues

Another area of implications for this study includes curricular design and teaching. It was clear in the research that the digital writers I examined did want to know more about copyright and other laws as well—so we definitely can demonstrate a need here for education. This should be considered in writing programs as they update their curriculums. The survey itself, specifically "Section E: Knowledge and Understanding" (appendix 2), is intended to be a portable, freestanding pedagogical tool to be used and changed over time.

Section E as embedded in the survey in appendix 2, is a record of my research. It, along with the answer key appearing in appendix 3, is an actual copy of the documents that were distributed. But section E can be extracted from the survey, and along with the survey answer key, can be used to teach in a number of ways I suggest here. The answer key was designed to be brief and timeless since I knew it would be distributed to a variety of research participants, including undergraduates and those who might have limited knowledge of copyright law. Since I wanted the answer key to remain timeless rather than become outdated as the law develops, I stayed mainly with citations to the U.S. copyright statute (Title 17) and U.S. Supreme Court opinions. Supreme Court opinions are precedent setting for the entire U.S., unlike U.S. federal district/appeals court opinions, which set precedent only within the jurisdiction covered by that particular court's circuit. Nevertheless, these courts always offer rich examples, are looked to by other courts in decision making-processes, and are all the interpretative case law we have unless the Supreme Court speaks on a particular issue. The Supreme Court cases I cited as authority in the answer key, such as *Stewart v. Abend*, *Campbell v. Acuff-Rose*, and *Harper and Row v. Nation Enterprises*, are virtually all of the U.S. Supreme court fair use jurisprudence we have in recent history (in addition to *Universal City Studios v. Sony Corp.)*—and at this writing are still good law.[1]

In the June 2010 recommendation written by Marybeth Peters, the register of copyrights, the extremely well-known and widely cited Supreme Court cases *Campbell* and *Harper and Row*, are cited with full authority. Of course, at the U.S. district court level, new cases will always occur offering new interpretations and examples that can help us understand copyright law. The United States Court of Appeals, Eleventh Circuit *Suntrust* case and the United States Court of Appeals, Second Circuit *Bill Graham* case are two examples of such lower court opinions, cited in the answer key, that can be used to understand copyright law. But it's actually been a significantly long time since a copyright or fair use case has made it to the Supreme Court. (The *MGM Studios v. Grokster* 2005 case was the most recent, but that case was about peer-to-peer file sharing rather than fair use; see Porter and Rife 2005). Documents like the June 2010 recommendation offer additional sources where we can extract examples to understand fair use and copyright.

As a teaching tool, students could use the survey and answer key in a couple different ways:

- Students, without seeing the answer key first, could try to develop their own written explanations to the questions, citing examples they obtain from their own research—and then match that up with the answer key. (In other words, I hope the survey questions and answer key will be used, reused, and transformed over time).
- Students could complete an activity where they conduct independent research in order to find if any of the answers in the answer key have changed, or if additional examples might be provided to extend our understanding. For example, question 7 in section E (appendix 2) asks whether remix writing in the particular instance given is likely a fair use. The answer key says this is probably a fair use, and outlines some key cases with examples. If students had read an excerpt of Peters's recommendation—and

were subsequently asked whether the recommendation provides anything to negate the fair use nature of the remix writing in question 7—they should be able to connect Peters's discussion on pages 50–51, where she discusses and cites various videos, like Luminosity's *Women's Work* and *Vogue/300* as contrastive examples of what is likely a fair use, and what is likely not a fair use. Using this same example, a few of the videos cited in the recommendation could be shown, and then based on the answer to question 7 as it appears in the answer key, students could discuss which video remixes are more or less likely to be fair uses.

- Students could also develop new scenario-based questions that they think might be interesting additions to the quiz. For example, none of the questions in section E addresses the DMCA or its exemptions. In light of the 2010 exemptions, students could construct a question that tests one's knowledge in this area. The new exemption for educators, noncommercial vidders, and documentary filmmakers specifically says that DVDs can have their anticircumvention technologies circumvented for criticism and commentary only if the DVD is "lawfully made and acquired." A new, student-created question might test one's knowledge of this:

> Under a reasonable belief she has no other available means of obtaining movie clips, a college teacher, in preparation for a class lecture, circumvents several CSS encrypted motion picture DVDs in order to gather numerous short portions. The short portions will be incorporated into a new video presentation, created by the teacher for students, which will allow the students to critique and comment upon racial stereotypes as they appear in the selected movies. The teacher obtained the various DVDs at issue, for $1.00 each from a street vendor in New York City who had certainly pirated and/or stolen the DVDs. The teacher's circumvention is legal under the 2010 DMCA exemptions.

Choices: True/False

Best Answer: False

While all the other requirements of the DMCA exemption seem to be met, i.e., a college teacher, with a reasonable belief of no other options, is taking short clips for purposes of critique and commentary in order to create a new work, the exemptions apply only if someone is using a "lawfully made" and "lawfully acquired" DVD. In this case, the DVDs are neither, so the teacher's subsequent circumvention is illegal under the DMCA.

Creating scenario based questions can be quite generative for students because they have to consider all the variables at work in the law. It really helps encourage close reading of the law, the statute, the exemption, and so on. In addition to using the survey as a teaching tool, the mediational-digital composing heuristic I derived from the study could be used as a mapping tool for program design. These are the issues that the writers of the twenty-first century are thinking about as they compose in digital environments. Therefore, someone designing a writing program might consider having coursework that covers all of the rhetorical topics that facilitate students' abilities to conduct probability thinking (similar to legal reasoning), and that complicates more traditional notions of authorship. I think placing an inventional heuristic at the center of a writing program responds in part to J. Lauer's (2009) detailing of a graduate program developed with rhetoric as its "cornerstone."

Since writing teachers care deeply about "the Author" and what that means, we need continued examination of authorship in the twenty-first century. My study only complicates our existing scholarship. If the author is not working in solitude even though he is "alone," if digital writing travels through space and time and collapses the past, present, and future all in a 10" × 15" screen, then we have to consider cross-cultural issues, issues of attribution and plagiarism, and issues of collaborative work in an entirely new light. We have to consider what it means for writing programs who insist on clinging to "the essay"—what I am suggesting here is that "the essay" in its paper form is functioning as a site of resistance for some writing programs and for students is becoming a "performance of authorship" rather than anything even partially analogous to the "authorship" students are experiencing in "real life" outside of school. I am not sure how helpful, if at all, the rendering of such performances is to students.

Further, spurred by Rob, the digital writer from India, I am very, very skeptical about any community that claims its knowledge is "community-owned." Every community and culture has methods that organize meaning, that say who is and is not permitted to have or grow certain types of information. I seriously call into question the label "community-owned" knowledge, which tends to be regularly applied to more marginalized peoples. We need a much more critical view here. The impact of a changed understanding of authorship, one where perhaps it does not matter who is speaking, the impact for teaching writing in the twenty-first century, especially in digital, networked environments, is overwhelming. We need to work together to unpack and organize this. Programs might consider developing a course that specifically looks at authorship in the academy, at making a transition to authorship in the workplace and at work-for-hire issues. This kind of course could also be meshed with a cross-cultural perspective on authorship. The composing heuristic could also, in turn, be used as a map for a single course within a more traditional writing program—a course specifically addressing issues of digital authorship. A single survey course could be built around these issues.

Another issue to consider when designing curriculum leading to a degree is the emphasis or lack of emphasis on students' digital portfolios and professional identity construction. From the interviews in this study, I surmise that students' digital portfolios and webtexts are amazingly permanent and have the potential to figure prominently in how a student might be perceived by others. Unlike the "senior project," "master's thesis," or "dissertation," the digital portfolio stays with the student and travels through space and time in amazing ways. For example, three years after she graduated with an undergraduate professional writing degree, a friend recently contacted me for advice because a faculty member in another discipline, whom she had never met, sent her an e-mail demanding that she take materials down from the web portfolio she had created when a student, posted to a webspace/URL provided by an educational institution. The faculty member at this institution accused my friend of both plagiarism, for failing to adequately attribute an author, and copyright infringement. This communication was sent totally out of the blue and took my friend by surprise. Based on the faculty member's inappropriate e-mail communication, she clearly did not understand copyright, fair use, or typical understandings around attribution. But this example illustrates how years after a web portfolio is constructed, the student can be held accountable or asked to justify choices. (In this case the former student attempted to instruct the faculty member that she was not doing anything illegal or inappropriate, but she ended up eventually moving her web portfolio to another digital space in order to satisfy the faculty member.) During the interviews, it became apparent that many of the webtexts I discussed with participants had existed for years prior to the interview. The practicality of spending all the time in degree coursework focused on the thesis or dissertation might be revisited—since ultimately the digital portfolio could have a more visible presence in a student's life than a document read by a few members of that student's committee, and then filed away.

Interesting international and global curricular issues arise due to this research as well. My research of these digital writers shows how difficult it is to define "original" due to authorship and composing practices in digital environments. If we ask, from whence did a text originate?—by unpacking some of the composing decisions writers made, how they were influenced, materials that were appropriated and then blended in to a text-in-progress, it becomes very difficult to discern a single originating point for that text. "Originality" thus is certainly a rhetorically constructed concept. To further emphasize the rhetorical nature of "originality," the legal definition of this concept varies by global jurisdiction at this writing; in the U.S., an artifact is original if it evidences a "modicum of creativity." The key opinion is the 1991 U.S. Supreme Court opinion *Feist Publications Inc. v. Rural Telephone Service Co.*, where at issue was whether material organized in a telephone directory constituted an "original" work thus subject to copyright infringement. The court espoused the U.S. view on originality: "Because Rural's white pages lack the requisite originality, Feist's use of the listings cannot constitute infringement. This decision should not be construed as demeaning Rural's efforts in compiling its directory, but rather as making clear that copyright rewards originality, not effort." In contrast, in the UK, originality is legally defined by "time and labor" or "sweat of the brow," while French law requires "skill and judgment" (Rife, 2009b). The various global definitions of "originality" provide cross-cultural views of a specific type of invention—invention that merits acknowledgment and protection by copyright law. More study of cross-cultural views on defining originality, and implications for teaching and curriculum, are in order.

Changing the Law

There are a number of ways we can work towards changing the law to be more conducive to digital learning environments—to cause less fear and chilled speech among digital writers working in educational contexts. Within our own institutions, we can work towards building a curriculum that helps students and teachers become more knowledgeable and savvy on issues at the intersection of law and writing. In the workplace, a professional development curriculum might work well for giving digital writers more awareness of legal issues like copyright. In the educational setting, work-for-hire policies and copyright/fair use guidelines should have input from teachers working with digital writing and web publishing—so that these guidelines reflect the state-of-the-art stances among the educational community towards corporate intellectual property stakeholders. We should work to assure that our institutions stand behind our choices as educators. Taking the notion of "actual law" and "proximate law" literally means that our proximate behavior can eventually shape the actual law—so if we keep at the cutting edge of appropriate and reflective use of copyrighted materials, and move forward as a group, we have more likelihood of actually inducing a change in the law. The strategy of using the proximate law to change the actual law is one that worked on the 2009 DMCA hearings.

When I testified with other educational stakeholders before the U.S. Copyright Office at the Library of Congress on May 6 and 7, 2009, the panelists (the register of copyrights and her team) hearing our testimony very much wanted to know our actual practices in the classroom, and the ways that the law circumscribed those practices, or the ways that students or teachers might be all but required, if not actually required, to break copyright law in order to accomplish learning objectives. The panelists wanted examples when law was pushed upon in order to achieve learning goals, and they wanted concrete, specific examples—they wanted vignettes and case studies of specific situations where the law circumscribed learning opportunities. "The submission of assorted hypothetical situations . . . speculation . . . mere conjecture" indicating certain users might be adversely affected in the future if an exemption was not granted, did not persuade the register (Peters, 2010, p. 64).[2] Peters demanded empirical evidence of possible harmful impact if an exemption was not granted. The panelists also of course wanted some evidence that these types of problems, imposed by law, impacted large numbers of people—that is, that there would be "substantial" harmful impact. While it might seem obvious, beginning a research project with a specific objective in mind—an objective of providing evidence to a public body in order to change law or policy—is an idea worth contemplating. During my graduate school experience, it was never suggested to me to design a study for purposes of using the research before, say, the U.S. Copyright Office or Library of Congress, although such a suggestion, I think, might have been very generative. Certainly, there are additional opportunities to be sought by researchers in rhetoric and composition and legal studies, where research could be customized to suit the information-needs of Senate hearings, Copyright Office hearings, and other public hearings. These opportunities are yet to be fully realized but appear very promising.

APPENDIXES

NOTES

REFERENCES

INDEX

Appendix 1. Institutions with Confirmed Participation ($N = 64$)

Arizona State University
Arizona State University East
Austin Peay State University
Ball State University
Baylor University
Boise State University
Briar Cliff University
Clarkson University
Clemson University
Coe College
Eastern Michigan University
Edison Community College
George Mason University
Georgia Institute of Technology
Grand Valley State University
Hilbert College
Illinois Institute of Technology
Illinois State University
Iowa State University
Ithaca College
Kutztown University of Pennsylvania
Louisiana Tech University
Lebanon Valley College
Massachusetts Institute of Technology
Mercer University
Miami University
Michigan State University
Milliken University
Minnesota State University, Mankato
Missouri State University
Missouri Western State University
Montana Tech of the University of Montana
Murray State University
Nazareth College of Rochester
New Jersey Institute of Technology
New Mexico State University
North Carolina State University
Oklahoma State University

Penn State University
Purdue University
Rensselaer Polytechnic Institute
Rocky Mountain College of Art and Design
San Francisco State University
San Jose State University
Southern Polytechnic State University
Texas State University
University of Arkansas at Little Rock
University of Baltimore
University of Central Florida
University of Cincinnati
University of Hartford
University of Illinois
University of Massachusetts
University of Massachusetts–Dartmouth
University of Minnesota
University of New Mexico
University of North Carolina Wilmington
University of Pittsburgh
University of Texas at San Antonio
University of Wisconsin–Milwaukee
University of Washington
University of Wisconsin
Utah State University
Washington State University

Appendix 2. Digital Survey

Cover Page

Welcome to: IS THERE A CHILLING OF DIGITAL COMMUNICATION? . . . click next to start the survey.

Section A: Informed Consent Agreement

Welcome! You have been randomly selected to participate in this survey, which hopes to generate important field knowledge on issues of copyright and digital composing. Your contribution is extremely valuable.

Survey Consent Form

Researchers at the WIDE Research Center at Michigan State University want your help with a survey on the topic of fair use/copyright and digital composing. We would like to gain a better understanding of how understanding of fair use/copyright interacts with digital composing. Even if you think you know little about fair use/copyright, we still need your input.

Participation in this survey is voluntary. The survey takes approximately twenty minutes to complete. The current survey consists of questions about knowledge, understanding, and attitudes on copyright and fair use. You may take the survey once. Your participation is strictly voluntary. You may refuse to participate or discontinue participation at any time without penalty. You're welcome to contact Martine Courant Rife, information on next page, at any time if you have questions about the survey. You may also contact the MSU IRB Office, information on next page, with your questions about research participants' rights. If you decide to complete the survey, your feedback will give us valuable information.

The survey is confidential. Any and all information we receive will be kept strictly confidential. If you wish to remain anonymous throughout the survey you may do so, and your answers will still be extremely valuable to us. Data gathered from the survey will be summarized in the aggregate, excluding all references to any individual responses. The aggregated results of our analysis will be shared with the technical and professional writing community and others interested in providing services to educate people about fair use. In the event analysis on individual responses is completed, pseudonyms will be assigned to describe participants.

At the end of the survey, student-participants are asked if they'd be willing to participate in a face-to-face or telephone interview. Please note that if you do not indicate that you are willing to do an interview then the survey is anonymous; However, if you do elect to participate in the interview by supplying your contact information, we will know your identity. But we will keep your identity confidential. Your answers on this survey are not necessarily relevant to selecting interviewees, and overall we will select very few individuals for interviews. If you are selected, we will contact you by e-mail in about 6 to 8 weeks. Again, you can stop participating at any time. Those who are selected for interviews and agree will go through a second consent process. Again, if you have questions please feel free to contact us.

You will not be compensated in any way, nor will you receive any course credit. Thank you for taking the time to help us with this important project.

By taking this survey, you have agreed to the terms above.

Section B: Questions or Concerns?

If you have any questions about the study, feel free to contact Martine Courant Rife, Rhetoric and Writing Program; WIDE Research Center, Michigan State University. Office: Suite 7 Olds Hall; cell phone: 517–294-xxxx; E-mail: courantm@msu.edu.

Martine will be happy to answer any questions you may have about this study and/or your participation in it. Please feel free to ask questions or express any concerns you may have at any time. Please keep the contact information provided on this page on hand for this purpose.

If you have any questions or concerns regarding your rights as a study participant, or are dissatisfied at any time with any aspect of this study, you may contact—anonymously, if you wish—Peter Vasilenko, Ph.D., Director of Human Research Protections, 517-355-2180; fax: 517-432-4503, e-mail: irb@ msu.edu; mail: 202 Olds Hall, Michigan State University, East Lansing, MI 48824–1047.

CLICK "I AGREE" to start survey.

Do You Agree?

> I agree
>
> No I do not agree

Section C: Digital Writing

The survey consists of twenty-eight short questions. The survey examines your knowledge, understanding, and attitudes about fair use/copyright and whether the law may have influenced your writing. Please select the best answer.

These first four questions ask for information about digital writing. (Note: If you answer no to either of the first two question, we thank you but do not need to collect further data. Thanks!)

1. Have you ever completed a web composition such as a webpage, web-space, wiki, blog, page on Facebook/Myspace or other social networking software application?

>Yes
>
>No

Section C (cont.): Digital Writing

2. Has the web composition been posted to the web such that it's available to at least some people (other than yourself or your teacher) with Internet access and a computer?

>Yes
>
>No

Section C (cont.): Digital Writing

3. In general, would you say that people should obey the law without exception, or are there exceptional occasions on which people should follow their consciences even if it means breaking the law?

>Can't answer
>
>Follow conscience even if break law
>
>Should obey without exception

4. Please pick the choice that best describes your *highest* educational level:

>Undergraduate student
>
>Master's student
>
>PhD student
>
>Undergraduate degree/certificate holder
>
>Graduate/professional degree holder
>
>Other/can't answer

Section D: How Chilled Is Your Speech?

The next six questions measure how law may have impacted your digital speech (how chilled your speech is Please pick the best answer.

1. Have you ever been asked to take down something (text, audio, image) you had posted to the web by a copyright holder or alleged copyright holder because the text, audio, image, etc. was allegedly infringing on the owner's copyrights (for example, via a communication by way of a takedown notice or a cease and desist letter, or even an e-mail)?

> Can't answer
>
> No
>
> Yes

2. If so, have you ever actually taken down such material because of this request?

> No
>
> Yes
>
> Can't Answer

3. Have you ever voluntarily taken something down, on your own initiative, that you had posted to the web because you felt you might be subject to copyright liability even though you never actually received a request to do so?

> Yes
>
> Can't Answer
>
> No

4. Have you ever not posted something to a web composition you were creating because of fear of copyright liability?

> Can't Answer
>
> No
>
> Yes

5. Have you ever felt that the purpose or message of a web composition you were creating would be better, clearer, or more aesthetically pleasing to the audience if you could use others' copyrighted materials without fear of legal liability?

> Can't Answer
>
> No
>
> Yes

6. Have you ever felt that you weren't really able to say what you wanted in a web composition because you were afraid if you said it the way you wanted, someone might sue you for copyright infringement?

> Can't Answer
>
> Yes
>
> No

Section E: Knowledge and Understanding

The next fourteen questions measure your knowledge and understanding of fair use. Each question has two parts—one that asks for a substantive answer, and one that asks for your attitude/confidence level towards that answer. Please choose the *best* answer.

Please calculate your answers based on current U.S. law.

1. Even though you have no permission, as long as you use less than three minutes of a legally obtained song, it is certainly fair use.

        True

        False

How sure are you that your answer is correct?

        Very certain

        Somewhat certain

        Undecided/Can't answer

        Not too certain

        Not certain at all

Section E (cont.): Next . . .

2. Using someone's "creative" work (i.e., fiction, drama, poetry, art, artistic designs, music) without their permission is just as likely to be a fair use as is using their "factual" work (i.e., nonfiction, unaltered photographic representations, news items) without permission.

        True

        False

How sure are you that your answer is correct?

        Very certain

        Somewhat certain

        Undecided/Can't answer

        Not too certain

        Not certain at all

Section E (cont.): Next . . .

3. If, without permission, you use someone else's copyrighted material in order to create a political parody, or otherwise conduct political commentary/criticism, it is more likely to be a fair use than if you were using the same material for simple decorative purposes.

        True

        False

How sure are you that your answer is correct?
>
> Very certain
>
> Somewhat certain
>
> Undecided/Can't answer
>
> Not too certain
>
> Not certain at all

Section E (cont.): Next . . .

4. The owner of a copyrighted novel has failed to make this novel into a play. You decide to do so without the copyright holder's permission. Your derivative work, the play, closely follows the plot and characters in the novel, but is likely to be a fair use because it is different than a novel.

> True
>
> False

How sure are you that your answer is correct?

> Very certain
>
> Somewhat certain
>
> Undecided/Can't answer
>
> Not too certain
>
> Not certain at all

Section E (cont.): Only Ten More Questions in This Section

5. Let's say you decide to, without permission, use a very small amount of a copyrighted work, incorporating it into your own web composition. The original copyrighted work is a text of two hundred thousand words. You use fifty words, but the fifty words you decide to use are key, and the very best and most financially valuable part of the original copyrighted work. In fact, the other 199,950 words are unanimously considered useless, mundane, and trite. Even so, since your use is so small, it is certainly a fair use.

> True
>
> False

How sure are you that your answer is correct?

> Very certain
>
> Somewhat certain
>
> Undecided/Can't answer
>
> Not too certain
>
> Not certain at all

Section E (cont.): Next . . .

6. In the event you have no permissions, using someone else's unpublished work is more likely to be a fair use than using someone's published work.

> True
>
> False

How sure are you that your answer is correct?

> Very certain
>
> Somewhat certain
>
> Undecided/Can't answer
>
> Not too certain
>
> Not certain at all

Section E (cont.): Next . . .

7. Without the copyright holders' permissions, you copy five copyrighted, freely available web-published images from five different authors. You mix these five images together, cropping them, and substantially changing their overall appearances such that they are totally unrecognizable from their original forms. You then blend in five of your own original images plus some original text you've written, creating a collage that is politically informative on an extremely urgent topic in current events. You publish your collage on your website for the Internet world to have free access to for educational and political purposes. In this kind of situation, your use of the five images you started with is probably a fair use even though you did not obtain permissions from the copyright holders of those first five images.

> True
>
> False

How sure are you that your answer is correct?

> Very certain
>
> Somewhat certain
>
> Undecided/Can't answer
>
> Not too certain
>
> Not certain at all

Section E (cont.): Next . . .

8. If you ask a copyright holder for permission to use their material in your own original web composition, and they say no, this means you absolutely cannot use the copyright holder's material under fair use.

> True
>
> False

How sure are you that your answer is correct?

> Very certain
>
> Somewhat certain
>
> Undecided/Can't answer
>
> Not too certain
>
> Not certain at all

Section E (cont.): Next . . .

9. The single most important thing U.S. courts look at when deciding whether or not a particular use is a fair use is whether or not the original author has been attributed and/or credited.

> True
>
> False

How sure are you that your answer is correct?

> Very certain
>
> Somewhat certain
>
> Undecided/Can't answer
>
> Not too certain
>
> Not certain at all

Section E (cont.): Only Five More Questions Left in This Section

10. If you use something with a Creative Commons license, it means you automatically get fair use.

> True
>
> False

How sure are you that your answer is correct?

> Very certain
>
> Somewhat certain
>
> Undecided/Can't answer
>
> Not too certain
>
> Not certain at all

Section E (cont.): Next . . .

11. Mary, a law-abiding citizen, is using a large chunk of text (one thousand words) in her webpage. The sole copyright holder of this text is her friend Tim. Tim's given her express written permission to use this text in her

webpage. Even so, as a conscientious, law-abiding citizen, Mary should still make sure she is within fair use when using Tim's text in her webpage.

> True

> False

How sure are you that your answer is correct?

> Very certain

> Somewhat certain

> Undecided/Can't answer

> Not too certain

> Not certain at all

Section E (cont.): Next . . .

12. When you were two years old, you drew an original Crayola drawing from your imagination. You've saved it all these years. Unbeknownst to you, your friend steals this from you, scans it, and posts it on her webpage as part of the design. You have no right to ask her to take this down based on copyright laws because such drawings are not copyright protected in the U.S. anyway.

> True

> False

How sure are you that your answer is correct?

> Very certain

> Somewhat certain

> Undecided/Can't answer

> Not too certain

> Not certain at all

Section E (cont.): Next . . .

13. Kim, a law-abiding citizen, does a search on the Creative Commons website for an image that allows her to use it as long as she attributes the original author and uses it for educational purposes. Kim decides to use this image for a 100 percent educational use. She clearly and prominently attributes the original author. Nonetheless, as a conscientious and law-abiding citizen, Kim should still carefully make a determination on whether she is within fair use.

> True

> False

How sure are you that your answer is correct?

Very certain

Somewhat certain

Undecided/Can't answer

Not too certain

Not certain at all

Section E (cont.): Next . . .

Please remember to choose the *best* answer.

14. Mary, a law-abiding citizen, decides to use five pages of a seven-page Ninth Circuit Court decision in her website. She legally obtains this unedited opinion directly from the court's website. She wants to cut and paste all five pages directly onto the html page she is composing. She will not edit or comment on the court opinion, nor does her webpage allow commenting by others. Before using the text in her website, as a conscientious, law-abiding person, she should be sure she is within fair use.

True

False

How sure are you that your answer is correct?

Very certain

Somewhat certain

Undecided/Can't answer

Not too certain

Not certain at all

Section F: Last Four!

These last four questions are just general in nature—you are almost done!

1. How important do you think it is, as a digital writer, that you have some knowledge and understanding of copyright and fair use laws in the United States?

Not very

Somewhat

Neutral/Can't answer

Important

Very important

2. How would you primarily describe yourself?

> Student
>
> Teacher
>
> Other

3. From the following list, please select your institutional name:

> [Institutions Listed]

Final Question

4. For *students* only: Would you be willing to supply your e-mail and name in order to be contacted for a follow-up interview (yes, you can change your mind later)? If no, leave blank; if yes, fill in information.

E-MAIL ADDRESS:

NAME:

Thanks for participating!!

Thank you very much. I will be posting results soon in a public place.

> Best,
> Martine Courant Rife
> WIDE Research Center
> Michigan State University
> courantm@msu.edu
> 517-294-XXXX

Appendix 3. Answer Key for Survey Section E: Knowledge and Understanding of Fair Use

Prompt: The next fourteen questions measure your knowledge and understanding of fair use. Each question has two parts—one that asks for a substantive answer and one that asks for your attitude/confidence level towards that answer. Please choose the *best* answer. Please calculate your answers based on current U.S. law.

The following are best answers based on the U.S. law in the fall of 2007. I have tried to keep the answers as brief as possible.

I begin by providing you with the text of Section 107, Title 17, USC.

§ 107. Limitations on exclusive rights: Fair use

Notwithstanding the provisions of Sections 106 and 106A, the fair use of a copyrighted work, including such use by reproduction in copies or phonorecords or by any other means specified by that section, for purposes such as criticism, comment, news reporting, teaching (including multiple copies for classroom use), scholarship, or research, is not an infringement of copyright. In determining whether the use made of a work in any particular case is a fair use the factors to be considered shall include—
(1) the purpose and character of the use, including whether such use is of a commercial nature or is for nonprofit educational purposes;
(2) the nature of the copyrighted work;
(3) the amount and substantiality of the portion used in relation to the copyrighted work as a whole; and
(4) the effect of the use upon the potential market for or value of the copyrighted work.
The fact that a work is unpublished shall not itself bar a finding of fair use if such finding is made upon consideration of all the above factors.

1. Even though you have no permission, as long as you use less than three minutes of a legally obtained song, it is certainly fair use.
Best Answer: False. The four-factor test requires that you look at more than just the quantity of the copyrighted work used, although that is one of the factors. In addition to "the amount and substantiality of the portion used in relation to the copyrighted work" you must also consider the nature of the copyrighted work, the purpose and character of the use, and the effect of the use upon the potential market of the copyright holder.

2. Using someone's "creative" work (i.e., fiction, drama, poetry, art, artistic designs, music) without their permission is just as likely to be a fair use as is using their "factual" work (i.e., nonfiction, unaltered photographic representations, news items) without permission.

Best Answer: False. One of the four factors looks at the nature of the copyrighted work; creative or fictional work receives greater copyright protection and is therefore less likely to allow fair use. Sometimes courts do not find factual material "original." In *Stewart v. Abend* (1990), the court upheld the copyright protection of the owner's exclusive right to create derivative works and did not find fair use. Cornell Woolrich, deceased at the time of the lawsuit, was the author of the story "It Had to Be Murder," and *Rear Window* was based largely on Woolrich's story. When MCA rereleased the film without accounting to Woolrich's successor, suit was brought by the successor. MCA argued the rerelease was a new work and acceptable under fair use. The court held against MCA, taking into account the four factors: the infringing work was commercial (factor one, purpose of the use); the original work was creative rather than factual (factor two, nature of the copyrighted work); and the rerelease harmed the copyright holder's ability to find new markets (factor four, effect on market). In this case, the creativeness of the infringed work was one of the factors that, added with the others, caused the court to find this use was not fair.

3. If without permission you use someone else's copyrighted material in order to create a political parody or otherwise conduct political commentary/criticism, it is more likely to be a fair use than if you were using the same material for simple decorative purposes.

Best Answer: True. The introductory matter in Section 107 points to the protection of a use for "purposes such as criticism, comment, news reporting, teaching . . . scholarship, or research." Political commentary and parody are areas where courts have made a special effort to protect a use from being deemed copyright infringement. Examples include the cases of *Campbell v. Acuff-Rose Music, Inc.* (U.S. Supreme Court 1994), and *Suntrust v. Houghton Mifflin Co.* (11th Cir. 2001).

4. The owner of a copyrighted novel has failed to make this novel into a play. You decide to do so without the copyright holder's permission. Your derivative work, the play, closely follows the plot and characters in the novel but is likely to be a fair use because it is different than a novel.

Best Answer: False. Turning a short story into a play is creating a derivative work, and the right to create derivative works is one of the exclusive rights granted to the copyright holder (*Stewart v. Abend;* Title 17, Section 106). The fact that this is a novel gives it more copyright protection as a creative work.

5. Let's say you decide to, without permission, use a very small amount of a copyrighted work, incorporating it into your own web composition. The original copyrighted work is a text of two hundred thousand words. You use fifty words, but the fifty words you decide to use are key, and the very best and most financially valuable part of the original copyrighted work. In fact, the other 199,950 words are unanimously considered useless, mundane, and trite. Even so, since your use is so small, it is certainly a fair use.

Best Answer: False. The landmark Supreme Court case on this issue is *Harper and Row, Publishers, Inc. v. Nation Enterprises* (1985). In *Harper,* the court applied the four factors and decided the use was not fair. In this case, seventy-five hundred words of President Gerald Ford's memoirs were prepared for publication by Harper and Row under a contract between Ford and the publisher. Meanwhile, Nation Enterprises published a magazine article containing a three-hundred-to-four-hundred-word excerpt of the entire memoir manuscript. Using a fact-specific analysis, the court held that the publication by *Nation* prior to the memoir's release by Harper and Row harmed the potential market. Even earlier in history, the court held a minimal use of George Washington's biography to be a copyright infringement rather than a fair use. In the 1841 case of *Folsom v. Marsh,* the defendant wrote a biography of George Washington but used 353 pages of the plaintiff's earlier published and copyrighted multivolume work to do so. Although the defendant's use amounted to less than 6 percent of the plaintiff's total work, the court held for the plaintiff, finding the defendant had copied the most important material (i.e., substantiality) in plaintiff's earlier volumes.

6. In the event you have no permissions, using someone else's unpublished work is more likely to be a fair use than using someone's published work.

Best Answer: False. Using work that is unpublished is less likely to be a fair use than using work that has already been published. However Section 107 states that even unpublished work can be used under the fair use doctrine: "The fact that a work is unpublished shall not itself bar a finding of fair use if such finding is made upon consideration of all the above factors."

7. Without the copyright holders' permissions, you copy five copyrighted, freely available web-published images from five different authors. You mix these five images together, cropping them, and substantially changing their overall appearances such that they are totally unrecognizable from their original forms. You then blend in five of your own original images plus some original text you've written, creating a collage that is politically informative on an extremely urgent topic in current events. You publish your collage on your website for the Internet world to have

free access to for educational and political purposes. In this kind of situation, your use of the five images you started with is probably a fair use even though you did not obtain permissions from the copyright holders of those first five images.

Best Answer: True. This use is probably a fair use. One of the key elements of this rather long question is that a lot of synthesizing has gone on by the new author (the one creating the remix described). Additionally, the proposed use is for "educational and political purposes." Plus, there is a concept in the law called "di minimus" use (see *Sandoval v. New Line Cinema Corp.*, 2d Cir. 1998)—indicative of a use that is minimal where copyrighted material is obscured or unidentifiable. Such a use is not copyright infringing. Also the cropping speaks to the fair use factor: "amount and substantiality" used. Another case that might inform is *Bill Graham Archives v. Dorling Kindersley* (2006) (see also "Remix as 'Fair Use': Grateful Dead Posters' Re-publication Held to Be a Transformative, Fair Use," http://www.ncte.org/cccc/gov/committees/ip/12/373.htm, from which the following explanation is taken). In *Graham*, the publisher, Dorling Kindersley, used without permission seven images of Grateful Dead concert posters or tickets in the book *Grateful Dead: The Illustrated Trip* (2003). Prior to the book's publication, the publisher had unsuccessfully attempted to negotiate permissions with the copyright holder, Bill Graham Archives. Due to what the publisher perceived as an unreasonable licensing fee, permission agreements were never reached. Nonetheless, the publisher used the seven images in the book, incorporating them into remixed compositions consisting of collages mixed with graphic art and textual explanations and commentary.

After conducting a careful four-factor fair use analysis, the Second Circuit Court of Appeals upheld the lower court's determination in favor of fair use. The Second Circuit found that with respect to the first factor, purpose and character of the use, the use of the Grateful Dead images was transformative since the images were used in a timeline and for historical purposes rather than for the posters' original purposes of concert promotion. On the second factor, regarding the nature of the copyrighted work, the court acknowledged this factor weighed against fair use because the posters were creative. Yet the court limited the weight of this factor because the biographical book did not exploit the creative aspects of the posters. On the third factor, amount and substantiality of portion used, the court said that even though entire images were used, their reduced size was consistent with Dorling Kindersley's transformative use. And finally, on the fourth factor, the court stated that Dorling's use didn't harm the potential market because no actual market harm was sustained, and, in this case, the court wouldn't find market harm based on "hypothetical loss" of revenue.

8. If you ask a copyright holder for permission to use their material in your own original web composition, and they say no, this means you absolutely cannot use the copyright holder's material under fair use.

Best Answer: False. Fair use applies to unauthorized use. Therefore if you ask permission and they say no, or even if the copyright holder were to agree to your use but ask an unreasonable price, you could still operate under fair use (see *Bill Graham Archives v. Dorling Kindersley*, 2006; *Campbell v. Acuff-Rose Music, Inc.*, 1994). Often, in the case of parody or satire, a use will not be agreed to by the copyright holder, and so fair use is the only option. In the case of the scenario in question 8, this is exactly the type of situation where you might have to rely on fair use.

9. The single most important thing U.S. courts look at when deciding whether or not a particular use is a fair use is whether or not the original author has been attributed and/or credited.

Best Answer: False. In the U.S., attribution is not an element of a fair use analysis. The only exception to this is if a work of "visual art" is used (Section 106A; Section 101 defines "visual art" as a painting, drawing, print, sculpture, or still-life photograph existing as a single copy, or in a limited edition of two hundred copies or fewer that are signed and consecutively numbered by the author). *Digital* visuals are not protected by Section 106A. Attribution is important for the ethical doctrine of plagiarism but is not part of a fair use determination. In fact, many fair use cases concern items where attribution is not important, such as in the case of parody or satire.

10. If you use something with a Creative Commons license, it means you automatically get fair use.

Best Answer: False. Fair use under Section 107 applies to unauthorized use. A Creative Commons license provides authorization for a use. It provides a license to use. And so using an item under a Creative Commons license means that you don't need to worry about fair use because you have a license.

11. Mary, a law-abiding citizen, is using a large chunk of text (one thousand words) in her webpage. The sole copyright holder of this text is her friend Tim. Tim's given her express written permission to use this text in her webpage. Even so, as a conscientious, law-abiding citizen, Mary should still make sure she is within fair use when using Tim's text in her webpage.

Best Answer: False. Since Tim gave Mary written permission, he's given her a license to use the text. Since Mary has a license to use it, she does not need to make a fair use determination as long as she uses within whatever terms he may have specified in his written permission. In this case, he gave her permission to use his text in her webpage, and that's what she is doing.

12. When you were two years old, you drew an original Crayola drawing from your imagination. You've saved it all these years. Unbeknownst to you, your friend steals this from you, scans it, and posts it on her webpage as part of the design. You have no right to ask her to take this down based on copyright laws because such drawings are not copyright protected in the U.S. anyway.

Best Answer: False. U.S. copyright law states that anything that is original and fixed is copyright protected. Section 102 states: "Copyright protection subsists, in accordance with this title, in original works of authorship fixed in any tangible medium of expression, now known or later developed, from which they can be perceived, reproduced, or otherwise communicated, either directly or with the aid of a machine or device." This includes the drawings of a two-year-old, as long as the drawing is original.

13. Kim, a law-abiding citizen, does a search on the Creative Commons website for an image that allows her to use it as long as she attributes the original author and uses it for educational purposes. Kim decides to use this image for a 100 percent educational use. She clearly and prominently attributes the original author. Nonetheless, as a conscientious and law-abiding citizen, Kim should still carefully make a determination on whether she is within fair use.

Best Answer: False. The Creative Commons site sets up a licensing scheme; in this particular scenario, the license requires attribution and educational use. As long as Kim uses within the stated license, she doesn't have to make a fair use determination. Fair use applies to unauthorized use. Since Kim has done everything required by the license, the use in this case is authorized and fair use is thus irrelevant.

14. Mary, a law-abiding citizen, decides to use five pages of a seven-page Ninth Circuit Court decision in her website. She legally obtains this unedited opinion directly from the court's website. She wants to cut and paste all five pages directly onto the html page she is composing. She will not edit or comment on the court opinion, nor does her webpage allow commenting by others. Before using the text in her website, as a conscientious, law-abiding person, she should be sure she is within fair use.

Best Answer: False. Federal government documents generally aren't copyright protected (see Section 105, Title 17, USC). The language in the question regarding editing or commenting is really a red herring. That might be relevant if the court opinion were copyright protected (nature of the use). Note that if a court opinion was taken from Westlaw or Lexis Nexis, where it may have been edited, enhanced with head notes or other annotations, summarized, etc., copyright and fair use would certainly be triggered. In this scenario though, the unedited text was taken directly from the governmental website.

Appendix 4. Interview Protocols: Sample Interview Questions

1. Can you tell me about this website?
2. Did you get paid to make this?
3. Did you come across any copyright issues as you wrote this?
4. How did you get these visuals?
5. For your slide show, would you consider including music as well?
6. Rather than including this thumbnail of the book cover, would you consider instead including a link to a PDF of the entire book?
7. Here where you talk about the book, would you consider including an excerpt from the book instead?
8. Would you consider including a larger, clearer image rather than this thumbnail?
9. Here you have included attribution to your coauthors; would you consider eliminating this attribution?
10. Here you have (don't have) copyright information on your web composition; would you consider deleting (including) this?
11. Rather than having a link here to an external site, would you consider instead creating a PDF and housing it on your own website, and then linking to that instead?
12. Would you consider packaging up your website and putting it on a CD and selling it at a profit? How about doing the same thing but giving the CD away at conferences?
13. Would you have done anything differently if copyright law didn't exist and everything was in the public domain?
14. Is there anything you want the readers of my study to know about issues of copyright and fair use as those issues impact teaching, learning, and web composing?

Notes

1. Copyright and Composing: Invention and Digital Writing

1. I am currently serving a two-year term as editor of the newsletter, with Jamie Thornton of Kaplan University as assistant editor.

2. See Emig, 1971; Flower and Hayes, 1981/2003; Perl, 1979/2003.

3. My study is "sequential" because I did the survey first, and then the interviews. It is transformative because instead of focusing on the quantitative data, I focus more on integrating the results of these two methods in my final interpretations (Creswell, 2003).

4. Twenty percent is not a magic number from any literature, but I initially predicted by selecting about 20% (fifty programs) of the entire number of programs I had a chance of obtaining over four hundred participants based on my formulation of possible participation. I thought that by requesting participation from fifty programs, I might get about ten participants per program, thus giving me an N of five hundred. However just in case this plan did not work, and in fact it did not, I made space for problems in recruitment by creating insurance samples to be taken in a total of three phases. The reason for three phases of population selection is that each phase of survey administration was successively conducted until I received an initial response to the survey (before attrition) of over four hundred participants. A survey sample population of over four hundred is desired in order to obtain a level of certainty of plus or minus 5% (Babbie, 2001; Lauer and Asher, 1988). However that number of survey participants was not achieved considering survey attrition. Since the online survey experienced attrition as participants progressed through the questionnaire, the number of individuals responding in my reported results in the following chapters will vary.

5. In order to analyze interviews, I transcribed them line-by-line based on the method described by Ding (2007) and read them multiple times both holistically and line-by-line for evidence of emergent patterns or themes (see also Barton and Stygall, 2002; Huckin, 1992).

6. All survey takers were permitted to voluntarily provide contact information if they wanted the answer key and study report. Those who provided contact information were sent a copy of the documents.

7. Heuristics and theories of rhetorical invention have been connected for a long time in the field of rhetoric and composition. A theory of rhetorical invention incorporating heuristics might speak to many disciplines. In the specialty area of technical writing, there already exists some research on how heuristics are used in evaluation processes (Donker-Kuijer, de Jong, and Lentz,

2008, pp. 392–93; see also Farkas and Farkas, 2000; Fu, Salvendy, and Turley, 2002; Hvannberg, Law, and Larusdottir, 2007; Nielsen, 1992, 1994).

8. Whether inventional heuristics provides strategies to both generate new knowledge and select and arrange existing information is historically a matter of dispute. In the 1970s, Janice Lauer (1970, 1972) and Ann Bertoff (1971, 1972) engaged in a scholarly debate on the issue of problem solving, heuristics, and the teaching of composition. Two decades later, Enos and Lauer (1992) acknowledged that "although there is no doubt that the meaning of heuristic has grown in sophistication and importance, its centrality to rhetoric and composition comes as no new phenomenon" (p. 79) (see also Selber, 2004).

9. See Enos and Lauer, 1992; Haller, 2000; J. Lauer, 1970, 1972; J. M. Lauer, 1979, 2004; McKeon, 1998; Miller, 2000; Scott, 1967; and R. E. Young, 1978.

10. Mediation is a particular mode of organizing behavior that coordinates between the behavior and a mediating structure that is not necessarily part of the inherent task domain (Hutchins, 1997, p. 338). So for example, knowledge and understanding of copyright law as a mediating structure (or a heuristic) might be coordinated through mediation when a human actor is composing a webpage. The copyright law heuristic is not part of the inherent domain of composing webpages. It does not necessarily show up in the finished product. Although copyright is a law, its mediational role depends on the logical affect the human actor allows it to have in her digital composing processes.

11. Vygotsky does not talk about "invention." He talks about "development."

2. The Meaning of Misunderstanding among Digital Writers

1. I did not collect demographics based on orthodox categories of gender, age, race, disability status, sexual orientation, etc. of participants, and in fact I change the gender of some interviewees in their vignettes, and so possible differences based on these subjectivities are not explored. My main reason for this purposeful stance is that I test knowledge; I want to avoid making inferences that one group knows more than another based on such subjectivities. The practice in the social sciences of asking survey questions on race, gender, ethnicity, and religion requires the operationalization of such "variables," and every metric reinscribes these institutionally sanctioned categories of "difference" again and again.

2. Since conducting my study, two large-scale surveys have been administered, and the results published—one survey was paper (see Tinberg and Nadeau, 2010) and examined community college students' and teachers' attitudes about writing, and the other was digital (see WIDE, 2010) and examined first-year writing students' writing practices. I am a member of the study group that executed the digital survey and authored the referenced white paper.

3. There might be a different answer if one were to take a judicial opinion from Lexis Nexis or Westlaw, where the opinion has elaborate footnotes,

headnotes, or annotations. In that case, the waters become a bit murkier when considering authorship. As the Wikipedia page on the *Feist* opinion reminds us: "Wikisource itself would be unable to present the text of this key Supreme Court decision to you, its readers, if companies could grab facts from the public domain (such as court decisions) and wrap them in a government-granted copyright monopoly" (http://en.wikipedia.org/wiki/Feist_v._Rural).

4. Statements, like authors, are not really just "things" according to Foucault—according to Foucault, both statements and authors are functions—products of the operation of power and activities within fields of discourse.

5. I am going to talk about Rob's interview and its contextualization of India in the most general fashion. I am not an expert on India or its religions. For purposes of providing the reader an example of how the use of scriptures might function in a culture, I am letting Rob, for these limited purposes, represent "India." Rob talked about the "word of God" in the singular, and I am letting Rob have all the agency in this discussion of religion, India, and authorship. I think further work exploring authorship and copyright in India is much needed and would be very timely considering India's economic rise in the world. I would love to see research and writing in this area.

It wasn't until reviewing the interview data that I knew what "Vedas" were. And still my knowledge is only the most limited. According to Wikipedia:

> The Vedas (Sanskrit, véda, "knowledge") are a large corpus of texts originating in Ancient India. They form the oldest layer of Sanskrit literature and the oldest sacred texts of Hinduism. According to Hindu tradition, the Vedas are apauruṣeya "not of human agency," being supposed to have been directly revealed, and thus are called śruti ("what is heard"). Vedic mantras are recited at Hindu prayers, religious functions and other auspicious occasions. The Sanskrit word véda "knowledge, wisdom" is derived from the root vid- "to know." This is reconstructed as being derived from the Proto-Indo-European root *u̯eid-, meaning "see" or "know." The Vedas are arguably the oldest sacred texts that are still used.

6. On the issue of respect, this study shows 73% of the population willing to disobey the law if it's wrong—perhaps there's not as much respect for the law as one might think.

3. The Rhetoric of Truth

1. The next few paragraphs are taken in part from: Rife (2008), "The 'Shock and Awe' of Digital Research Design: Rhetorical Strategies As Mediational Means in Digital Survey Research." *Conference proceedings, IEEE-IPCC.*

2. See figure 6.2 for a diagram of the typical activity theory triangle.

3. The tri-annual rulemaking proceedings are statutorily authorized and

occurred previously in 2000, 2003, and 2006. The Copyright Office maintains the most useful and excellent website as a DMCA resource (Rulemaking, 2010). This website maintains just about all of the filed documents as well as audio and text transcripts of all hearings. The rulemaking process includes proposing initial classes of works to be exempted, submitting comments and responses to comments, submitting requests to testify, testifying, and participating in the question and answer period following the hearing. The hearings are open to any person or organization that wishes to participate as long as they follow posted procedures. In 2009, thirty-seven witnesses testified on twenty-one proposed classes of works (Peters, p. 20, 2010). I became involved in the hearings as a witness and participated in the intense and extended question and answer period following the hearing. On June 19 and 22, 2009, the Copyright Office sent out the first question set, and on August 21, 2009, it sent out the second question set. My response to the first question and the joint statement I signed are posted online, as is my response to the second question and the additional joint statement I signed. While the 2010 exemptions cover six areas, I'm just discussing the exemption I contributed to—that exemption focused on colleges and universities, and permitting educational/noncommercial uses of DVD clips for remix writing.

As a resource, the following is a list of documents I either filed or signed jointly:

Rife's Request to Testify
http://www.martinecourantrife.com/DMCA/0Arife_request_FI-NAL_4–1–09.pdf
Rife's Handout
http://www.martinecourantrife.com/DMCA/01Rife_handout_4–30–09.pdf
Rife's Summary of Audiovisual Demonstration
http://www.martinecourantrife.com/DMCA/02Rife_representative_handout4–30–09.pdf
A couple of samples of Rife's testimony from the Copyright Office's transcripts:
May 6 Sample
http://www.martinecourantrife.com/DMCA/Pages_from_may6.pdf
May 7 Sample
http://www.martinecourantrife.com/DMCA/Pages_from_may7.pdf
Posthearing Q & A, June 19 and 22, 2009; Copyright Office Question
http://www.copyright.gov/1201/2008/questions/questions-for-dvd-related-panelists.pdf
Rife's Response
http://www.copyright.gov/1201/2008/answers/7_10_responses/final-rife_response-to-questions-july-10–2009.pdf
Rife also signed this joint statement:

http://www.copyright.gov/1201/2008/answers/7_10_responses
/joint-response-jonathan-band.pdf
August 21, 2009, Copyright Office Question
http://www.copyright.gov/1201/2008/answers/9_21_responses
/questions-panelist.pdf
Rife's Response
http://www.copyright.gov/1201/2008/answers/9_21_responses/rife.pdf
Rife also signed this joint statement:
http://www.copyright.gov/1201/2008/answers/9_21_responses
/joint-supporters.pdf

4. This particular interviewee participated in the pilot study. Her name is "Shauna," and I will discuss her more in chapter 4 because she provides some very good examples.

5. Under the DMCA, every three years the librarian of Congress, register of copyrights, and assistant secretary for communications and information of the Department of Commerce follow certain procedures to decide what persons/users of copyrighted work "are, or are likely to be . . . adversely affected by the [anti-circumvention] prohibition" of the DMCA. The librarian of Congress (LoC) issues the final exemptions, but the register of copyrights writes the recommendation (in 2010, a 262-page document), which is adopted by the LoC. So while the LoC literally issues the exemptions, it's really the register who crafts the exemptions.

4. Seven Digital Writer Multimedia Vignettes

1. Five interviews were conducted in a conference room at a midwestern university, another in a student's office at this same university, and one by telephone.

2. The concept of tacit knowledge derives from the work of Polanyi (1962).

3. J. Law (2003) might describe what I've done as overcoming the resistance of "heterogeneous materials" and placing them into ordered networks (p. 2).

4. The statute of limitations limits the time within which the copyright holder must bring suit. USC Title 17, Section 507 provides a three-year window. The time period usually runs from the date of the most recent infringing act—publication. Web publishing is problematic because items on the web are continuously published. There is some case law supporting the idea that the first date of publication on the web is when the statute begins to run (see *Ben-Tech v. Oakland University*, 2005). Other courts refused to reach the question of whether or not "publishing" to the web is "publishing" in the fullest sense of the term under U.S. copyright law and other international treaties (see *Moberg v. 33T LCC*, 2009). Generally courts will look at when the copyright holder had a reasonable chance to discover the infringement and begin counting the

years from that point. Once the three years have passed, the copyright holder can bring suit, but the case will be dismissed if the defendant successfully raises the defense of the statute of limitations. Under the statute, criminal proceedings for copyright infringement must be brought within five years. Criminal copyright liability requires willful intention to violate copyright law and make a profit from that violation (17 USC 506).

5. A Remixed Theory of (Digital) Authorship

1. These two senses are based on information provided in the *Oxford English Dictionary Online* (2nd ed., 1989).

2. I could also have pictured a group of blue-eyed, blonde-haired Paris Hilton lookalikes—I acknowledge the sameness and difference in attire originates from a certain gaze. A colleague who studies Jewish history and culture reviewed this chapter and caused me to switch out my original image of Hasidic Jewish men. I had selected a picture that was commonly known among Jewish scholars to depict something politically charged. I wanted to avoid that. But because I lacked the same common knowledge as my colleague, I was unaware of the possible faux pas I was about to make by including the wrong picture—by essentializing. One of the dangers of ANT is that when you make things radically symmetrical, when you flatten things, you in effect must essentialize many experiences and differences into one thing. But it is just a research stance, not a stance for living.

3. Why Foucault attributed Nietzsche in the first instance and not the second can be only speculated upon. It would be common sense, however, to draw from this example the idea that at some point, the words or ideas taken from another become one's own—when one has transformed those words and ideas sufficiently.

6. Toward a Metatheory of Rhetorical Invention in Digital Environments

1. The survey data showed misunderstandings about the government-document exception to copyright, confusion between the legalities of fair use and the ethic of antiplagiarism's requirement for attribution, and the failure of a majority of respondents to acknowledge that creative works receive more copyright protection than factual works. Based on these misunderstandings, for this population, copyright law functioned to impede the flow of government information, require attribution, and equally protect creative and factual work. In some ways, all of the misunderstandings actually benefit digital writers by supporting the author-function in a value-added way to this community. Impeding the flow of government information gives both teachers and students, perhaps, greater likelihood of using design heuristics, ethics,

rhetoric, or other motivations for composing choices, rather than laws and regulations. Seeing fair use as requiring attribution when it does not sustains the economy of symbolic capital via attribution, a beneficial stance for this community. Imagining equal protection for both creative and factual work again benefits digital writers, who are often involved as creators of the technical or factual rather than the "creative." If these key misunderstandings are braided together, they illustrate how misunderstandings in this case potentially align as cultural operations and activities that better support the work of digital writers than the actual law. The misunderstandings make attribution requirements have the force of law, give equal protection to creative and factual work, and place unnecessary hesitation before using government work (because it might be copyrighted). These misunderstandings, the "proximate law," fit the value system of contemporary writing students and their teachers and transcend the actual law.

7. Implications for the Future

1. *Feist Publications* is another Supreme Court opinion sometimes cited in discussions of fair use—but it's mainly thought of as a copy case defining "originality" in the U.S. (see http://en.wikipedia.org/wiki/Feist_v._Rural).

2. In this area of the recommendation, the register was addressing a proponent of an exemption for K–12 teachers and students. This particular proponent was not successful in her arguments to extend the exemption for that group of users, but the register did note that once the proponent gathers the proper evidence, she may be able to obtain the exemption in the future.

References

7 things you should know about . . . the P2P provisions of the HEOA. (2010, May). Educause. Retrieved Aug. 13, 2012, from http://net.educause.edu/ir/library/pdf/EST0901.pdf.

Ad Hoc Committee on Fair Use and Academic Freedom, International Communication Association. (2010). *Clipping our own wings: Copyright and creativity in communication research.* Center for Social Media at American University.

Apte, V. S. (1965). *The practical Sanskrit dictionary* (4th ed.). Delhi: Motilal Banarsidass.

Atwill, J. M. (1998). *Rhetoric reclaimed: Aristotle and the liberal arts tradition.* Ithaca: Cornell University Press.

Aufderheide, P. (2010). Fair use victories on the DMCA. Center for Social Media. School of Communication. American University. Retrieved Oct. 5, 2010, from http://centerforsocialmedia.org/blog/fair-use/fair-use-victories-dmca.

Babbie, E. (2004). *The practice of social research* (10th ed.). Belmont, CA: Wadsworth.

Backstrom, C., and Hursh-Cesar, G. D. (1981). *Survey research* (2nd ed.). Evanston, Ill.: Northwestern University Press.

Barton, E., and Stygall, G. (2002). *Discourse studies in composition.* Cresskill, NJ: Hampton.

Bazerman, C. (1999). *The languages of Edison's light.* Cambridge, MA: MIT Press.

Ben-Tech Industrial Automation et al. v. Oakland University and Donald Mayer, and Eric Kaczor. State of Michigan Court of Appeals. (2005). Oakland Circuit Court, N. 247471.

Bertoff, A. E. (1971). The problem of problem solving. *College Composition and Communication, 22*(3), 237–42.

———. (1972). Response of Janice Lauer. Counterstatement. *College Composition and Communication, 23*(5), 414–16.

Bill Graham Archives v. Dorling Kindersley Limited, et al. USCA (2nd Cir.). (2006, May). Retrieved Aug. 13, 2012, from, http://fairuse.stanford.edu/primary_materials/cases/GrahamKindersley.pdf.

Bizzell, P., and Herzberg, B. (1990). *The rhetorical tradition: Readings from classical times to the present.* Boston: St. Martin's.

Black's law dictionary with pronunciations (5th ed.). (1979).

Booth, W. C. (1974). *Modern dogma and the rhetoric of assent.* Chicago: University of Chicago Press.

Bracewell, R. J., and Witte, S. P. (2003). Tasks, ensembles, and activity linkages between text production and situation of use in the workplace. *Written Communication*, 20(4), 511–59.

Bright Tunes Music Corp. v. Harrisongs Music, Ltd., No. 71 Civ. 602, United States District Court for the Southern District of New York (1976) 420 F. Supp. 177; 1976 U.S. Dist. LEXIS 13423,.

Britton, J. (1982/2003). Spectator role and the beginnings of writing. In V. Villanueva (ed.), *Cross-talk in comp theory: A reader* (2nd ed.) (pp. 151–73). Urbana, IL: NCTE. Reprinted from M. Nystrand (ed.), *What writers know: The language, process, and structure of written discourse*. New York: Academic, 1982, pp. 149–69.

Brockmann, R. J. (1988). Does Clio have a place in technical writing? *Journal of Technical Writing and Communication*, 18, 297–304.

———. (1998). *From millwrights to shipwrights to the twenty-first century: Explorations in a history of technical communication in the United States.* Cresskill, NJ: Hampton.

———. (1999). Oliver Evans and his antebellum wrestling with theoretical arrangement. In T. C. Kynell and M. G. Moran (eds.), *Three keys to the past: The history of technical communication* (pp. 63–89). Stamford, CT: Ablex.

Bruffee, K. A. (1984). Collaborative learning and the "conversation of mankind." *College English*, 46(7), 635–52.

Bulun Bulun and Anor v. R and T Textiles Pty Ltd. (1998). *Australian Indigenous Law Reporter.* Retrieved Mar. 26, 2009, from http://www.austlii.edu.au/au/ journals/AILR/1998/39.html.

Burchell, G., Gordon C. and Miller P. (eds.). (1991). *The Foucault effect: studies in governmentality.* Chicago: University of Chicago Press.

Burke, K. (1966). *Terministic screens. Language as symbolic action: Essays on life, literature, and method.* Berkeley: University of California Press.

Burns, H. (2009). It still takes Phronesis: Thirteen ways of looking at practical wisdom in online teaching for global learning. In S. Borrowman, S. Brown, and T. P. Miller (eds.), *Renewing rhetoric's relation to composition: Essays in honor of Theresa Jarnagin Enos* (pp. 53–67). New York: Routledge.

Campbell v. Acuff-Rose Music, Inc. (1994). 510 U.S. 569.

CCCC IP Caucus letter. (2010). Letter to United States Intellectual Property Enforcement Coordinator. NCTE CCCC Committee Website. Retrieved May 23, 2010, from http://www.ncte.org/library/NCTEFiles/Groups /CCCC/Committees/cccc-ip_caucus-committee-ltr-03–24–10.pdf; Also published on the Whitehouse.Gov website. Retrieved Oct. 10, 2010, from http://www.whitehouse.gov/sites/default/files/omb/ IPEC /frn_comments/ConferenceCollegeCompositionCommunication.pdf.

Charney, D. (1998). From logocentrism to ethnocentrism: Historicizing critiques of writing research. *Technical Communication Quarterly*. Retrieved Aug. 13, 2012, from http://www.cwrl.utexas.edu/~charney/homepage/Articles/Charney_ethocentrism.pdf.

———. (2004) Empiricism is not a four-letter word. In J. Johnson-Eilola and S. A. Selber (eds.), *Central works in technical communication* (pp. 281–99). New York: Oxford University Press.

Cloatre, E. (2008). Socio-TRIPS and pharmaceutical patents in Djibouti: An ANT analysis of socio-legal objects. *Social Legal Studies*, 17, 263–81.

Collins, R. (2007, Dec. 5). Deference to authority in Canada and the U.S. Blog. Retrieved Feb. 3, 2008, from http://www.igloo.org/shortpieces/deferenc.

Committee on the Major in Rhetoric and Composition (Mar. 2010). (2009). Conference on College Composition and Communication. Retrieved Oct. 30, 2009, from http://www.ncte.org/cccc/committees/majorrhetcomp.

Connors, R. J. (1982). The rise of technical writing instruction in America. *Journal of Technical Writing and Communication*, 12(4), 329–52.

Constitution of the United States. (1787/1991). Washington, DC: Commission on the Bicentennial of the United States Constitution.

Copyright and You. (n.d.). York University. Retrieved Mar. 3, 2008, from http://www.yorku.ca/univsec/documents/copyright/text4.htm.

Copyright Law of the United States (Title 17, United States Code). (2003). Retrieved May, 17 2007, from http://www.copyright.gov/title17/.

Creswell, J. W. (2003). *Research design: Qualitative, quantitative, and mixed methods approaches* (2nd ed.). Thousand Oaks, CA: Sage.

Curtis, A. (2008). Orphan works 2008: House and Senate bills introduced. *Public knowledge*. Retrieved Mar. 26, 2009, from http://www.publicknowledge.org/node/1537.

Darrell v. Joe Morris Music Co. (1940). 113 F. 2d 80 (2nd Cir.).

DeJoy, N. (2005). *Process this: Undergraduate writing in composition studies*. Logan: Utah State University Press.

Detienne, M., and Vernant, J. (1978). *Cunning intelligence in Greek culture and society*. Trans. from the French by J. Lloyd. Sussex: Harvester.

DeVoss, D. N., and Porter, J. E. (2006a). Rethinking plagiarism in the digital age: Remixing as a means for economic develop? WIDE Conference paper. Retrieved June 24, 2006, from http://www.wide.msu.edu/conference/ wide_conference_speakers/.

———. (2006b). Why Napster matters to writing: Filesharing as a new ethic of digital delivery. *Computers and Composition*, 23(2), 178–210.

DeVoss, D. N., and Webb, S. (2008). Media convergence: Grand theft audio: Negotiating copyright as composers. *Computers and Composition*, 25, 79–103.

Digital Millennium Copyright Act (DMCA). (1998). Public Law 105-304— Oct. 28, 1998. Retrieved Oct. 5, 2010, from http://www.copyright.gov /legislation/p1105-304.pdf.

Digital Rhetoric Collective. (2006). Teaching digital rhetoric: Community, critical engagement, and application. DigiRhet.org. *Pedagogy: Critical Approaches to Teaching Literature, Language, Composition, and Culture,* 2(1), 231–59.

Ding, H. (2007). Confucius's virtue-centered rhetoric: A case study of mixed research methods in comparative rhetoric. *Rhetoric Review,* 26(2), 142–59.

Dobrin, D. N. (1983). What's technical about technical writing? In P. V. Anderson, R. J. Brockmann, and C. R. Miller (eds.), *New essays in technical and scientific communication: Research, theory, practice* (pp. 227–50). Farmingdale, NY: Baywood.

Donker-Kuijer, M. W., de Jong, M., and Lentz, L. (2008). Heuristic web site evaluation: Exploring the effects of guidelines on experts' detection of usability problems. *Technical Communication,* 55(4), 392–404.

Durack, K. T. (2001). Research opportunities in the U.S. patent record. *Journal of Business and Technical Communication,* 15(4), 490–510.

———. (2004). Gender, technology, and the history of technical communication. In J. Johnson-Eilola and S. A. Selber (eds.), *Central works in technical communication* (pp. 35–43). New York: Oxford University Press.

———. (2006). Technology transfer and patents: Implications for the production of scientific knowledge. *Technical Communication Quarterly,* 15(3), 315–28.

Dush, L. (2009). Beyond the wake-up call: Learning what students know about copyright. In S. Westbrook (ed.), *Composition and copyright: Perspectives on teaching, text-making, and fair use* (pp. 114–32). New York: State University of New York Press.

Emig, J. (1971). *The composing processes of 12th graders.* Urbana, IL: NCTE.

Engestrom, Y. (1990). When is a tool? Multiple meaning of artifacts in human activity. In Y. Engestrom (ed.), *Learning, working and imagining: Twelve studies in activity theory* (pp. 171–95). Helsinki: Orienta-Konsultit Oy.

———. (1999). Activity theory and individual and social transformation. In Y. Engestrom, R. Miettinen, and R. Punamaki (eds.), *Perspectives on activity theory* (pp. 19–38). New York: Cambridge University Press.

Enos, R. L., and Lauer, J. M. (1992). The meaning of heuristic in Aristotle's rhetoric and its implications for contemporary rhetorical theory. In S. P. Witte, N. Nakadate, and R. D. Cherry (eds.), *A rhetoric of doing: Essays on written discourse in honor of James L. Kinneavy* (pp. 79–87). Carbondale: Southern Illinois University Press.

Erickson, F. (1986). Qualitative methods in research on teaching. In M. C. Wittrock (ed.), *Handbook of research on teaching* (3rd ed.) (pp. 119–61). New York: Macmillan.

Espinel, V. A. (2010). 2010 joint strategic plan on intellectual property enforcement. Executive Office of the President of the United States. Retrieved Oct. 5, 2010, from http://www.whitehouse.gov/sites/default/files /omb/assets/intellectualproperty/intellectualproperty_strategic _plan.pdf.

Farkas, D. K., and Farkas, J. B. (2000). Guidelines for designing web navigation. *Technical Communication*, 47, 341–58.

Feather, J. (1994). *Publishing, piracy and politics: An historical study of copyright in Britain*. London: Mansell.

Federal register. (2010). Coordination and strategic planning of the federal effort against intellectual property infringement: Request of the intellectual property enforcement coordinator for public comments regarding the joint strategic plan. Office of Budget and Management. Executive Office of the President. Retrieved May 23, 2010, from http://edocket.access.gpo.gov/2010/2010-3539.htm.

Feist Publications, Inc., v. Rural Telephone Service Co. (1991). 499 U.S. 340.

Fisher, W. W., and McGeveran, W. (2006, Aug.). The digital learning challenge: Obstacles to educational uses of copyright material in the digital age. A Foundational White Paper. The Berkman Center for Internet and Society at Harvard Law School. Research Publication No. 2006–09. Retrieved Nov. 18, 2006, from http://cyber.law.harvard.edu/ home /research_publication_series.

Flessas, T. (2008). The repatriation debate and the discourse of the commons. *Social & Legal Studies*, 17, 387–405.

Flower, L., and Hayes, J. R. (1981/2003). A cognitive process theory of writing. In V. Villanueva (ed.), *Cross-talk in comp theory: A reader* (2nd ed.) (pp. 273–97). Urbana, IL: NCTE. Reprinted from *College Composition and Communication*, 32(4), 1981, Dec., 365–87.

Foucault, M. (1965/1988). *Madness and civilization: A history of insanity in the age of reason*. New York: Random House.

———. (1970/1994). *The order of things: An archaeology of the human sciences*. New York: Random House.

———. (1972). *The archaeology of knowledge and the discourse on language*. Trans. by A. M. Sheridan Smith. New York: Pantheon.

———. (1972/1977). *Power/knowledge: Selected interviews and other writings, 1972–1977*. C. Gordon (ed.). New York: Pantheon.

———. (1977). *Discipline and punish: The birth of the prison*. Trans. by A. Sheridan. New York: Random House.

———. (1978/1990). *The history of sexuality*. Vol. 1., *An introduction*. New York: Random House.

————. (1979/1984). "What is an author?" *The Foucault reader*. Paul Rabinow (ed.). New York: Pantheon.

————. (1985/1990). *The history of sexuality*. Vol. 2, *The use of pleasure*. New York: Random House.

————. (1986). *The history of sexuality*. Vol. 3, *The care of the self*. London: Penguin.

————. (1991). Politics and the study of discourse. In Burchell, G. Gordon, C., Miller, P. (eds.), The Foucault effect: studies in governmentality (pp. 53–104). Chicago: University of Chicago Press.

Fu, L., Salvendy, G., and Turley, L. (2002). Effectiveness of user testing and heuristic evaluation as a function of performance classification. *Behavior and information technology*, 21, 137–43.

Gates, H. L., Jr. (2003). Phillis Wheatley on trial: In 1772, a slave girl had to prove she was a poet. She's had to do so ever since. *New Yorker*, 78 (43), 82.

Gaylor, B. (2008). Rip! A remix manifesto. National Film Board of Canada. Retrieved June 13, 2010, from http://films.nfb.ca/rip-a-remix-manifesto/.

Geisler, C., and Slattery, S. (2007). Capturing the activity of digital writing: Using, analyzing, and supplementing video screen capture. In H. A. McKee and D. N. DeVoss (eds.), *Digital writing research: Technologies, methodologies, and ethical issues* (pp. 185–200). Cresskill, NJ: Hampton.

Gellar, P. E. (2000). Copyright history and the future: what's culture got to do with it? *Journal of the Copyright Society of the U.S.A.*, 209–64. Retrieved Aug. 13, 2012, from http://www.criticalcopyright.com /Geller-Copyright_History%26Future.pdf.

Gill, R. (1999). *Churchgoing and Christian ethics*. Cambridge: Cambridge University Press.

Glick, J. (1997). Prologue. In R. W. Rieber (ed.), *The collected works of L. S. Vygotsky*. Vol. 4, *The history of the development of higher mental functions* (pp. v–xvi). New York: Plenum.

Gordon, C. (1991). "Government rationality: an introduction." In Burchell, G. Gordon, C., Miller, P. (Eds.) *The Foucault effect: studies in governmentality* (pp. 1–51). Chicago: University of Chicago Press.

Grabill, J. T. (2001). *Community literacy programs and the politics of change*. Albany: State University of New York Press.

————. (2007). *Writing community change: Designing technologies for citizen action*. Cresskill, NJ: Hampton.

Grabill, J. T., and Hicks, T. (2005, July). Multiliteracies meet methods: The case for digital writing in English education. *English Education*, 37, 301–11.

Greene, J. C. (2007). *Mixed methods in social inquiry*. San Francisco: Jossey-Bass.

Groves, R. M., Cialdini, R. B., and Couper, M. P. (1992). Understanding the decision to participate in a survey. *Public Opinion Quarterly*, 56, 475–95.

GSSDIRS General Social Survey 1972–2000. (2005) Cumulative Codebook. (2005). Retrieved Apr. 24, 2007, from http://www.icpsr.umich.edu/GSS.

Gutting, G. (2005). *Foucault: A very short introduction.* New York: Oxford University Press.

Hacking, I. (1991). How should we do the history of statistics? In G. Burchell, C. Gordon, and P. Miller (eds.), *The Foucault effect: Studies in governmentality: With two lectures by and an interview with Michel Foucault* (pp. 181–95). Chicago: University of Chicago Press.

Hafner, K. (2008). Publishers sue Georgia State on digital reading matter. Technology. *New York Times.* Retrieved May 24, 2010, from http://www.nytimes.com/2008/04/16/technology/16school.html?_r=2.

Haller, C. (2000). Rhetorical invention in design constructing a system and spec. *Written Communication,* 17(3), 353–89.

Haraway, D. (2004). *The Haraway reader.* New York: Routledge.

Harper and Row, Publishers, Inc. v. Nation Enterprises (1985). 471 U.S. 539.

"Harry Potter" author J. K. Rowling wins copyright claim. (2008). *New York Daily News.* Retrieved Aug. 13, 2012, from http://articles.nydailynews.com/2008-09-08/local/17906163_1_rdr-books-rowling-and warner-bros-potter-encyclopedia.

Hart-Davidson, W. (2007). Studying the mediated action of composing with time-use diaries. In H. A. McKee and D. N. DeVoss (eds.), *Digital writing research: Technologies, methodologies, and ethical issues* (pp. 153–70). Cresskill, NJ: Hampton.

Haswell, R. (2005). NCTE/CCCC's recent war on scholarship. *Written Communication,* 22(2), 198–223.

Heins, M., and Beckles, T. (2005, Dec.). Will fair use survive? Free expression in the age of copyright control. A public policy report. Brennan Center for Justice. Retrieved Feb. 27, 2006, from http://www.fepproject.org/issues/copyright.html.

Henry, J. (2000). *Writing workplace cultures: An archaeology of professional writing.* Carbondale: Southern Illinois University Press.

Herrington, T. K. (1997, Spring). The unseen "other "of intellectual property law or intellectual property is not property: Debunking the myths of IP law. *Kairos,* 3(1). Retrieved June 11, 2007, from http://kairos.technorhetoric.net/3.1/coverweb/ty/kip.html.

———. (1998).The interdependency of fair use and the first amendment. *Computers and Composition,* 15(2), 125–43.

———. (2001). *Controlling voices: Intellectual property, humanistic studies, and Internet.* Carbondale: Southern Illinois University Press.

———. (2003). *A legal primer for the digital age.* New York: Pearson Longman.

Hobbs, R., Jaszi, P., and Aufderheide, P. (2007, Oct.). The cost of copyright confusion for media literacy. Retrieved Nov. 9, 2007, from http://www.centerforsocialmedia.org/resources/publications/the_cost_of_copyright_confusion_for_media_literacy/.

Howard, T. W. (2004). Who "owns" electronic texts? In J. Johnson-Eilola and S. A. Selber (eds.), *Central works in technical communication* (pp. 397–406). New York: Oxford University Press.

Huckin, T. (1992). Context sensitive text analysis. In G. Kirsch and P. Sullivan (eds.), *Methods and methodology in composition research* (pp. 84–104). Carbondale: Southern Illinois University Press.

Hutchins, E. (1995). *Cognition in the wild.* London: MIT Press.

———. (1997). Mediation and automatization. In M. Cole, Y. Engestrom and O. Vasquez (eds.), *Mind, culture, and activity: Seminal papers from the Laboratory of Comparative Human Cognition* (pp. 338–53). Cambridge: Cambridge University Press.

Hvannberg, E. T., Law, E. L. C., and Larusdottir, M. K. (2007). Heuristic evaluation: Comparing ways of finding and reporting usability problems. *Interacting with Computers,* 19, 225–40.

"I will be heard!"(2002). In Their Own Words: Slave Narratives. *Abolitionism in America.* Cornell University Library Division of Rare and Manuscript Collections. Retrieved August 3, 2012, from http://rmc.library .cornell.edu/abolitionism/narratives.htm.

IP Watchlist 2010. (2010). Consumers International. Retrieved May 23, 2010, from http://a2knetwork.org/watchlist.

Jaszi, P. (2010). Worth the wait—installment #1. ©ollectanea. Retrieved Oct. 5, 2010, from http://chaucer.umuc.edu/blogcip/collectanea/2010/07 /worth_the_wait_-_installment_1.html.

Johanek, C. (2000). *Composing research a contextualist paradigm for rhetoric and composition.* Logan: Utah State University Press.

Johnson, R. R. (1998). *User-centered technology: A rhetorical theory for computers and other mundane artifacts.* New York: State University of New York Press.

Johnson-Eilola, J., and Selber, S. A. (2007). Plagiarism, originality, assemblage. *Computers and Composition,* 24, 375–403.

Kaufer, E. (1989). *The economics of the patent system.* Chur, Switzerland: Harwood Academic Publishers.

Kennedy, G. (1963). *The art of persuasion in Greece.* Princeton, NJ: Princeton University Press.

Kinney, J. (1979). Classifying heuristics. *College Composition and Communication,* 30(4), 351–56.

Knight, A., et al. (2009). About face: Mapping our institutional presence. *Computers and Composition,* 26, 190–202.

Kolowich, S. (2010a). Hitting pause on class videos. *Inside Higher Ed.* Retrieved May 24, 2010, from http://www.insidehighered.com/news/2010/01/26 /copyright.

———. (2010b). Movie clips and copyright. *Inside Higher Ed.* Retrieved Oct. 5, 2010, from http://www.insidehighered.com/news/2010/07/28 /copyright.

Kuhn, T. (1996). *The structure of scientific revolutions* (3rd ed.). Chicago: University of Chicago Press.

Laster, J. (2010). UCLA pulls videos from course sites after copyright challenge. Wired Campus. *Chronicle of Higher Education.* Retrieved May 24, 2010, from http://chronicle.com/blogPost/UCLA-Pulls-Videos-From-Course/21013/.

Latour, B. (1988). Mixing humans and nonhumans together: The sociology of a door-closer. *Social Problems,* 35(3), pp. 298–310.

———. (1992). Where are the missing masses? The sociology of a few mundane artifacts. In W. E. Bijker and J. Law (eds.), *Shaping technology/building society: Studies in sociotechnical change* (pp. 225–58). Cambridge, MA: MIT Press.

———. (1993). *We have never been modern.* Cambridge, MA: Harvard University Press.

———. (2005). *Reassembling the social: An introduction to actor-network theory.* Oxford: Oxford University Press.

———. (2010). *The making of law: An ethnography of the counseil d'etat.* Trans. by M. Brilman and A. Potage. Malden, MA: Polity.

Lauer, J. (1970). Heuristics and composition. *College Composition and Communication,* 21(5), 396–404.

———. (1972). Response to Ann E. Bertoff. *College Composition and Communication,* 23(2), 208–10.

———. (2009). Rhetoric: The cornerstone of a graduate program. In S. Borrowman, S. Brown, and T. P. Miller (eds.), *Renewing rhetoric's relation to composition: Essays in honor of Theresa Jarnagin Enos* (pp. 104–16). New York: Routledge.

Lauer, J. M. (1979). Toward a metatheory of heuristic procedures. *College Composition and Communication,* 30(3), 268–69.

———. (2004). *Invention in rhetoric and composition.* West Lafayette, IN: Parlor.

———. (2008, June 1). Tracing theories of teaching writing. Presentation at Michigan State University.

Lauer, J. M., and Asher, J. W. (1988). *Composition research: Empirical designs.* New York: Oxford University Press.

Law, J. (1992/2003). Notes on the theory of the actor network: Ordering, strategy, heterogeneity. Centre for Science Studies, Lancaster University. Retrieved Aug. 13, 2012, from http://www.lancs.ac.uk/fass/sociology/papers/law-notes-on-ant.pdf/.

———. (2003). Networks, relations, cyborgs: On the social study of technology. Centre for Science Studies. Lancaster University, Lancaster LA1 4YN, UK. Retrieved Mar. 4, 2008, from http://www.comp.lancs.ac.uk/sociology/ papers/Law-Networks-Relations-Cyborgs.pdf.

Leont'ev, A. N. (1978). *Activity, consciousness and personality.* Englewood Cliffs, NJ: Prentice Hall.

Lessig, L. (2004). *Free culture: How big media uses technology and the law to lock down culture and control creativity.* New York: Penguin.

———. (2008). *Remix: Making art and commerce thrive in the hybrid economy.* London, Bloomsbury.

———. (2010). Getting our values around copyright right. *EDUCAUSE Review* 45(2), 26–42. Retrieved August 1, 2012, from http://www.educause.edu/ero/article/getting-our-values-around-copyright-right.

Librarian of Congress announces DMCA Section 1201 rules for exemptions regarding circumvention of access-control technologies. (2010). News from the Library of Congress. Retrieved Oct. 5, 2010, from http://www.loc.gov/today/pr/2010/10–169.html.

Lincoln's Gettysburg Address. (1863). Abraham Lincoln Online. Retrieved Mar. 3, 2008, from http://showcase.netins.net/web/creative/lincoln/speeches/gettysburg.htm.

Lindquist, J. (2004). Class affects, classroom affectations: Working through the paradoxes of strategic empathy. *College English*, 67(2), 187–209.

Litman, J. (2004). Sharing and stealing. *Hastings Communications and Entertainment Law Journal*, 27, 1–50.

Logie, J. (1998). Champing at the bits: Computers, copyright, and the composition classroom. *Computers and Composition*, 15, 201–14.

———. (2005). Parsing codes: Intellectual property, technical communication, and the World Wide Web. In M. Day and C. Lipson (eds.), *Technical communication and the World Wide Web* (pp. 223–41). Hillsdale, NJ: Lawrence Erlbaum.

———. (2006a). Copyright in increasingly digital academic contexts: What it takes. WIDE paper #7. Retrieved June 24, 2006, from http://www.wide.msu.edu/widepapers.

———. (2006b). *Peers, pirates, and persuasion: Rhetoric in the peer-to-peer debates.* West Lafayette, IN: Parlor.

Luminosity. (2008). Vogue/300. YouTube. Retrieved Sept. 2, 2010, from http://www.youtube.com/watch?v=QNRjzUB7Afo.

———. (n.d.). Women's work. Blip.tv. Retrieved Sept. 2, 2010, from http://www.blip.tv/file/2299910/.

MacNealy, M. S. (2009). Concepts basic to quantitative research. In S. Miller (ed.), *The Norton Book of Composition Studies* (pp. 874–96). New York: Norton.

Mandich, G. (1948). Venetian patents (1450–1550). *Journal of the Patent Office Society*, 30, 166–223.

McKeon, R. (1998). *Selected writings of Richard McKeon.* Vol. 1, *Philosophy, science, culture.* Z. K. McKeon and W. G. Swenson (eds.). Chicago: University of Chicago Press.

Melton, J., Jr. (2009). Going global: A case study of rhetorical invention, packaging, delivery, and feedback collection. *IEEE Transactions on Professional Communication*, 52(3), 229–42.

MGM Studios v. Grokster (2005). 545 US 913. Retrieved August 5, 2012, from http://supreme.justia.com/cases/federal/us/545/04-480/.

Miles, M., and Huberman, M. (1994). *Qualitative data analysis: An expanded sourcebook* (2nd ed.). Thousand Oaks: Sage.

Miller, C. R. (2000). The Aristotelian Topos: Hunting for novelty. In A. G. Gross and A. E. Walzer (eds.), *Rereading Aristotle's Rhetoric* (130–48) (e-book). Carbondale: Southern Illinois University Press.

Mittell, J. (2010). Letting us rip: Our new right to fair use of DVDs. ProfHacker. *Chronicle of Higher Education.* Retrieved Oct. 5, 2010, from http://chronicle.com/blogPost/Letting-Us-Rip-Our-New-Right/25797/.

Moberg v. 33T LCC. (2009). U.S. District Court District of Delaware. Civil No. 08–625.

Nguyen, N. (2011). Intellectual property instruction in first year writing classes. In M. C. Rife, D. N. DeVoss, and S. Slattery (eds.), *Copy(write): Intellectual property in the writing classroom* (295–307). WAC Clearhouse /Parlor Press. Retrieved Aug, 13, 2012, from http://wac.colostate.edu /books/copywrite/chapter16.pdf.

Nielsen, J. (1992). Finding usability problems through heuristic evaluation. In P. Bauersfeld, J. Benet, and G. Lynch (eds.), *Proceedings of the SIGCHI conference on human factors in computing systems* (pp. 373–80). New York: ACM.

———. (1994). Heuristic evaluation. In J. Nielsen and R. L. Mack (eds.), *Usability inspection methods* (pp. 25–62). New York: John Wiley.

North, S. (1987). *The making of knowledge in composition: Portrait of an emerging field.* Portsmouth, NH: Boynton/Cook.

Odell, L., Goswami, D., and Herrington, A. (1983). The discourse-based interview: A procedure for exploring the tacit knowledge of writers in non-academic settings. In P. Mosenthal, L. Tamor, and S. Walmsley (eds.), *Research on Writing* (pp. 221–36). New York: Longman.

Ong, W. (1988). *Orality and literacy.* London: Routledge.

Ostrom, E. (1990). *Governing the commons: The evolution of institutions for collective action.* New York: Cambridge University Press.

Perelman, C. (1963). *The idea of justice and the problem of argument.* New York: Humanities.

Perelman, C., and Olbrects-Tyteca, L. (1971/2006). *The new rhetoric: A treatise on argumentation.* Notre Dame: University of Notre Dame Press.

Perl, S. (1979/2003). The composing process of unskilled college writers. In V. Villanueva (ed.), *Cross-talk in comp theory: A reader* (2nd ed.) (pp. 17–39). Urbana, IL: NCTE. Reprinted from *Research in the Teaching of English,* 13(4) (1979), 317–36.

Peters, M. (2010, June). Recommendation of the register of copyrights in RM 2008-8: Rulemaking on exemptions from prohibition on circumvention of copyright protection systems for access control technologies. Retrieved Sept. 2, 2010, from http://www.copyright.gov/1201/2010 /initialed-registers-recommendation-june-11-2010.pdf.

Phelps, L. W. (1988). *Composition as a human science: Contributions to the self-understanding of a discipline.* New York: Oxford University Press.

Plambeck, J. (2010, May 13). Court rules web site infringed copyrights. *New York Times.* p. B10.

Polanyi, M. (1962). *Personal knowledge: Towards a post-critical philosophy.* Chicago: University of Chicago Press.

Porter, J. E. (1997). Legal realities and ethical hyperrealities: A critical approach toward cyberwriting. In S. Selber (ed.), *Computers and technical communication: Pedagogical and programmatic perspectives* (pp. 45–73). Greenwich, CT: Ablex.

———. (1998). *Rhetorical ethics and internetworked writing.* Greenwich, CT: Ablex, 1998.

———. (2005). The chilling of digital information: Technical communicators as public advocates. In M. Day and C. Lipson (eds.), *Technical communication and the World Wide Web in the new millennium* (pp. 243–59). Mahway, NJ: Erlbaum.

Porter, J. E., and Rife, M. C. (2005). *MGM v. Grokster:* Implications for educators and writing teachers. WIDE paper #1. Retrieved Feb. 26, 2006, from http://www.wide.msu.edu/widepapers/grokster/ republished on NCTE-CCCC, retrieved Aug. 13, 2012, from http://www.ncte.org/cccc/committees/ip/2005developments/mgmvgrokster.

Portewig, T. C. (2008). The role of rhetorical invention for visuals: A qualitative study of technical communicators in the workplace. *Technical Communication,* 55(4), 333–42.

Powell, M. (1999). Blood and scholarship: One mixed-blood's story. In K. Gilyard (ed.), *Race rhetoric and composition* (pp. 1–16). Portsmouth, NH: Boynton/Cook.

Prior, P. (2004). Tracing process: How texts come into being. In C. Bazerman and P. Prior (eds.), *What writing does and how it does it: An introduction to analyzing texts and textual practices* (pp. 167–200). Mahwah, NJ: Lawrence Erlbaum.

Prioritizing resources and organization for intellectual property act of 2008, Public Law 110–403. (2008) Retrieved Aug. 13, 2012, from http://www.gpo.gov/fdsys/pkg/PLAW-110publ403/pdf/PLAW-110publ403.pdf.

Raphael, D. D. (2001). *Concepts of justice.* Oxford: Clarendon.

Ratliff, C. (ed.). (2007–2010). Top Intellectual Property Developments. NCTE CCCC Committee website. Retrieved May 23, 2010, from http://www.ncte.org/cccc/committees/ip.

Ray, A., and Graeff, E. (2008). Reviewing the author-function in the age of Wikipedia. In C. Eisner and M. Vicinus (eds.), *Originality, imitation, and plagiarism: Teaching writing in the digital age* (pp. 39–47). Ann Arbor: University of Michigan Press.

Reyman, J. (2006). Copyright, distance education, and the TEACH Act: Implications for teaching writing. *College Composition and Communication*, 58(1), 30–45.

———. (2010). *The rhetoric of intellectual property: Copyright law and the regulation of digital culture*. New York: Routledge.

Ridolfo, J., and DeVoss, D. N. (2009). Composing for recomposition: Rhetorical velocity and delivery. *Kairos: A Journal of Rhetoric, Technology, and Pedagogy*, 13(2). Retrieved Oct. 25, 2009, from http://www.technorhetoric.net/13.2/topoi/ridolfo_devoss/intro.html.

Ridolfo, J., and Rife, M. C. (2011). Rhetorical velocity and copyright: A case study on the strategies of rhetorical delivery. In M. C. Rife, D. N. DeVoss and S. Slattery (eds.), *Copy(write): Intellectual property in the writing classroom* (223–43). WAC Clearhouse/Parlor Press. Retrieved Aug. 13, 2012, from http://wac.colostate.edu/books/copywrite /chapter12.pdf.

Rife, M. C. (2005). The visual rhetoric of the family photo: One cyborg's story. Master's thesis Michigan State University.

———. (2006, Fall). Why Kairos matters to writing: A reflection on our intellectual property conversation during the last ten years. *Kairos Tenth Anniversary Issue* 11(1). Retrieved Oct. 7, 2006, from http://english .ttu.edu/KAIROS/11.1/

———. (2007a). The fair use doctrine: History, application, implications for (new media) writing teachers. *Computers and Composition*, 24(2), 105–226.

———. (2007b). Remix as "fair use": Grateful Dead posters' re-publication held to be a transformative, fair use. NCTE CCCC IP Caucus. Retrieved July 27, 2007, from http://www.ncte.org/cccc/gov/committees /ip/127373.htm.

———. (2008). The "shock and awe" of digital research design: Rhetorical strategies as mediational means in digital survey research. Conference proceedings IEEE-IPCC.

———. (2009a, May 6). DMCA Tri-Annual Rulemaking Hearing. PTX Transcript. Retrieved Oct. 22, 2009, from http://www.copyright.gov/1201 /hearings/2009/transcripts/.

———. (2009b). Ideas towards a fair use heuristic: Visual rhetoric and composition. In S. Westbrook (ed.), *Composition and copyright* (pp. 133–53). New York: State University of New York Press.

———. (2010a). Copyright law as mediational means: Report on a mixed methods study of professional writers. *Technical Communication*, 57(1), 44–67.

———. (2010b). Ethos, pathos, logos, kairos: Using a rhetorical heuristic to mediate digital survey recruitment strategies. *IEEE-Transactions on Professional Communication*, 53(3), 260–77.

———. (2010c). Making legal knowledge in global digital environments: The judicial opinion as remix. In D. Starke-Meyerring (ed.), *Writing in the knowledge society. Research Network on Interdisciplinary Studies in Rhetoric and Writing.* Book chapter for peer reviewed digital book. Forthcoming from Parlor.

———. (2010d). New copyright "combat" regulations for colleges and universities go into effect July 1. June CCCC IP Caucus Report. Retrieved Oct. 5, 2010, from http://www.ncte.org/cccc/committees/ip/ipreports/combat.

———. (2010e). Part one: The new DMCA exemption for college teachers and students. Sept. CCCC IP Caucus Report. Retrieved Oct. 5, 2010, from http://www.ncte.org/cccc/committees/ip/ipreports.

Rife, M. C., and Hart-Davidson, W. (2006). Is there a chilling of digital communication? Exploring how knowledge and understanding of the fair use doctrine may influence web composing. Pilot Study Report. SSRN Working Paper Series. Retrieved Nov. 18, 2006, from http://papers.ssrn.com/s013/papers.cfm?abstract_id=918822.

Rife, M. C., Westbrook, S., DeVoss, D. N., Logie, J. (guest eds.). (2010). *Copyright, Culture, Creativity, and the Commons*, 27(3), 161–246.

Rose, M. (1988). The author as proprietor: *Donaldson v. Becket* and the genealogy of modern authorship. *Representations*, 23, 51–83.

Roth, W. M., and Lee, Y. J. (2007). "Vygotsky's neglected legacy": Cultural-historical activity theory. *Review of Educational Research*, 77(2), 186–232.

Rowntree, D. (2004). *Statistics without tears.* New York: Scribner's.

Rulemaking on exemptions from prohibition on circumvention of technological measures that control access to copyrighted works. (2010). U.S. Copyright Office. Retrieved Oct. 5, 2010, from http://www.copyright.gov/1201/.

Rutter, R. (1991). History, rhetoric, and humanism: Toward a more comprehensive definition of technical communication. *Journal of Technical Writing and Communication*, 21(2), 133–53.

Samuelson, P., et al. (2010). The copyright principles project: Directions for reform. *Berkeley Technology Law Journal*, 25, 1–68. Retrieved Oct. 5, 2010, from http://www.law.berkeley.edu/files/bclt_CPP.pdf.

S.B. 2913: Shawn Bentley Orphan Works Act of 2008. (2008). Public Knowledge. Retrieved June 5, 2008, from http://www.publicknowledge.org/bill/110-s2913.

Schillewaert, N., Langerak, F., and Duhamel, T. (1998). Non-probability sampling for www surveys: A comparison of methods. *Journal of the Market Research Society*, 4(40), 307–13.

Scott, R. (1967). On viewing rhetoric as epistemic. *Central States Speech Journal*, 18, 9–17.

Seidman, I. E. (1991). *Interviewing as qualitative research: A guide for researchers in education and the social sciences.* New York: Teachers College Press.

Selber, S. (2004). Technological dramas: A meta-discourse heuristic for critical literacy. *Computers and Composition, 21,* 171–95.

Singh, A., Taneja, A., and Mangalaraj, G. (2009, June). Creating online surveys: Some wisdom from the trenches. *IEEE Transactions on Professional Communication, 52*(2), 197–212.

Spinuzzi, C. (2003). *Tracing genres through organizations: A sociocultural approach to information design.* Cambridge: MA: MIT Press.

———. (2007). Texts of our institutional lives: Accessibility scans and institutional activity. *College English, 70*(2), 189–201.

St. Amant, K., and Rife, M. C. (guest eds.). (2010). Legal issues in global contexts. *Technical Communication, 57*(4).

Statement of the librarian of Congress on the anticircumvention rulemaking. (2006). Retrieved May 24, 2010, from http://www.copyright .gov/1201/2006/index.html.

Stewart v. Abend. (1990). 495 U.S. 207.

Sturcke, J. (2010). Harry Potter plagiarism lawsuit could be billion dollar case, says claimant. *The Guardian.* Retrieved May 24, 2010, from http://www.guardian.co.uk/books/2010/feb/18/harry-potter-jk-rowling -willy-wizard.

Sullivan, P. (2008). "Mixing methods into a rhetorically-based, flexibly driven, 21st-century methodology." CCCC's Presentation. New Orleans.

Suntrust Bank v. Houghton Mifflin Company. (2001). 268 F.3d 1257; 2001 U.S. App. LEXIS 21690.

Swoboda, S. J., Muehlberger, N., Weitkunat, R., and Schneeweiss, S. (1997). Web-based surveys by direct mailing: An innovative way of collecting data. *Social Science Computer Review, 15*(3), 242–55.

Terrill, R. E. (2004). *Malcolm X inventing radical judgment.* East Lansing: Michigan State University Press.

Tiersma, P. (2008). Writing, law, and text. In C. Bazerman (ed.), *Handbook of research on writing: History, society, school, individual, text* (pp. 129–41). New York: Lawrence Erlbaum.

Tinberg, H., and Nadeau, J. (2010). *The community college writer: Exceeding expectations.* Carbondale: Southern Illinois University Press.

Title 35—Patents. (1952/2012). USC. Retrieved Aug. 13, 2012, from http://uscode .house.gov/download/title_35.shtml.

Tushnet, R. (2010) I put you there: User-generated content and anticircumvention. *Vanderbilt Journal of Entertainment and Technology Law,* 12, 889–946. Retrieved Oct. 5, 2010, from http://papers.ssrn.com/so13 /papers.cfm?abstract_id=1652211.

United States Government Accountability Office. (2010). Observations on Efforts to Quantify the Economic Effects of Counterfeit and Pirated Goods. Report to Congressional Committees. Intellectual Property. Retrieved Apr. 25, 2010, from http://www.gao.gov/new.items/d10423.pdf.

"Vedas." (2009). *Wikipedia: The free encyclopedia.* Retrieved June 1, 2008, from http://en.wikipedia.org/wiki/Vedas.

Vygotsky, L. S. (1978). *Mind in society: The development of higher psychological processes.* M. Cole, V. John-Steiner, S. Scribner, E. Souberman (eds.). Cambridge, MA: Harvard University Press.

———. (1997). *The collected works of L. S. Vygotsky.* Vol. 4, *The history of the development of higher mental functions.* R. W. Rieber (ed.). New York: Plenum.

———. (1999). *The collected works of L. S. Vygotsky.* Vol. 6, *Scientific Legacy.* R. W. Rieber (ed.). New York: Plenum.

Waller, R. D. (2006a). Fair use. Ethics Case. *Intercom* (In John G. Bryans, column ed.). Retrieved Nov. 23, 2006, from http://www.stc.org.

———. (2006b). Responses to "fair use." Ethics Case. *Intercom* (In John G. Bryans, column ed.). Retrieved Nov. 23, 2006, from http://www.stc.org.

Watson, J., and Anderson, N. (2005). Pinnacles and pitfalls: Researcher experiences from a web-based survey of secondary teachers. *E-learning,* 2(3), 276–84.

Westbrook, S. (2006). Visual rhetoric in a culture of fear: Impediments to multimedia production. *College English,* 68(5), 457–80.

——— (ed.). (2009). *Composition and copyright: Perspectives on teaching, text-making, and fair use.* New York: State University of New York Press.

WIDE Research Center Collective. (2005) Why teach digital writing? *Kairos,* 10(1). Retrieved May 23, 2010, from http://endora.wide.msu.edu/10.1/coverweb/wide/index.html.

WIDE Research Center Study Group. (2010, Sept.). Revisualizing composition: Mapping the writing lives of first-year college students. White Paper. Retrieved Sept. 13, 2010, from http://wide.msu.edu/special/writinglives/.

Witte, S. P. (2005). Research in activity: An analysis of speed bumps as mediational means. *Written Communication,* 22, 127–65.

Woodmansee, M., and Jaszi, P. (eds.). (1994). *The construction of authorship: textual appropriation in law and literature.* Durham: Duke University Press.

Woodmansee, M., and Jaszi, P. (1995). The law of texts: Copyright in the academy. *College English,* 57, 769–87.

Wyatt, G. (1986). *The economics of invention: A study of the determinants of inventive activity.* New York: St. Martin's.

Yancey, K. (2009). Writing in the 21st century: A report from the National Council of Teachers of English. Retrieved Mar. 29, 2009, from http://www.ncte.org/library/NCTEFiles/Press/Yancey_final.pdf.

Young, I. M. (1990). *Justice and the politics of difference.* Princeton, NJ: Princeton University Press.

Young, R. E. (1978). Paradigms and problems: Needed research in rhetorical invention. In C. R. Cooper and L. Odell (eds.), *Research on composing: Points of departure* (pp. 29–47). Urbana, IL: NCTE.

Yun, G. W., and Trumbo, C. W. (2000, Sept.). Comparative response to a survey executed by post, e-mail, and web form. *Journal of Computer Mediated Communication*, 6(2). Retrieved Jan. 26, 2008, from http://jcmc.indiana.edu/vo16/issue1/yun.html.

Zhang, Y. (2000, Jan.). Using the Internet for survey research: A case study. *Journal of the American Society for Information Science*, 51(1), 57–68.

Zimmerman, Traci A. (2009). "It's a hard knock life": The plight of orphan works and the possibility of reform. In Clancy Ratliff (Ed.), *College Composition and Communication IP Caucus: Top intellectual property developments of 2008*. Retrieved August 3, 2012, from http://www.ncte.org/cccc/committees/ip/2008developments/hardknocklife.

Index

100 different pieces, 68, 78

abandoned or lost materials, 112
activity theory, 11, 17–19, 22, 54,
    120–21, 125, 129–32, 140, 142,
    152–53, 191; rules, view of, 120,
    128–30, 135, 137; tools, view of, 18,
    119–20, 128–30, 135–37, 147, 152
actor network theory, 11, 19–22,
    92–96, 103, 114, 125, 130–33,
    137–38, 194n2
alternative hypothesis, 45–46
*Archaeology of Knowledge and the
    Discourse on Language, The*
    (Foucault), 37, 92, 94
architecture for writing, 3, 20, 74,
    111, 115–16
argument from probability, 27,
    125–26
Aristotle, 11, 13–15, 147–50, 156
artifacts, 17–18, 65, 89, 90, 92,
    103–10, 121, 130–31, 135
art of rank, 114
Association of Teachers of Techni-
    cal Writing, 2
attribution, 32–33, 36, 75–76, 84, 100,
    102, 108, 111, 121, 124, 143, 151, 160–
    61, 184–85, 194–95n1 (chap.6)
Atwill, Janet M., 146
author, 4–5, 11–12, 20–21, 34–35, 38,
    74–75, 88, 90, 93–105, 108, 112–13,
    116–17, 160–61; and citation, 34;
    and common knowledge, 110–11;
    as construct, 93; as filter, 5, 110; lit-
    erary, 36, 92, 104, 122; as founder
    of discursivity, 36–37; in a net-
    work, 20, 93, 131; and origins, view
    of, 11–12; and work-for-hire, 148

author-function, 20–21, 33–36,
    92–107, 112, 115–16, 137, 154, 194n1
    (chap.6)
author-heavy, 37–38, 74, 100, 107,
    111
author-light, 37–38, 74, 83, 100, 107,
    108, 110–11, 156
authorship, 5, 17, 38, 57, 83, 96, 99,
    104, 112–13, 121–22, 140, 143–44,
    146; and common knowledge,
    110; corporate, 10, 101, 148; in
    digital contexts, 91, 96–97; God
    as, 102; of government docu-
    ments, 35; and *metis*, 150; and
    originality, 161; as a search for
    origins, 19, 90; performance of,
    160; and Phillis Wheatley, 105,
    115, 157; remixed theory of, 22,
    92–93, 96, 103, 112, 118–19, 130–32;
    traditional notions of, 160

Bazerman, Charles, 3, 13
Ben-Tech v. Oakland University,
    193n4 (chap.4)
Bertoff, Ann E., 190n8
beyond a reasonable doubt, 44, 46,
    126
*Bill Graham Archives v. Dorling
    Kindersley Limited*, 24, 81–82,
    109, 158, 183–84
Bizzell, Patricia, 11
Booth, Wayne C., 126
Bracewell, Robert J., 120
*Bright Tunes Music Corp. v. Harri-
    songs Music, Ltd.*, 34, 104, 106
Britton, James, 140–41
Brockmann, R. J., 3, 13
Bruffee, Kenneth A., 152

Martine Courant Rife is a professor at Lansing Community College, where she teaches writing. Her work has most recently appeared in *Technical Communication*, *Computers and Composition*, *Kairos*, *Teaching English in the Two-Year College*, and *E-learning and Digital Media*. Rife is the 2007 recipient of the Frank R. Smith Outstanding Journal Article Award from the Society for Technical Communication.